BRYAN COONEY began his journalistic life on the *Press & Journal* in 1963. As a racing sub-editor and tipster taking the pseudonym of The Colonel, he won the 1965 Sporting Chronicle naps table. Fleet Street and a post as a sports sub-editor on the *Daily Mail* beckoned. He was appointed as *The Scottish Sun*'s chief sports writer in 1974, but an eventful lifestyle ended this association 17 months later. He worked on oil barges and selling penny insurance policies, and then joined the *Daily Express*. He went on to become Chief Sports Writer of the *Daily Star*, before being head hunted by the *Scottish Daily Mail* as Sports Editor in 1995. He was appointed Head of Sport of the *Mail* in London two years later.

He has written five books, won three Scottish Sports Writer of the Year awards, has covered three World Cups and myriad Wimbledons and Open Championships, presented several sports series for BBC Radio Scotland (picking up a Sony bronze) and for the celebrated BBC Radio 4's *Archive Hour*. Now retired, he lives with his wife of 42 years in Glasgow. He has been an Aberdeen fan all his life.

Contents

Prologue

IDEALLY, PESSIMISM SHOULD NOT have a place in the lexicon of football. Yet, today, during the preliminaries at the Betfred Scottish League Cup final, negativity is overriding every other emotion. I mean, I'm wondering whether Aberdeen can beat Celtic, and the inescapable conclusion, derived from recent history, is that there's more chance of Colombia being declared a drug-free zone. I've just seen the Dons team sheet and winced: there's nothing in the line-up that suggests aggression, or even a desire to attack; players seem to be out of their positional comfort zones.

Off the pitch, it's a different matter altogether. Here, on Sunday 27 November 2016, I find myself in the middle of a flag day extraordinaire. Twenty-two thousand Dons fans have been presented with either red flags or white flags. Some admirable souls have spent hours the previous day ensuring that there will be an awesome display. And now, 15 minutes before the scheduled 3pm kick off, people unfurl those flags and start waving them, frenziedly, above their heads. I join in. Hey, you don't look particularly cool waving a flag, but I'm 72 years of age and cool belongs to another lifetime. The extravaganza endures for another 15 minutes and is an awesome flourish of faith and solidarity, one that so far has been unanswered over on the other side of the ground. Before they finally get their acts together, the Celtic brigades seem to be staring, awestruck, at the guys they love to denigrate as sheep shaggers. Well, we are certainly ahead in terms of these terracing mind games. But what will happen when the real spectacle begins?

My mind drifts back a couple of years, where we found ourselves in a similar Cup final situation, this time against Inverness CT. I wrote about it in the *Cooney and Black* blog…

The ascent to Area 410, Row N, Seat 12 of Celtic Park's North stand upper might have been acceptable to a man possessing not only the lung power of a Chris Bonington but also his mountaineering pedigree. This old fella, without having the benefit of either, was consequently looking for an oxygen tent only a couple of minutes into the climb. The compensatory factor was reaching the summit and finding himself besieged by a red and white bedlam. Two important points were proved. Firstly, 43,000 Aberdeen fans, 150 miles from home, were demonstrating that if Scottish football is close to self immolation, then the potential North East obituarists have yet to be notified. And secondly, joy of joy, those roistering, raucous, rambunctious fans seemed intent on ridiculing the indictment that they suffer badly from inhibition and are dedicated rustlers of sweetie papers. Hey, legendary producer Phil Spector once nurtured what was described as the Wall of Sound, an impenetrable, multi-layered onslaught of orchestra-inspired music to monopolise the senses and the pop charts in the early '60s. He should have been in the East End of Glasgow on Sunday afternoon to record something that came very close to his concept of noise. This was one that steamrollered the senses and made you inordinately proud to be an Aberdonian.

Now, I have pursued the fortunes of this wildly idiosyncratic team for 65 years, most times fanatically, occasionally almost apologetically. I have never heard anything like this before – even on a night of Pittodrie mayhem which I shall return to in due course. Suddenly, all supporter sacrifice made sense. The myriad tears, disappointments and disaffections were forgiven if not forgotten. And this, you should note, was before the League Cup final between the Dons and Inverness CT had even begun.

But let's go back to those 65+ years: if this promised to be an occasion for nostalgia, I determined to indulge myself. I remembered the 1949 day my dad took me to Pittodrie for the first time. Soon, he was wishing he hadn't troubled himself. How do you constrict the conduct of a venturesome four-year-old who was fascinated by everything aside from the football? The denouement came when I heard Dad complaining about someone fiddling. I began looking around, perhaps expecting to see a string quartet in the immediate vicinity. My father became agitated, possibly because of the home team's shortcomings, most probably because of my finite attention span, and he signalled he'd had enough. He grabbed my hand and marched me down the stairs of the main stand. As far as I know, he never called in at Pittodrie again.

But sometimes it takes only one visit to be infected with the football virus. And so, within three years, I became a Pittodrie regular. I began to identify my own heroes and there was not a fiddler among them. Their names adorned my autograph book: Archie Glen, Jackie Hather, of the double shuffle, Paddy Buckley, Harry Yorston and ultimately Graham Leggat. They won the First Division championship in 1954-55 with a manager called Dave Halliday. They added a League Cup victory a year later with a new man: Davie Shaw. There was victory on the pitch and spoils on the terracing. My entrepreneurial instincts were satisfied: I'd wait for the crowd to disperse and then collect the beer bottles in a carrier bag. I'd swap them for a couple of shillings in the licensed grocer's in Merkland Road. Perhaps I'd been blessed with foresight – my dear brother John eventually bought that shop in the late sixties.

Paradoxically, in spite of this success, we were destined to occupy the football boondocks for more years than I care to remember. This was no deterrent to a few young men from Aberdeen Academy who were willing to accept equal dosages of rough and smooth. Guys like Ivor Finnie, Gordon Donald, John Dingwall and I decided to join the official supporters' club, which comprised a handful of men from another generation and a couple of highly emancipated women. The chairman, a lovely yet intensely garrulous guy, had a serious speech impediment and if you were in the front row at a meeting, you had to duck, bob and weave, like a professional boxer, to avoid taking direct hits from his saliva. You required dedication to be in our small gang. Think of today's Red Army and its impressive infiltration of away ends. Ours didn't even constitute a platoon as it made its way all over Scotland, kitted out in red and white caps and scarves. We even bought ourselves blazers and badges at a later, more sophisticated, date.

Campbell's, of Bon Accord Square, provided our transport and, normally, one bus was sufficient for our needs. Our travels were not without incident, however: we left Ibrox one year with a hail of stones bouncing off the framework of the bus; we retreated from Kirkcaldy severely depleted of our numbers. We invaded the pitch when a Cup defeat proved unacceptable; the local police were unforgiving. On another Cup adventure, this time under the managerial custody of Eddie Turnbull, we took a respectable following to Easter Road, and only a last-minute equaliser secured us a replay at Pittodrie. By now, I was working in the *Press & Journal* editorial but was granted a night off. I squeezed myself into the Merkland Road end as 44,000 rolled up that Wednesday evening. The crowd groaned collectively as it was announced that the pugnacious Ernie Winchester would be playing: in some quarters, he was slightly less popular than a visit from the bailiffs. Those sceptics changed their minds, temporarily, at least, when he scored twice. Winchester, who died last year, was an inspiration, but not as far as Hibs centre half John Madsen was concerned.

He later informed anyone who would listen, 'Tonight I met a madman!'

But pay attention, if you will, to that figure of 44,000 on a hysterical night in March of 1967. It brings me back to the hysteria of Sunday and the pretty surreal fact that 43,000 of my ain folk had converged on Glasgow to ostensibly take over the city. Was it all worthwhile? Not, perhaps, in my highly critical book. The football game began, but to call it a game is taking a liberty with the English language. Thankfully, as far as this person was concerned, it was over fairly quickly, not of course before Jonny Hayes had been carted off to hospital, nails had been gnawed to the quick and penalties had been missed (by Inverness) and converted (by our lot). We won, but it was a victory that delivered little in terms of satisfaction. Still, as we prepared to leave Celtic Park, my eyes were drawn to the seats immediately in front of us and a little boy clad, like his father, in red. He was bright-eyed and pumped full of mischief, sticking his tongue out at anyone who looked his way. It was pretty obvious that it was of very little concern to him what was going on down on the pitch. Considering the paucity of the play, he could have been forgiven. Perhaps this was his first football match. His initiation. Perhaps he was looking for a fiddler in the stand, just to remove the edge from the boredom. There again, maybe, just maybe, he'd caught the virus that makes professional football so compulsory – the one that infected me 65 years ago. I wondered whether he'd still be supporting his team in the year 2079.

We're right up to date and, unfortunately, back at Hampden. The pessimism – maybe prescience is a better word – has been justified. The players are disporting themselves in a manner that might suggest their rectal hairs have been tied together. Their performance is abysmal, going on abject, and they look petrified of Celtic's presence. They have a semblance of an excuse, of course. The fans are becoming restless: they are targeting their natural victim. Why has the manager put a right-footed player, aka Anthony O'Connor, as left-side centre back? Why has the manager placed the faithful servant Andrew Considine in a situation (left back) that illustrates his weaknesses? Why is Graeme Shinnie being persevered with in midfield and not his natural niche of full back? Why is James Maddison, a welcome and intuitive loanee from Norwich, playing ostensibly on the left wing and not in central midfield? There are no answers to these questions because Derek McInnes is someone who allegedly has an abhorrence of justifying himself.

This is the same manager who declared himself satisfied with his squad back at the end of the 2016 summer transfer window when it was apparent, to anyone barring the myopic, that he required two robust players to stiffen the centre of defence and midfield. Anyway, the goals go in – one, two three – and once again we are occupying the roles of the oppressed. Why are we giving Celtic such space? Why are we standing off them as if we are David Attenborough's cameramen and they (Celtic) are a rarefied species? I have had enough humiliation around the three-quarter-time mark. Yet there are vestiges of guilt as I file out of Hampden, in the manner of a carpetbagger who has been denounced. Still, the paying customer is invariably right. Being short-changed in this life demands a response. Mine is a silent protest. Well, perhaps a few profanities short of silent. As for those players, well, the thing is if you come to Glasgow and occupy the roles of frightened sheep, then you're going to get a spanking. Jesus! It all started so well with those flags. But, am I surprised by another anti-climactic event in the history of Aberdeen FC? Of course I'm not. In some ways I'm inured to disappointment. Supporting and writing about Aberdeen FC over seven decades prepares you for anything that the Good Lord can fling at you.

But enough of the present. We'll return there soon enough. It's time to explore those idiosyncrasies of the past. There will be no over-concentration on facts, figures and games played. This book will be more about personalities, significant flashpoints and 'inside' stories. Let's start on a positive note with a closer look at the team that cantered through the serried ranks of Scotland's finest football teams in the 1950s. It was a time when Aberdeen FC were feared by everyone.

CHAPTER I

A Plot by the Old Firm?

IN SOME WAYS, THE REASON FOR Aberdeen's inexorable rise to the pinnacle of Scottish football in the mid-1950s can be laid at the educated feet of two men: Paddy Buckley, from Leith, Edinburgh, and local lad Harry Yorston. Scoring goals represented no problem to them, but there was a problem for all that. A major one which we shall come to presently. They were contrasting units in style, if not in height. Buckley, a 5ft 6in centre forward, was a veritable flying machine. Over the vital first five to ten yards, it was as if someone had applied a blowtorch to his backside, and that searing pace took him past opponents and on to confront chittering goalkeepers. His Pittodrie goal ratio, much the same as that at his previous club, St Johnstone, was to be located at the top end of the market: 92 goals in 153 matches.

Yorston, half an inch taller, blond and handsome and given the somewhat challenging sobriquet of 'golden boy', operated in the W-formation of a five-man forward line and therefore further back at inside right. He didn't belong to the streamlined class as far as speed was concerned, but there were compensatory factors. Most of the time, his spirit belonged to the never-say-die society and the way he worked ensured that his socks were ritually discarded. Equally impressive was his appetite for goals. Owing to the absence of official records burned in the Pittodrie grandstand fire of 1971, there are two quite different versions of that appetite. On the player's personal page in Wikipedia, he is said to have scored 98 goals in 201 outings. But the same organisation, on its Aberdeen FC page, stipulates that he accumulated 278 appearances and hit the sweet spot 141 times. The one certainty is that he derived considerable pleasure from scoring goals, something that today's contemporaries would do well to digest and indeed work on. Sometimes, in current matches at Pittodrie, a spectator can count himself lucky if he sees two or three shots of worthwhile calibre in 90 minutes from the home brigade. Yet, they play with a ball that is so light it almost begs to be blootered. In contrast, away back when, they were playing with what might be considered an alternative to the medicine ball – a ball that, when saturated with rainwater, could test the durable properties of your ankle ligaments if you were unlucky enough to mis-kick it.

In terms of scoring, then, there was little to separate Buckley and Yorston when, in 1955, Aberdeen won the Scottish First Division title for the first time. And, yet, in the eyes of the paying public, or at least more than a few members of this fraternity, they were leagues apart in delivery of satisfaction. Buckley, who joined the club in 1952, was simply incapable of misconduct in the fans' books. Former colleague Bobby Wishart illustrates that statement:

'There was a funny incident with him at Inverurie one night. He was guest of honour at some function and, while he was sitting on the platform, he fell asleep. When he woke up, he was somewhat disoriented and didn't realise there was a microphone near him. He said something like, "I suppose I'll have to thank these bastards!" Would you believe, the crowd just burst out laughing? And, for some reason, there was a never a squeak of that back in town. Can you imagine what would have happened if that had been today? You cannae get away with anything these days.'

So, you would be borrowing from hyperbole only slightly if you said Buckley's popularity with everybody concerned was such that he might have careered up Union Street, buck naked, and received no more than a token admonishment from either the constabulary or indeed the magistrates.

With Yorston, it was radically different. You suspect this player – he had been at Pittodrie since 1947 and established himself as a first-team regular a year later – would not have been so fortunate had he embarked on a similar escapade. It seemed that, on the Pittodrie playing surface, he was only a footfall away from reprimand and the derision of hundreds, if not thousands. Whatever, this attitude eventually helped him make the decision to forfeit the putative glamour of football and plunge himself into a far more exacting existence: he retired at the age of 28 and, following his father's lead, spent a portion of his working life as a porter, hefting stinking boxes at the fish market. The Dons, in turmoil due to his decision and other defections, disappeared into a tailspin. But, returning to my theme: what, do you imagine, affected the dichotomy between the two men? Why did the crowd generally favour one and frown on the other, particularly when they were delivering proportionate parcels of aid and assistance to the team?

The answer, or more correctly, one rather controversial interpretation of the answer, comes from Wishart. The latter became a vital member of the championship winning team of 1954-55. He was to be found at the second base of the W formation, at inside left. Even more helpful, for this particular narrative, he became Harry's pal. He was also on good terms with Buckley. Now in his 84th year, Wishart's insights into events that occurred 60 years ago are as sharp as they are revealing:

'The fact was that half the crowd loved Harry, the other half hated him,' he recalls. 'He had that sense of humour that some people understood, while others thought he was big headed. Sometimes, maybe something he said in the newspapers was misinterpreted. In Aberdeen, anything happening through the football went round the city like a bush fire. The bigger the scandal, the quicker it went round. There was only one team to concentrate on. I always had the feeling that a lot of people came up to work in Aberdeen but weren't Aberdeen supporters. You'd get Rangers and Celtic guys who worked in the city and went to Pittodrie for their football. A lot of the stuff went on – players getting picked on and barracked – but I don't think they were the true Dons fans. I think they were Old Firm people who didn't want Aberdeen to win. And, indeed, I think over the years these fans kinda got Harry down.'

Even today, the reason behind Yorston's defection to harbour life has never been made public. Certainly, the constant carping seemed to occasionally deflate and discombobulate Yorston, not that he was a man for appending his angst to sandwich boards and parading them in the city. Was it, as Wishart suggests, a covert, terracing-inspired Old Firm conspiracy? If so, it was a devious tactic that eventually paid a handsome dividend for the critics. There again, was the genesis of it all far more simplistic? Was envy the main player here? There is, after all, repeated evidence in football of local lads being unable to satisfy the standards set by their own townspeople. Friendship or not, Yorston did not reveal his inner thoughts on the issue even to his closest colleague. Wishart remembers a deep, sometimes impenetrable, often paradoxical guy who thought about the game of football far more than most of his contemporaries. But, if he was not more forthcoming about his personal problems, he was pleased to fulfil the role of mentor.

When Wishart had performed well in one game and perhaps indicated that he had arrived as a player, Yorston cautioned him against believing that this guaranteed a long-term future. His advice was far more prosaic but weighted with wisdom: wait for three months and see if the crowd's attitude remained the same.

'He was an old soldier,' is the Wishart assessment. Indeed, an old soldier in so many respects. On the day of a pre-season trial, when the first team took on the reserves, Yorston told Wishart that a trip to the hairdresser's was an imperative. The younger man protested that he'd had a haircut two weeks previously. Yorston insisted that having a trim made a man look his best. 'And when the crowd see me tonight, they'll say, "See Yorston, he's looking younger than ever!"'

Yorston was an enthusiast of the tricks of the football trade long before they became fashionable. And his young protégé learned quickly:

'I'd weigh up the running ball and if I didn't think I could catch it, I let it go out of play. Harry didn't advocate taking things so easy. "That's not the way to do it," he'd say. "You knock your pan in trying to catch it, even although you know you'll not succeed. Then you get up, having just failed in your mission, and you spring back to your position, then wait for the goalkeeper's kick. The fans will say, "Christ! Look at Yorston – he can't wait to get back into the game again." These were the wee touches that Harry had. What he said was right: it could put a fine polish on things.'

But, of course, if the theory sounded perfect, the practice occasionally was blighted by imperfection. Yorston could be happy go lucky at times and, added to that, he had a smile that could outperform the sun. Some folk, suspicious folk in the Granite City, felt that he occasionally disappeared into a mood of indifference – and rushed to an inevitable conclusion: 'See that Yorston, he's no botherin' himself, he couldna care less.' This was in contrast to Buckley, Wishart insists. 'Paddy could get away with smiling when he missed an open goal. He was forever shrugging and putting his hands up to the crowd. Harry simply couldn't get away with that.'

On the field of play, Buckley did not look for hiding places, yet, off it, he seemed to favour the abrogation of responsibility. Wishart's still handsome features form a smile. 'I remember Paddy got a contract for the Daily Express while we were on tour in Canada and America, and they (the Express) were one of the better payers. Aberdeen Journals, in contrast, weren't good payers and I was writing for them all year round. Mind you, I think they gave me a little bit extra for sending stuff from Canada. Anyway, the upshot was I wrote Paddy's articles for him as well. He picked up the cheques and I did the donkey work.'

Wishart appears reluctant to adjudicate on Buckley's writing skills, but adds, significantly, 'Some lads didn't seem to know what was acceptable and what wasn't. I remember there was an article one of the guys wrote. The headline was: Does a Manager Manage? They (the directors) stopped all the journalism (from players) after that – and probably quite rightly. I mean, you cannae come away with stuff like that and not upset either the manager or the directors. But, anyway, Paddy was a bright little fella. When we were coming back from games, we used to play solo whist – Alec Young, Archie Glen, Paddy and myself. I would say Paddy was the best player of the four. Remember, Archie was a B.Sc and all. But Paddy was streetwise.' Wishart might have added: most of the time. 'You know, after games, he and I used to go for a drink at the Royal Hotel, for it was the quietest place in Aberdeen at the time. He wasn't a big drinker, but he was a guy who never looked sober after a couple of pints. He always loosened his tie and took his false teeth out – and his hair fell down like bead curtains on both sides of his face. He could look dishevelled in no time at all and always seemed half-canned. But, put him on a football field and the fans really liked him; he never stopped trying, he chased everything and gave 110 per cent.'

Yorston, in contrast, found that Pittodrie was a forbidding place even in the early fifties as people were still attempting to clear the dust and smell of World War II from their throats. He therefore enjoyed life more on his days off.

The ladies were attracted to his chiselled features. Wishart recalls, 'When he went to the local Palais in Diamond Street, he would tell his dance partner not to stand on his toes, or kick his shins, because he reckoned those feet were worth £25,000 each. He would make the ladies smile. So, yes, he was a great guy – but he also was a great gambler. He'd gamble on all sorts – horses, mainly, and the dogs at Garthdee, You couldn't really gamble on football at that time – it was frowned upon – but he was a student of gambling. He used to have a notebook full of all the dog tracks in Britain, complete with the numbers (traps) that won. He was forever looking for a system – I don't know if he ever got one.

'But the laugh of the thing was that I used to tell him that he should pack it up: that it was a mug's game. I never had a flutter, but I was a smoker. He replied, "Well, look at you – you use fags and they just go up in smoke. Meanwhile, I spend money on dogs and horses and I might get a return some time." And years later he won, I think it was £175,000, on the pools, so I said to him, "You were right after all, and I was wrong." That was after he stopped playing for Aberdeen.'

Yorston, who disappeared into the less demanding reaches of Highland League football, took a more understandable decision when he received that massive windfall in 1972: he quit the stench of the fish market and began to ingest the more attractive aroma of pound notes. It is only fit and proper, at this juncture, that we concentrate, more on the man who is contributing to the composition of this opening chapter.

Wishart was a notable donor to the Dandies' cause from 1953 to 1961, before he finally decamped, most probably disillusioned, to near neighbours Dundee. There, he helped the Dappers win the title a year later. He initially stepped into Pittodrie on a bright August day in 1951. His was what might be considered a whirlwind signing. He'd played only two trial games, one against Celtic at Parkhead, the second against Brechin. Wishart turned out at outside left in the second match and remembers doing nothing of any great account in a no-scoring draw. 'I didn't score and I didn't make a goal.' Yet director John Robbie was at the game and saw something beyond the obvious, and so plans were hastily drawn up to make the 18-year-old an instant Don.

Aberdeen, allegedly the highest-paying club in Britain at the time (£14 per week, with a £2 win bonus: this rose incrementally to £20 a week, plus bonuses, over the years), did some things in style. They travelled first class on the train and accommodated players in grand hotels. The young Wishart and his dad were put up at the Caledonian, in Union Terrace, before signing. They were impressed. A cursory inspection of the Pittodrie dressing room impressed him even more, but caused him to wonder whether he had taken the right decision. He discovered a football club almost bloated by icons and legends, some of them old enough be his father: Jimmy Delaney, Tommy Pearson, Gentleman George Hamilton, Tommy Bogan, Pat McKenna, Don Emery, Archie Baird; and then a host of others: Hughie Hay, George Kelly, Yorston, Joe O'Neill, to name but four. 'They had that many players,' he remembers. 'And there were not many bad ones. At that time, they had virtually three guys for each position, including inside forwards and left wingers in abundance.' There had been a plan to field a third team in the Highland League, but this had failed to materialise. Where was he going to fit in to what was an overcrowded situation?

The solution was provided with an almost immediate call-up to National Service. Wishart was sent to Ireland and subsequently played with Portadown, who turned him into a scoring centre forward. 'I was a nobody with no reputation, a wee guy coming in from nowhere. If it hadn't been for National Service, I don't think I'd have made the grade at all.' Back in the North East of Scotland, the nobody had altered the script: now he was a seasoned player with a reputation. He found everything had changed. The Dad's Army brigade had been 'demobbed' – with the greatest of respect, you imagine – and there was an infusion of new blood. There were changes, too, other than personnel. 'Originally, there had been no equipment at all. The cure for all injuries was a hot cloth. Hey, you weren't surprised that no-one was injured in those days, for the treatment was worse than the injury. But now they brought in this machine that you could give you infra-red and ultra violet rays. The latter was most popular because the guys could not wait to get under it to get a sun tan.'

Football occupied an alternative planet back then as opposed to now. The riches, the baubles and fashion statements, upon which today's players seem to place so much emphasis, scarcely existed. 'There were only three or four guys at Pittodrie who had a car – and I'm talking about when we were winning the championship. George Hamilton had one, so did Harry, Jackie Hather and Jimmy Mitchell. I didn't. I always looked upon it as a waste of money. I lived right in the middle of town and could walk anywhere. Most people travelled by bus. And it all meant that you were consequently in touch with your public. You couldn't avoid them, as you were sitting next to folk on the bus. It wasn't the glamorous occupation that it is now.'

Wishart wanted more than fancy wheels and a bronzed countenance; he sought a speedy graduation into the first team. He had two things in his favour. First, Davie Shaw, who had gone from player to coach in 1953, spent a lot of time educating the young players: 'In those days, the manager managed from his office, and the coach or trainer was the guy who tried to help you with your game. Shaw was of great assistance to me.' Second, Wishart was a clever passer and, allied to this, possessed a shot that could blister goalkeepers' fingers.

Essential to the force was a short back-lift which didn't offer goalies a sporting chance of spotting from whence the danger was coming.

So let's return to Wishart's assertion that managers managed from their offices. What of the Dons leader? David Halliday was familiar with the contours of a football pitch: as a player for Dundee, Sunderland, Arsenal and Manchester City, he had scored a phenomenal 303 goals in 396 matches. The scoring flamboyance did not translate to his job as manager, however. He appears to have been the ostensibly silent type. Yet the silence was effective. Since his arrival from the quaintly-entitled Yeovil and Petters United, he had piloted Aberdeen to a win over Rangers in the Scottish League Cup in 1945-46 (prior to its recognition as a fully-fledged competition) and lifted the Scottish Cup in 1947. And, of course, he would be charge in the halcyon days of 1955. But what of him as a man? Wishart recalls, 'He wasn't the kind of manager or coach you have nowadays who works with the players every day. He appeared on a Tuesday for the practice match between the first team and the reserves. He would stand at the tunnel, watching from afar. He hadn't a tracksuit on; he wore a suit and, no, he wasn't a snappy dresser. He didn't shout or pass comments, he just observed. On Saturdays he was there to give team talks. Really, he was the kind of fella you never got to know because you weren't in touch with him. I remember one day I was dropped and I went to see him to register my disquiet. He told me simply, "Bobby, you were in my team" (an indication that the directors interfered). I wasn't surprised, mind you. But, hey, even suppose he had picked the team, what a good get-out! I mean, you went in there, pretty annoyed, and thinking you had something to impart, but you were immediately deflated with what he was saying. And he was saying, "I think you're a good player and you should have been playing, but..." You landed back in the passageway without really saying very much at all.'

The time is appropriate to inspect the board of directors who, if you swallow the Halliday line, were intent on sticking their fingers in the playing pie. At that time, Willie Mitchell, the managing director of a licensed grocer's, was the chairman. His deputy was Charlie Forbes, a rather austere schoolteacher. Dick Donald, who had played for the Dons for five years before the War, brought a bit of warmth to their directorial number, and John Robbie perhaps a sprinkling of notoriety. Apart from being vital to Wishart's signature, he was the SFA man who had Rangers stalwart Willie Woodburn placed in the sine die cell in 1954: the offence? A head butt on a Stirling Albion player. 'Those directors were very much aloof,' says Wishart. 'We always travelled first class, but they were in their own compartment, so you never spoke to them. They didn't come in the dressing room, apart from Dick Donald, who'd appear before games and wish you well. No, you were very much left to your own devices; you were the player, you knew what you had to do, so you just had to get out there and do it. You also knew your place. It was very much a case of the Upstairs, Downstairs syndrome. At Dundee, Bob Shankly used to talk of 'Them Upstairs' as a necessary evil. But the other thing was that you never knew what was going on in the world of football, because no-one told you anything. You read in the newspaper that Leeds United were interested in you, or Chelsea. This all happened to me. In fact, Newcastle United came up and made a £25,000 offer for me, but I never even got consulted or told. But I knew first hand because I had been semi tapped. A guy who was very friendly with the manager, Stan Seymour, asked me if I would be interested in going down there.'

Wishart, possibly remembering how he'd failed to achieve a result in the manager's office, ignored any temptation to reprise the situation: 'Besides, it didn't bother you much because you knew that you were playing for the highest paying club in Britain.'

No-one at that time, it should be pointed out, dared take liberties with Aberdeen. Alex Young, nicknamed 'The Golden Vision' by Hearts fans because of his sublime skills, later confided to Wishart that the Dons had become the most feared team in the land. And this, despite the fact that there were several seasoned outfits around at the time. Aside from the traditional contenders, Celtic and Rangers, people talked in awe of Hearts' front three, Conn, Bauld and Wardhaugh. Hibs, meanwhile, were blessed with the Famous Five of Smith, Johnstone, Reilly, Turnbull and Ormond. Dundee, Clyde and St Mirren had good players. It was an exceptionally difficult league to win, then, far more so than today's premiership. But, as a collective, Aberdeen proved superior to anyone that 1954-55 season and that made me inordinately proud. A pupil of Kittybrewster primary school, I believe I was probably more proficient at rhyming off the Aberdeen team than I was my mathematics tables: Martin; Mitchell, Caldwell; Allister, Young, Glen; Leggat, Yorston, Buckley, Wishart and Hather.

I could not wait for my weekly visit to the South terracing. Preferably, I was stationed against the perimeter stone wall and thus within touching distance of my heroes. Weekly? My loyalty was such that I attended reserve matches as well, watching young men like Jim Clunie, Ian McNeill and George Mulhall beginning to shape their careers. First-team affairs were the ultimate delight, of course. If I were late in arriving, having walked from my home in Hilton Drive and perhaps having lingered too long salivating over notable additions to my autograph book, the crowd would pick me up and hand me down over their serried, cloth-capped ranks until I reached the safety of that wall. Here, there was a temporary relief from the fug of cigarette smoke – smoking being a fashion that seemed to fascinate everyone back then.

The tannoy system – a prototype of today's one that encourages you to 'Come on you Reds' – would spew out the popular music of the day. Trumpeter Eddie Calvert's 'Oh, Mein Papa' was a particular favourite, sending chills scurrying down my spine. Then the teams would emerge to the accompaniment of the delightful 'Bluebell Polka' – a tune I practised with great gusto on my dad's piano. The appreciation of the crowd sometimes obscured parts of the Jimmy Shand hit, but that was a small and acceptable negative. Then, with my preparation complete, it was match time: I owned a rattle (a product of my bottle-selling enterprise); I had a set of lungs to provide shrill support. Now it was up to those players to perform. But these were magical performers. I shut my eyes and can visualise them all now, particularly Graham Leggat sprinting in on goal from the right wing; Buckley stealing in like a whippet and making capital out of even bad passes; Hather introducing full backs to the innovative double-shuffle, a trick that inevitably left them floundering. Otherwise known as 'The Hare', Hather was the fastest man Wishart ever saw on a park, and yet he coupled speed with excellent ball control: 'You know, I heard the odd comment about how he wasn't the bravest winger they ever saw. But if they'd known that he was playing with one kidney. That was brave enough in itself, never mind the attentions of a couple of burly full backs. He was a very courageous wee fella.'

Aberdeen would need a generous helping of Hather's courage if they were to win the title. They had done nothing to enhance their league status in 1953-54 when they finished a distant ninth, ten points behind winners Celtic. But they were beginning to warm up in other ways, appearing in the 1953 and 54 Scottish Cup finals. They were beaten in both, first by Rangers (1-0, after a 1-1 draw) and Celtic, by 2-1. That second final was when I truly formalised my relationship with Aberdeen FC and became a fan for life. The minutiae surrounding that match is deeply implanted in my memory.

I am positioned, for once not at the Pittodrie perimeter wall, but in the living room of my home in Hilton Drive. Excitement dictates that I cannot sit down, but prefer to pace, nervously, from wall to wall. I look out on a lovely front garden that might have been designed by Capability Brown, and see the tall figure of my father. He is a schoolteacher by profession, but a horticulturalist by nature. The HMV radio is turned on and hope courses through my heart because we won our semi-final in a canter, slaughtering the mighty Rangers, 6-0. Then comes a team announcement. Joe O'Neill, whom my brother Michael professes to know, scored a hat-trick in that Rangers game, but he had fractured his skull and is missing from the line-up. Jim Clunie, Aberdeen's reserve centre half, suddenly finds himself in the alien position of inside left. I knew nothing of tactics in those days – perhaps I still don't – but the metrological office in my head informs me that a storm is imminent. Alec Young gives confirmation of the bad news when he puts through his own goal in the 50th minute. But this is football and the course of a match can alter very quickly. And so it unfolds: the inimitable Paddy Buckley equalises within 60 seconds. If there are wild scenes of jubilation in a sizeable portion of the 130,000 crowd, there is commensurate chaos in that Aberdeen living room on that day of 24 April 1954.

I go ape, jumping around the room in a frenzy of delight. I can see my father's face now. It is pressed hard against the front window. It's a concerned face, one that doesn't have an answer to the present conundrum. He's mouthing the words, 'What's wrong with you?' I'm too busy screaming to deliver an effective response. He rushes into the house, possibly intent on calling the emergency services. But soon his fears are becalmed: I'm telling him that the only problem is to find a cure for sheer elation. He returns to his garden. I return to the inevitable. Celtic, through the capabilities of Sean Fallon, make it 2-1 and take the Scottish Cup back to Parkhead. The day ends in tears. Rivers of them. My father, horticulture over, is presented with another conundrum: the kid he took to Pittodrie a few years ago –the kid who did everything but concentrate on the football – has obviously formed a deep attachment with the club in a short time. He is only nine years old.

But if that match impacted on me, it possibly slaughtered Wishart. Somewhat inexplicably, he found himself 12th man that day. His old pal, Harry Yorston, was similarly overlooked. His recollection comes at the expenditure of pain. 'They had the choice of two inside forwards, one very experienced in Harry, then myself, a natural in that position, left foot and all that. They gambled, took a chance. They had no need to do that. They must have had a rush of blood to their heads. I'm pretty sure it wouldn't have been Davie Halliday that came up with that one. Anyway, I reckon that's what lost them the game. Of course, I was a wee bit biased because I was sitting it out. Harry was out, too. That was the sad thing because Celtic weren't really a force to be reckoned with at that particular time. You had more concerns with Rangers and Hibs. But it was unfortunate. I'll put it that way.'

Wishart claims that this wasn't a defensive tactic and that Clunie was out to fulfil the forward role. Big Jim, he says, did not pursue the style of conventional centre halves: he was a guy who could put his foot on the ball and look to direct it to someone in a more influential position. A John Stones prototype, if you like. Without the price tag, of course. 'But there's a big difference to being where you can see the ball coming to you, and playing a team with your back to the enemy. It's a different concept altogether. Yes, there were two disconsolate guys that day. Harry and I were obviously hoping Aberdeen would win, but let's say we were a bit disappointed that we couldn't take part.'

Perhaps the lesson had been learned. Wishart and Hather were restored to the front line in the new season and Aberdeen began to put down their league marker so forcibly that the ground trembled. Four successive victories, over Stirling Albion, Dundee, Hibs and Motherwell gave them an impetus that they would rarely lose. Thirty-eight thousand fans subsequently came to Pittodrie to see if their heroes could eclipse the then current champions, Celtic. Unfortunately, they couldn't, the Glasgow team recording a 2-0 win and their centre half, Jock Stein, attempting a new method of defending: ripping Buckley's shorts from his backside. But this, the defeat, not the shorts shearing, was only a flaw on the radar screen: the Dons were soon returned to winning ways and their home form, in particular, removed the threat of Rangers and Hibs as authentic challengers. Rangers, in fact, were destroyed, 4-0, at Pittodrie, with a Buckley hat-trick and a typical Leggat counter delighting the home crowd. Aberdeen, requiring three points from their final three games, travelled down to Clyde in early April. A win would give them their first title in 52 years, provided Hearts did not leave Ibrox, their faces wreathed in smiles. An Archie Glen penalty gave the Dons victory. Over the city, Hearts were snarling rather than smiling. Defeat makes you snarl. Aberdeen were champions.

So, what changed from one season to the next? Why did a hitherto rather mercurial Dons side suddenly blossom into title winners? 'Modesty prevents me from saying,' a smiling Wishart recalls, 'I hadn't been playing in the team all that often but I came into the scheme of things in 54-55. That's not the whole story, though, or even a fraction of it. One thing I remember is that we didn't have many injuries. We were able to put the same team out week after week. And that helped a lot. That's why you could rattle off the team because the team picked itself. And there were no subs. With the pool system nowadays, folk will not be remembering teams as such. Another thing: we also had a very good home record.'

The celebrations that night were confined to a few bottles of champagne and a homecoming at Aberdeen's Joint Station that was somewhat low on fervour. Estimates differ as to the number of fans that greeted them, but it's probably safe to say it was anything between ten and 30. But were those fans who didn't attend simply acknowledging, if only subliminally, that they were nearing the end of a delicious lollipop? Everything was about to change and, unfortunately, not for the better. Halliday was first to abscond. He took over at Leicester City after having allegedly being told by the parsimonious directorship that no advancement in his salary was imminent. But the parsimony had equally damaging tendrils. The players who had performed with such distinction asked the directors for more finance and, like latter-day Oliver Twists, were sent away as if they had been guilty of ingratitude. 'Aberdeen stuck to the rule book,' Wishart remembers, 'In spite of their status as the highest paid club in Britain, they never paid over the odds.'

Discontent, owing to the short-sightedness of the Pittodrie board, proliferated among the playing staff. In spite of this disaffection, they managed to finish second to Rangers in the 1955-56 season and win the Scottish League Cup by beating St Mirren, this under the guidance of the newly-elevated Davie Shaw. The Aberdeen populace, possibly eager to atone for their embarrassing absence earlier that year, turned up in multitudes, and it's said 15,000 formed the welcoming committee. But trouble is never far from the surface when money, or more appropriately, the lack of it, is concerned. In the close season of 1956, the team went on a whistle-stop tour of Canada (principally) and New York. They sailed up the St Lawrence River on The Empress of France. It has been described as a very good tour. 'There wasn't any skulduggery going on,' Wishart claims. 'But we had a lad looking after us from the Canadian Football Association. He was in charge of the purse strings.' Presumably he had received a fiscal tutorial from the Aberdeen board of directors. 'He came from Fraserburgh, and I can tell you we had a helluva job getting money out of him. I'll never forget him.'

Neither would the Canadian press forget the new Aberdeen manager. Shaw was comfortable on the training pitch, but found it difficult to strike up an equally satisfactory relationship with sports reporters. They christened him Davie 'No Comment' Shaw. This, however, was only the beginning of the manager's woes. The ship was anything but happy. Mutinous thoughts prevailed. Harry Yorston lobbed a grenade into the boardroom by retiring from football, aged 28. The punishment that had been inflicted on Buckley's knees took its toll the same year. He went for a cartilage operation and it proved unsatisfactory. He retired. Age tapped on the respective shoulders of Alec Young and Jimmy Mitchell and both were released in 1958. Wishart reckons that both Fred Martin and Jackie Allister had their differences with Shaw. The influential Leggat departed for Fulham in 1958. It's as if a wrecking ball had been at work. Pittodrie became a demolition site. 'Apart from Fred Martin and Davie Caldwell,' he remembers, 'we were left with the left-wing triangle of Glen, Hather and I. The side just disintegrated and we didn't have the good, experienced reserves because we had sold most of them. Jackie Allister was a volatile kind of guy and I think Davie felt he wasn't going to fit in with his plans – that maybe he would be difficult to control. They fell out and we'd lost another good player. So, by the time we got to 1959, we were left with only five of the title-winning squad. By some freak – the draw favoured us greatly – we went to the Cup Final that year, only to lose 3-1 to St Mirren.'

League form had slipped ominously by then: sixth place in 56-57; 13th in 57-58; a similar performance in 58-59. The stench of disaster was in the air for a team now replete with pale imitations of the legendary figures of old. Was Shaw capable of leading the fumigation squad? Sadly, the answer was in the negative. Luckily for Shaw, however, there was no firing squad: Aberdeen, until recent times, have never been associated with sacking managers. Tommy Pearson, a former stalwart, came in as boss despite flourishing a curricula vitae that contained this alarming message: NPE – No Previous Experience. Shaw moved back to his role as trainer. Would Aberdeen pull themselves up by their jockstraps, or would they find their testicles squeezed even further?

CHAPTER 2

Ally, the Ultimate Warrior

IN TERMS OF GRANDEUR AND excess, the pre-season trial at Pittodrie – first team versus reserves – was a sepia-tinged event and therefore quite unable to compete with anything as colourful as the Lord Mayor's Show. But, if it scarcely stirred the senses, it occasionally delivered a sound bite as to the team's possible progression or, for that matter, regression. The 1960-61 event, however, simply scattered any negative preconceptions to the four winds. Charlie Cooke, a month or so short of his 18th birthday, delivered a calling card that was embossed in gold. Not only did he steal the show on 'stage', but he also bloody well produced and directed the production. These days, television pundits talk endlessly about the No. 10 slot. It's become the precious position, as if it never existed previously. Well, here, before our very eyes in the year of 1960, the definitive No. 10 was unveiled. Charlie had it all and then some more besides. His looks were such he might have pursued his luck in Hollywood, but the gifts didn't end there: he had wondrous ball control, a vast range of passing options, and a plethora of dribbling skills that made the mouth water and beg for more.

The unlucky soul in immediate receipt of this tour de force was Ian Burns. Now Burns, a part-timer and a committed and aggressive replacement for Jackie Allister, had a career in insurance, but no short-term policy could equip him for what was on offer that evening. Exertion often encouraged Burns' face to assume a reddish hue. By the end of these proceedings, his face replicated the colour of an Aberdeen pillar box. He had tried to deny Charlie Cooke space; he would have had more chance subduing an affray in Craiginches. The crowd, for their part, wanted to know the identity of this magnificent specimen who betrayed not even a semblance of first-night nerves. Not quite believing their luck, they wondered why he had arrived at a club that, at the time, was virtually auditioning for an appointment in the breakers' yard. The story should have been, like Cooke, complex. Instead, it was simple and over, indeed, before an eye blinked. Bobby Calder, the extraordinary little man who scouted so many stars for Aberdeen, had worked the oracle again: 'Just think Aberdeen, Charlie. Don't let it leave your mind. You'll love it there – and be in the first team in no time at all.' In effect, by convincing this adopted Greenockian (Charlie was born in St Monans, Fife) to ignore overtures from nearly every club in the land and travel north from Renfrew Juniors, he had completed his life's work. As far as we Dons fans were concerned, we had found a legitimate hero and also confirmation of our wildest dreams. A few thousand of us went home that night drooling over an envisaged golden future.

Today, over half a century later, I still wonder what in damnation went wrong, because it did go wrong. But, there were mitigating circumstances in that Charlie was a law unto himself and, on occasion, was living life to its limits. Long-serving full back Jim Whyte recalls the inconsistency in his make-up. 'Some days, he'd go out for a couple of laps to warm up; he'd be away like the clappers, a full lap in front of everybody. The next time, he'd be a lap behind. So one day he was busting a gut, the next he couldn't be bothered.' It was the same in competitive games; brilliance one day, average or worse the next. Could it have been that the rather irregular lifestyle was responsible?

But, rather than focusing on what would be a rather unfortunate ending, for the club if not the player, let us first examine the credentials of the other man who was responsible for the signing of Cooke. If sporting history had a face, it would most likely frown on Tommy Pearson. Although he'd enjoyed a charmed existence as a footballer with Newcastle United and latterly Aberdeen, the charm forfeited its sheen after six years as manager of the Dons. Those years mirrored life living on a switchback: it was Cooke-esque: exhilarating at times, tortuous at others. The training, let's say, was scarcely exemplary. Whyte illustrates a typical Friday session. 'You didn't need to get stripped. You'd just take off your jacket, roll up your trousers and put your spikes on. Then it was a couple of shuffles down the grandstand side and that was it. Honestly, that was training under Pearson. Some of the players stripped, some didn't, Jimmy Hogg, for instance, used to roll up his trousers, saying, "F*** this..."'

Nevertheless, there was a side to Pearson that was comfortably distanced from incompetence. Some of today's managers are apprehensive of youth. It would appear we have one at Aberdeen at the moment. Pearson, though, had undeniable bravery and a sense of adventure: he may have been a managerial tenderfoot, but he pledged to give the young ones their chance and, by God, he did just that. In doing so, he signed two of the most influential players who would ever wear the red jerseys. Cooke, in spite of his foibles, was one. Alistair Stewart Shewan, who joined in 1959, was the other. I shall come back to him in a moment.

First, I am anxious to talk to Cooke, who now runs a coaching school in Cincinatti. I believe I first met him in Valencia back in 1975 when Scotland were trying to qualify for the European Championships, and I was attempting to hold

on to my job with the *Scottish Sun*. Neither Scotland nor I succeeded. I cannot
remember the exact exchange between us because I was comprehensively pixilated when I fell upon a reception for the international team. But I fear time
and strong drink had removed the gloss from my adolescent hero worship and
perhaps I was not as respectful as I should have been. Hoping to atone, all these
years later, I send an email to the soccer school's Ohio headquarters and their
response is delivered in the time it takes to trim an eyebrow. They promise to
send the missive on. There is no reply. Cooke, I can only assume, doesn't appreciate my anxiety. Perhaps he remembers Valencia. I don't. What I do recall is
sleeping in the wrong room and keeping an SFA selector out of his bed – a story
delineated in full in an e-book of mine, *Fingerprints of a Football Rascal*. There
again, considering the wild stories that pursued Cooke in his four years at Aberdeen, maybe he cares not to remember that segment of his past. The story, I'm
confident, will manage without him.

Engaging with Shewan presents no such problems. He is an old friend and I
travel to Peterhead to find him. It might be said I've been an infrequent visitor to
the Blue Toun, the infrequency amounting to one visit in seven decades. It was
a memorable one, however, co-ordinated by the chief officer at the local prison.
My memory fails to sort out the fine details: he was uncle of my then girlfriend,
or perhaps the uncle of my girlfriend's friend. No matter. It's still clear what
occurred. We were having dinner and debating what might happen were hanging to be abolished. A tough and resolute old hombre, he recommended that the
miscreants should be loaded onto cargo planes, flown across the Atlantic and
deposited over the rainforests of the Amazon. Without parachutes, he added.

Now, I'm back in Peterhead all these years later. My host this time is no less
uncompromising than the previous one, by reputation, anyway. Shewan's 75
years on earth should not be allowed to belie his capabilities. He was, and still
is, you suspect, a serious force and the suspicion is that anyone attempting to be
cheeky with him cares nothing of his personal longevity. He was not the kind
of professional footballer you find flouncing around in iridescent boots and
claiming hamstring injuries at any given moment. He belonged to the variety
who refused to recognise the properties of pain, or acknowledge the legacies of
injury.

So if Cooke provided the flamboyance, Shewan weighed in with durability,
reliability and of course a spirit that was truly irrefrangible (sic). The stats supplement the compliments. He played 320 consecutive games for Aberdeen from
the January of 1962 to 1969. This included friendlies and testimonial matches.
Admittedly, he was slower off the blocks than Cooke, who was pitched feet first
into the team after that historic trial match. The lad from Cummingston would

have to wait until the club was satisfied that he had served his apprenticeship. But he was proficient in the art of catch-up and, ultimately, he would be of far greater assistance to all around him than Cooke.

The salutary tale of Ally Shewan unfolds, sometimes emotionally, one winter's afternoon, in his lovely bungalow on the fringes of the town. His beloved father, he admits, was responsible for putting in the foundations for that long and (mostly) distinguished career at Pittodrie. 'We were close but families were always close in those days. We used to go for a walk on a Sunday – some days we'd wear a tie. We were never church-going people, but us kids went to Sunday school. You learned how to live and how to behave early in life.'

His father encouraged him to love and respect sport and never to give up, however prohibitive the cost. An inveterate Dons fan, he took the young Ally to see them at every opportunity. The youngster's enthusiasm sometimes overtook him. He kicked every ball and had to be restrained from kicking those fans in front of him, in the south terracing. His father died when Ally was 15, but the dream of becoming a footballer suddenly became more alive than ever. A two-footed player, modelling himself on Graham Leggat, he turned out first for Cuminestown in the Banff and Welfare league and became their top scorer. Then it was onwards and upwards to Formartine United.

Soon, the team's needs dictated a switch to centre half, and Shewan began to experience the life of pain common to those who deposit their bodies on the line. One day he hurt his ankle badly. Typically, he insisted in playing on. Nothing in the prognosis included optimism, but his manager, Eddie Edmonds, developed a plan that included driving him 60-plus miles from his home to Aberdeen for an appointment with a physiotherapist in Torry. 'What he did to that ankle, I don't know,' says Shewan. 'But I passed oot wi' the pain. And, you know this, I came oot o' there walkin' normally. Oh, I started limpin' but he told me I didnae need tae limp. So Eddie says, "Right, we'll see ye on Saturday." And he did. We never missed one game with Formartine. My father had told me if I was doing a job, I had to stick in. That was me stickin' in. Oh, I remember some bloke rattlin' me in a tackle and sayin' that I'd get plenty o' that in this game. So I just started rattlin' back.'

With 'rattlin' back' a speciality, it might have been a declaration from the tarot cards that Shewan was destined for Pittodrie. Teddy Scott, Aberdeen's reserve trainer-cum coach, came to lodge with the Shewans and Scott really helped to push him on after a successful trial. The great George Hamilton would come in on afternoons and encourage the youngster to join him. Ally was shown how to head a ball properly. 'I was 5ft 9in and yet I was beating the six footers for high balls.'

Another conversion was ahead of him – this time to left back. His rhythm never missed a beat. 'I was in digs with a Mrs Robertson in Great Western Road, along with Gordon Sim, Dessie Herron, Charlie Cooke and Willie Callaghan. Ma sister came in to see me play left back in one game. She phoned me and said, "There was a mannie sittin' beside me in the stand, and he was telling me to look at that player, kicking the ball with either foot. The mannie described it as perfect and beautiful." He was Gordon Sim – I had taken his place! Oh, how my father would have loved to see me playing for Aberdeen.'

It's inevitable that we'll arrive at his relationship with Charlie Cooke sooner rather than later. So let's get it on. I ask Shewan if he liked him. You imagine he's trying – and succeeding – to keep the enthusiasm out of his response. 'Well, he was in digs wi' me, but he was difficult to get through to. I think he was going around with a bit of stuff, mostly: he was never with the crowd. He was a boy in Aberdeen, that's for sure; always last in at the digs. But then, it takes all types. There's nobody perfect. As a player, he was good, really good, and he was a great dribbler. Mibbe I shouldna say this, but he wisna a team player. He only passed the ball when he couldna find a way through. He played for himself. I remember in one match he passed to me three or four times when I was covered by people. The crowd were shoutin', "Oh, come on, Shewan, you're a hopeless bastard!" I always remember Charlie for that. I told him after the game, "See if you do that to me again, I'll break yer leg!" He just looked at me.'

In order to escape what would have been instant retribution from a greater power, there was no alternative but for Cooke to keep his counsel. 'He went away to Dundee not long after that. Maybe he was glad tae get oot! You know, I think Charlie got off with a lot because the crowd loved him. Tommy Pearson wisna really able to control him. If Eddie Turnbull had been there, he wid have just put him in his place right away. There again, Charlie wouldn't have done for Eddie, 'cos he was too much of a ball player, but greedy with it.'

In spite of the greed, Shewan is still ready to acknowledge the virtuosity. 'We were down training at the Bridge of Don barracks. A wee Chinese ball juggler came down from His Majesty's Theatre, where he was appearing, to entertain us. Charlie took over and did everything that the Chinese did – and more besides.'

Cooke, it was said at the time, had a voracious appetite for the good life. The allegations of heavy drinking were confirmed some years later when he admitted to Jeff Powell of the Daily Mail that he filled in a questionnaire on alcoholism – and given up when he'd answered the first few questions in the affirmative. He was playing for Chelsea then. He is in Cincinatti now, teetotal and somewhat embarrassed by his eventful past. Or so it's claimed.

Shewan, in contrast, enjoyed a couple of pints after matches, but his preference was for recreation other than elbow bending. His colleague, Martin Buchan, who went on to captain Manchester United, was never short of a witty word. He had two for Shewan: 'Hello, Shagger!' The nickname chimed effortlessly with reality. Shewan liked his women – and they in turn liked him. 'I remember I took a bit of stuff hame and we went through to the kitchen. We were just about t'get there when Mrs Robertson came in. "Get that slut out of here," she roared. I was just young at the time. So, next morning, I apologised. "We don't allow that in here," she said. She was a fantastic landlady who kept us all in order. And she was quite right when she pit her fit doon. It wid have been a hoo-ers' hoose otherwise!'

Shewan later decamped to another landlady in Donbank Terrace, where, ironically, I spent my formative years. He lived next door to Jimmy McGregor, a delightful little guy who was a compositor in the Press & Journal, where I made my first tentative steps in journalism as a racing sub-editor. All the co-incidences came together in the mid sixties when Jimmy introduced me to Ally and his colleague and best friend, Ernie Winchester, in the Palace, that subterranean coffee shop in Union Street. Shewan fretted over one of his team mates who also shared the Donbank digs. George Kinnell played centre half for Aberdeen but, being a cousin of Jim Baxter, there were times when he was more interested in playing the field. 'He was a boy. He used to come in on a Friday night, late. He'd been oot at Bucksburn: his wife Christine came from there. You could smell the drink on him. "George, you have tae stop that, man," I'd say. Yet he'd go oot the next day and play a stormer. He was a great centre half. One Friday, he says, "Ally, I took yer advice – I hivnae had a drink the night!" The next day, that was the worst game I'd ever seen him play!'

The Kinnell anecdote prompts a personal visit to that area in the brain where memories are stacked.

The sixties have begun swinging. Me? I'm swinging on the star of Aberdeen FC, even though it's a falling star. My lust for all things Dons is no less than it was when I nearly gave my father heart failure back in 1954. In fact, it's grown exponentially. I now go to matches wearing the full paraphernalia of fanaticism. I mean, I've got the scarf, the red and white bonnet and red socks. My mates are similarly attired. When funds permit, we travel all over the country watching our team. Oh, and I have a blazer with an Aberdeen supporters' club (AFC SC) insignia on the breast pocket.

Good, old George Kinnell is a hero and a leviathan in the centre of defence. Even in my sleep, I can hear his encouragement echoing all over Pittodrie. The Fife accent is compelling and exhorts players to battle. 'Way N-O-W-W-W!'

He can do no wrong in my star-struck eyes. At Christmas, he is invited to the Aberdeen supporters' club dinner-dance, which is being held in the Imperial hotel. He and Norrie 'The Skull' Davidson are guests of honour. They are positioned at either end of the top table. They seem to be enjoying themselves, judging by the cargo of beer they are shifting. George stands up and clears his throat. Is he about to make a speech? Yes, it appears he is. I'll wager it'll be a memorable one, straight out of the General McArthur textbook. It's memorable all right. 'Norrie!' he shouts down the table, 'I'm gaun for a pish!'

Before we return to the Shewan narrative, let's monitor what was going on with the Pearson-led Aberdeen. Yes, he had a youth policy, but there were worrying signals that he had a fixation for footballing greybeards. Hugh Baird, brought back from Leeds by Shaw, had left his best in England but was retained to play until 1962. A 34-year-old Tommy Ring came in for one season only in 1963 and figured twice; Andy Kerr, 33, managed two campaigns but was picked on only 14 occasions. These were not the players for a restoration job.

Then there was the embarrassment of the Armando Maskarennis affair. Aberdeen announced that they had signed an Indian superstar. The fans couldn't wait for his arrival. But when he arrived, he immediately disappeared and his future became swathed in mystery. Finally, one foggy Saturday, he made his debut in a bounce game. Stirling Albion were due to call, but had been held up in the fog. Those present wished the fog would shroud Pittodrie and mask the deficiencies of Maskarennis. He was beyond hopeless. Soon, we were informed that he was an international hockey player and not a footballer. We had worked the latter part out for ourselves.

Now, there was a carnival just off the beach promenade but, if memory serves, it was a rollercoaster short of being the real deal. No matter. Pittodrie provided a more than rocky ride. Aberdeen finished sixth in Pearson's first full season of 1960-61. Cooke, demon of the dribble, scored ten times. Gleefully, I watched them slaughter Rangers, 6-1, in the second last home game of the season. But the glee dissipated the following term. The highlight was a 10-3 victory over Clyde in the Scottish Cup. I was one of thousands of fans who marched up King Street and into Broad Street, home of the Press & Journal, and obliged the photographers to get busy. The low spots? Two back-to-back 3,000 home crowds, against Falkirk and then Kilmarnock. You wondered how a club could exist on such paltry attendances.

The next season, manure still figured prominently on the digest. We beat Raith Rovers, 10-0, in the league, then lost, 2-1, to them in the Scottish Cup, at Kirkcaldy. There was crowd trouble, as I mentioned in the prologue, and several arrests. My pal Ivor Finnie was apprehended but, fortuitously, escaped when two policemen hurled him against a door. It opened and Ivor ran free.

Mediocrity continued to run amok in 63-64: fans' apathy turned to anger the next season when Cooke, having proved himself a flawed superstar, was sold to near neighbours Dundee for £40,000. We all knew that his genius would flourish one day, provided he took a grip on himself. But, sadly, this would not happen at Pittodrie. So, we gave him away for a pittance. The bottom of the glass was reached in February of 1965. East Fife were held to a 0-0 draw away, in the Scottish Cup first round, then they came north and slapped their hosts in the face, 1-0. Tommy Pearson was officially toast.

We're back with Shewan, the ultimate warrior, for two amusing moments concerning Baird. 'I remember in one practice game, he missed an open goal at the Beach End – at that time there was just terracing there. He picked up the ball, vaulted over the wall, ran up the terracing to the top, ran along it and then down the other side. Then he threw the ball back to us. Davie Shaw asked him what he'd done that for. Hugh replies, "Ah needed a bit of training!" Another day we were doin' spikes in sprints. Hughie went up in the stand, above the players' entrance, and when Davie came out, he threw a bucket of cold water over him. That was Hughie. What a man he was – what a character!'

Baird, luckily for him, was long gone by the time Eddie Turnbull arrived. Turnbull's six years of managerial bombast and brilliance will be dealt with in some appropriate depth in the next chapter, but it's critical that we discuss his relationship with Shewan at this juncture. The pugnacious Shewan was Eddie's kind of fella, the kind who accepted that brick walls were built to be run through. Pearson had made him team captain in 1964, and Turnbull saw no reason to tamper with the status quo. Sadly, in 1967, he was given a reason to change his mind. This is a matter that Shewan is slightly reluctant to talk about, but I remind him that this is a book about the truth. I put it to him that he was in a cinema with a lady – whilst he was married to his first wife. 'Yes, I misbehaved,' he laughs. And Turnbull was waiting outside in his car? 'No, he wisna. It was ma father in law. Me and this lady went to wait for a bus after leavin' the Odeon. The next thing is my father-in-law – he was a policeman – came up and took us both by the ear doon to the car (this must have been one brave guy). I told him to get to hell. I had t'fight him off, really. Anyway, he went doon t'Eddie and told him about it. That's why I lost my captaincy. Harry Melrose took over. It didn't make a lot of difference. Eddie always told me to look after the defence. We still had a great relationship. Hey, he was good about it and, what's more, he was right in what he did. It's not the done thing if you're captain of a team.'

So, now, Aberdeen had a new leader in Melrose. But it was still Shewan to whom many looked for leadership, particularly on the sand dunes of Balmedie. But not everyone appreciated the pace that was set. 'Eddie used to say to me, "Ally, take them round." I was always leader of the pack. He'd also say,

"See that sand dune o'er there (the highest een, of course). I want you to take them tae the top, right back down again and back tae here." Oh, the complaints. The hill was a massive thing – hundreds of feet high. I was lucky. I was born fit and I loved ma training. A lot didn't. Tubby Ogston would say, "F***'s sake, slow doon!" Tubby had a big stature and wisna fit. But I wisna going to slow doon. I wisna the fastest but I wisna slow. And I had stamina. Martin Buchan and Ian Taylor told me a couple of years ago that they called me after some horse. Can't remember its name. But it was a fast horse.'

As already stated, Shewan's dedication to his profession was not universally appreciated. On the 1967 evening of Aberdeen's 2-0 Scottish Cup final defeat by Celtic, the club retreated to their Gleneagles lair. Turnbull had missed the match through illness, but two of the younger players didn't miss with what they considered a jape. Jinky Smith and Frank Munro, both of whom had joined Aberdeen since the Turnbull revolution, offered Shewan a sip of beer. 'I spat it out. One of them had pissed in it. I said to them, "By Christ, if I ever come across either of you on a football field again, whether you're on my side or no', I'll break yer necks – aye, and yer legs." Fancy doin' that to your friend. But that was their bit o'fun. Ye see, a lot of them took umbrage at me being sae professional, if you like. But, remember, I was just doin' it a' for ma dad.' Shewan admits it was fear that fine-tuned such professionalism and set up this incredible record of consecutive games played. 'I was always scared that I would miss a game and that somebody could go in my place and keep it. We once played Dunfermline in the Scottish Cup. I broke two toes in a tackle – I'd kicked somebody's boot. Next night, we had a replay because of the weather. Eddie asked me how I was. I told him I was alright, that I'd be there. And I was. That's why they called me the Iron Man – the nickname I got in America when I played for the Washington Whips.'

Shewan, who cannot countenance false modesty, continues, 'I still canna understand this injury that the modern players get: the hamstring. There was nothing like that back then. Ridiculous! I laughed when some stupid reporter called Ryan Jack the Iron Man. He was aff with a hamstring injury! I pit something on Facebook. I was bein' interviewed and this guy asked if I'd ever had a hamstring. I said, "It's something you get in the butcher's, isn't it?" Honest t'God, you get a wee strain, you run it off. I think it's doon to the kind of trainin' they get. They run about and it's what like girls do. Oh, it really annoys me. And what about the celebrations? When we scored, we wis a' delighted; we used to shake each other hand's and that was it. There was none of this carry on, slidin' along on knees, dancin' at corner flags. I think it incites people, apart from makin' themselves look stupid. They practice these things; mebbe they should concentrate on practicing their skills. A lot of modern players seem to say, "Look at me: best dressed, lovely boots." You know something: they couldna lace m'boots!

'And what about this carry-on in the penalty box? Half of them are no' lookin' at the ball, but at their opponents. Referees should get the gither and have a blether about it, because it's makin' life difficult for them. Start takin' their names. Second time, send them off! And if they have any problems with the SFA, they should get together and go on strike. Away back, you just looked at the ball comin' from a corner kick. You either headed it away, or the boy beat you. That's the way it should be done, but none of this jersey pullin' or whatever. You know, that put me right off football. It's not the game as I knew it any more. Honestly, I wouldna bother if I saw another game again. It's horrible to watch. I remember we played Blackpool in a friendly, and I was playin' against Stanley Matthews. I was just young at the time. He came up to me afterwards, and says that I had the right attitude and to stick in. That sort of thing made me a better player, and gave me a better idea about the game and what it should be.'

These recollections are stirring memories of days gone down. By this time, I've moved on from my fantasies and I'm content with my lot. I have my job in the Press & Journal, and a colleague called Peter Brown and I have just won the Sporting Chronicle naps table. My share of the prize money – 50 quid – goes on a sapphire ring for the girl to whom I've become engaged. For various reasons, principally my quest for journalistic stardom, she will not become my wife – my eyes are set firmly on the bedlam of Fleet Street – but I don't know this at the time. Jimmy Forbes, a legendary sports writer on the Evening Express, is putting rumours around that I've been seen emerging early morning from a big house in the Chanonry, Old Aberdeen, where a professor's daughter has been entertaining me. What if my fiancée hears of this? I rush up to Forbes' office and confront him and indeed tell him he'll be exiting by the second-floor window if there is any repetition of this scurrilous gossip. His brother, Gordon, who is my immediate boss on the subs' table, hears of the dispute and takes me to task over it. Now there is a thoroughly strained atmosphere in the office.

Yet there is an antidote to all this: my devotion to the Dons. A couple of times a week, just before starting my evening shift in Broad Street, I meet the guys – Ally, Ernie and Jimmy McGregor, who really is a treasure. When I'm working late in Broad Street, he runs me home on his red motor bike. On one Palace occasion, we discuss everything from Ernie Winchester's new car – it's a red Vauxhall VX 4/90 – to a centre half who has incurred Ernie's displeasure. Roy Barry, of Hearts (it may have been Dunfermline) is the unfortunate subject. There is a score to settle on Saturday, says an emphatic Ernie, punching his hand. The score is duly settled on the day. My memory tells me Barry is duly poleaxed.

Back in the Shewan parlour, I tiptoe lightly around the next subject, and suggest to my host that he and Ernie were a couple of mean buggers. Ally is perhaps not exactly thrilled by this suggestion. 'I would never call us that. I was never a dirty player, but a player who looked after himself. I learned early on that if you didna look after yourself, you would land on the sidelines. There were a lot of mean players around, you know. Some fantastic players, but they had that bit of go about them.' Did any players scare him? 'I didn't worry who I was playin' against. If it was a 50-50 ball, I'd always be there. Right in. I says: if it's goin' to happen, it will happen. I got stuck right in. And then a lot of people began to get scared of me! I remember Willie Henderson sayin', "Oh, my God, I'm gettin' out of here and goin' over to the other side (wing)." '

Jimmy Johnstone? 'The first time I saw him, it was a bad winter and we'd missed about four games. Pittodrie was playable and there was this reserve match against Celtic. So Eddie's put on half his first team. I wanted to play just to keep myself fit. I had a habit of always looking at the No.7 just to see what like they were early on. I see Wee Jinky come and I thought, "It'll be a good game today, seeing the size of him." Oh, my God, that was the only time I got the run-around. In my career. What a player! Fantastic! I went up to him at the end and shook his hand. I told him he'd played well, but added, "You won't do that to me again." He recalled that later when we met again. What I did was stand a bit closer. I wisna dirty with him – I got the ball, but I got the man as well. It was allowed back then. The same with Willie Henderson. People used to love coming to see me bounce Willie off the wall. He went across the track a few times. Nothing dirty, just hard. I couldna be dirty to anyone.'

Shewan smiles. Even the smile is formidable. So, I tell him how I once interviewed a rugby league forward called Doug Laughton and he'd told me how he and his cohort, Jim Mills, enjoyed hurting fellow players. It was a case of Mills and swoon. I go back to a corollary of my original question: did Shewan enjoy inflicting the pain? Shewan is as resolute as he was when confronted by a wing magician. 'My enjoyment came from getting the ball. I don't think I hurt anybody – just Derek Dougan (Los Angeles Wolves), when I was playing for the Whips, in the final of the USA championship. Eddie Turnbull told me to hurt him. Tommy McMillan was getting a hard time off Derek. Eddie says, "Ally, get in the middle and sort that bugger out." The first time the ball came down, it was Dougan who headed it. Came the shout, "Ally, what did I put you in there for?" The next time the ball came down, my fist went right in to the solar plexus. He was winded for a while. Eddie was delighted. They won their section and we won ours, so we had a grand finale which, unfortunately, they won, 6-5 (a Shewan own goal settled matters). Derek and I shook hands before the game. Eddie had told me to sort him out at the first corner. Same again. Down he went. It was done in such a way that the referee didn't see. Anyway, at the next corner, I woke up on the ground. He'd stuck the heid on me and then stood on m'fingers. Broke three of them! This was early on in the game. So, he came and helped me up. "Now, Ally, let's get on with the f***in' game," he says. We did, but there wis a few scrimmages in that final. Wee Paddy Wilson was involved. The next thing I saw was him and Chalky White running up the terracing after one of their players. There was real bad blood that night. It was some game, though. Oh, my God, Frank Munro was just magnificent. He scored a hat-trick. He wisna much of a trainer and had a problem with his weight. But he was a great player and no mistake.'

Talk of great players brings us, organically, to a tale about Bertie Auld, of Celtic. Shewan cannot remember the exact score, but it was one of those ritual humiliations that Aberdeen experienced on occasion at Parkhead. There was ice on the park and, to all intents and purposes, the game should have been postponed. Big Yogi Hughes was adapting to conditions by playing in a pair of baseball boots, and consequently was the only player who could retain his balance. Shewan watched Auld out on the right wing. He was sitting on the ball, arms cheekily folded. The situation was intolerable. 'I ran out there and he was laughin' at me. I slid right in on the ice and he went right up in the air. It wisna even a foul because I got the ball. In fact, he was actually booked for sittin' on the ball. That was my experience of Bertie Auld. He wisna very happy. At all. "Ya bastard!" he shouted. I got a right mouthful. I didn't want to hurt him, really, but it was my style. My thigh was red raw afterwards; it was worth it.'

I'm studying the vitality of my old friend and marvelling at it. He originally modelled himself on Graham Leggat and the decision served him well. But, what if he had chosen to simulate the career of other, less dedicated, players? Had he done this, he might have left the rails and tumbled down the embankment of life. 'I modelled myself on people's antics on the field, not their social antics. Oh, I could take a few beers, but that was it. I wasna for going' out and havin' a session with the boys.' I relate the Imperial hotel story about Kinnell and Davidson. He laughs. 'What a pair they were! When we were over in America, Jim Baxter and George were playing with Sunderland. We took them on. Afterwards, we went for a couple of beers. That's all we had. But every night they got absolutely pissed. The manager, Ian McColl, tried to send them home, but they wouldn't go. When we played them, one of the local boys told us there was a nice, quiet wee lounge if we wanted to drink. We invited George and Jim along. Which was a mistake. And yet the talent they had – fantastic!'

We return to the man who was most compatible with Shewan, despite their respective strong personalities. Eddie Turnbull imported discipline and consistency to Aberdeen. 'We were very unpredictable before he came. Whose fault was it? I think it was the manager's; Eddie used his authority and you wouldn't cross him. Tommy was too soft and Davie (Shaw) was a bit soft as well. They were nice men. But, say, Alex Ferguson, you wouldn't cross him, either. He must have modelled himself on someone like Eddie. But Eddie's theory was so good. He always said that if you've got no defence, you've got nothing and that if the defence looks after everything, the forwards will score. I remember playing The Swivel. If I was up the park and someone kicked the ball the other way, Chalky White would be behind the centre half, Tam McMillan. Similarly, if Chalky was up the park and the ball came over Tam's heid, I'd be there t'get it. It worked a treat.'

I'm taking breaks whilst writing this chapter. During one of them, I turn on the television and watch Stewart Regan being photographed with his new performance director, Malky Mackay. Regan is the man who, in my opinion, has cursed Scottish football with his lack of vision. You suspect he would have difficulty identifying illness in a hospital. The SFA has plunged itself into another needless controversy – with the appointment of the author of text messages that were considered to be racist, sexist and homophobic. Meanwhile, there's Ally Shewan, 320 games not out, six years never missing a game; the love of the game and the fear of rejection keeping him going. Yet he is missing from the hallowed room that is the SFA Hall of Fame. Will this ridiculous lot ever learn? Why is our ruling body so purblind to matters of real importance?

It's fast approaching the time I must leave Shewan and Peterhead. We have explored the nice memories, visceral times, embarrassing moments. But what about the most unpleasant chapter of them all? By this, I'm referencing She-wan's premature departure from Aberdeen at the end of the 1968-69 season. He was 29. We have studiously avoided this, but it cannot be ignored any longer. He tells me he could have gone on playing for another six years at least. Instead, after the shortest of stints in Australia, he returned to play and manage for another six in the Highland League. It's not that Shewan is afraid of relating the end-game story; it's just that he's unwilling to over-dramatise the situation.

'It wasn't unpleasant, but I found it very difficult to digest. At the end of that season, they asked me to sign another contract. I says, "no." They asked why. Charlie Forbes was the chairman. I says, "It's just like this, Mr Forbes, there's a lot of guys leaving here and they're getting free transfers, going to another club and getting three or four thousand pounds in their hands to sign. What am I getting to sign?" He told me they didn't do that. I went on, "Well, I havena had a testimonial, or benefit match, nothing like that. It's ten years since I signed provisional. The last six years, I've never missed a game." I was really proud of that. Well, they didn't count "provisional" and wouldna pay.

'Ernie Winchester had gone to Australia just before this. He got in touch with me and said it was fine over there. So I went over, with the proviso that if I came back, Aberdeen got first choice. It didna really work out for me because it wisna very well organised; they promised me a part-time job, but it didna come to fruition. So I telt them I was leavin' Sydney and going home. I was only there for a couple of months.'

Shewan returned, disillusioned. But there was another roadblock of disillusion ahead. He went down to Pittodrie and told them he was back. Eddie Turnbull took him aside and informed him he didn't think Shewan would be playing for them again. 'That man (Charlie Forbes) spoiled everythin' for ye,' he said. 'Eddie must have said something to him. He wisna a very popular man after that, was Charlie Forbes. I told Eddie it was okay, as long as I knew the score. The board didna like me leavin'. The only one who spoke to me was Chris Anderson, a really nice man. Hey, heartbreak didna come into it, but I was really disappointed, because these guys weren't as good as me and they were away and getting four, five or six thousand pounds, a lot of money back then. Yet they wouldna give me a testimonial. "We don't do that at Aberdeen." Oh, no? What they did do was hand out plenty of tickets for the cinemas, though. Dick Donald owned them all.'

Alistair Shewan, aside from a few unfortunate memories, is a man at peace. He is married to his third wife, Isobel, and describes her as a wonderful woman. They travel the world together and have been to Hong Kong, Singapore, Bali and, most recently, Vietnam. They plan to visit Colditz this year and also Indonesia. Aberdeen FC remains close to his heart, but he insists on being objective about the team. I ask him if he thinks we'll win on Sunday. We are talking, you'll note, two days before the 2016 League Cup final. 'I hope they win, but I canna see it,' he begins. 'The manager is too careful – I think Derek does this every game: the first half he's always too wary. Players like Ash Taylor; he's nae good enough and has given away a lot of goals. There are always mistakes and that's what has cost them. They were doin' a lot of sittin' back. The square passin'…'

They say it takes all sorts to make this life. By this token, my old friend Alistair Stewart Shewan is the sort of the earth.

CHAPTER 3

You're in Eddie's Army Now

RESTORATION WORK ON the famous Aberdeen began in the February of 1965. It came quickly, spectacularly and violently, like a storm blowing in from the near-by North Sea. The project manager was Eddie Turnbull, once a member of Hibs' Famous Five forward line, now a pejorative football boss from Queen's Park. He offered everything that was sorely required: dynamism allied to despotism, reality as opposed to delusion, industrial language in contrast to sophistry. The players, even those with a potential for cluttered thinking, realised they now were occupying a different world, a professional world. They knew their lives would be subject to irrevocable change. The words of Chalky Whyte perhaps best described the metamorphosis. 'That's when I realised I was playing for a professional fitba club. Up until then, I'm no' saying it was a glorified junior team, but it had been run more or less like that.'

On the first morning of the new regime, it wasn't long before the grounds-man was looking for a darkened room in which to lay his fevered brow. Turn-bull ordered shuttles across the park. This prompted an observation from Ernie Winchester, who told his new boss they weren't allowed on the pitch after a Wednesday. Ernie was to learn that observations were discouraged. Turnbull provided a rhetorical question. 'Do you want a good f***ing park, or a good f***ing team?' There was a noticeable absence of footballs. Someone was sent to Peter Craigmyle's sports shop in King Street and, suddenly, each player had a ball. The weights and dumb-bells, so beloved by the previous regime, were immediately discarded on the orders of the manager. The word went out: body circuits only.

The sea change, as far as methods and equipment were concerned, then, was quite dramatic. What occurred on the personnel side of it might have been contracted for a lengthy run at the local Tivoli theatre. Tubby Ogston, the goalkeeper who had become a fixture and fitting at Pittodrie, was immediately and perhaps unfairly identified as a passenger and one who didn't pay his fare. Whyte recalls, 'Ach, Eddie couldnae stand Tubby. I'd just got into the first-team pool: there were nae substitutes, but I was the 12th man. Turnbull took me down to Hearts and I was sitting in the dug-out with him. He's saying, "F***in' Ogston – the useless bastard! I'm getting Robert Clark up. He's comin' here – I'm no' pittin' up wi' that." And, true to his word, he brought Bobby up from Queen's Park within weeks. Maybe another reason for his dislike of Tubby was because of training. We were doing circuits and Tubby was about half a mile behind everybody. Tubby says, "Mr Turnbull, I don't do that. I'm a goalkeeper!" Turnbull rounded on him. "A goalkeeper my arse – you're a fitba player!"'

Ogston, of course, was not the only target for the trenchant tongue of Turnbull, and this leads us, organically, to the Nun's Story. This one, you are warned, does not have the beauty or elegance of Audrey Hepburn to embellish it. The team were training at nearby Linksfield Stadium. A creche was being held there simultaneously, with nuns supervising the children. The players were occupied with a drill known as 'The Circle'. As soon as the ball got knocked out of 'The Circle', another one was thrown in. At one point, a ball landed at a child's foot. Turnbull shouted to the kid. 'Kick it!'

A nun was standing beside the kid, who appeared oblivious to Turnbull's entreaty. 'For f***'s sake, kick it!' Turnbull shouted, ignoring the need for diplomacy. Still no action was being taken. 'For f***in' f***'s sake, kick it!' screamed the enraged Dons boss. 'The nun and the kid were away like the clappers,' Whyte recalls. 'Thereafter, it was complaint, complaint, complaint (to the club). Oh, dear, what a man!'

What a man, indeed. Turnbull became infamous for the clear-out he effected in his first close season. Seventeen players were adjudged to be surplus to stringent requirements and therefore pointed towards the dole queue. Ogston's demise could be likened to a public flogging. The Dons were on their annual golf day to Aboyne. On that same day, there was an exclusive in a national newspaper about some new playing method devised by the manager. Turnbull was apoplectic. He allowed the players their golf constitutional, then took them back to Pittodrie and herded them into the dressing room. His opening words might have been lifted from a James Cagney gangster film: 'There's a rat in this dressing room!' The alleged whistleblower, in Turnbull's eyes, was Ogston and the outsize goalkeeper was on his way to Liverpool and Billy Shankly before the latter had time to suggest that football was more important than life itself. Bobby Clark, as forecast by the manager in that Tynecastle dug-out, had been drafted in. Even all these years later, Ian Taylor is unsure if the charge against was justified. 'Tubby was a big, amiable guy. I don't know if he gave that information to the newspaper.' Ogston, however, was not alone in his humiliation. The Bobby Hume affair was scheduled to last for more than just a few minutes.

Taylor, the left-wing speed merchant who joined the Turnbull revolution in 1965, picks up what is by any standards an extraordinary story. I ask Taylor if

Turnbull scared him. He gives an involuntary shudder. 'I was absolutely terrified. He was the composite disciplinarian. I remember I was still at school after
signing provisional forms, but Martin (Buchan) and I trained three nights with
the part-timers. During the Easter holidays, you'd go down to the ground and
do a few odd jobs, cleaning boots, etc. One afternoon, there was what we called
a functional, getting the ball wide, the winger taking it and whipping in a cross.
Bobby Hume shanked this ball behind the goal. Eddie, when he wasn't happy,
had a habit of spitting, although nothing came out. So he spits and tells Bobby
to go back and take another one. Bobby jogs back. "Aye, a bit quicker," says
Eddie. You could see he was rattled. Bobby shanks again. "Last chance," says
Eddie. "Son, make it count this time, eh?" Hume shanks for a third time. Eddie
tells him to go away and he'd see him back at Pittodrie.

'That was the last time Bobby Hume ever played for Aberdeen. There used
to be a big tea urn in the corridor at Pittodrie. We were sitting there, having a
cup of tea, remember, I'm still a school kid. Eddie comes out of his office and
tells Hume that his contract has been paid up. He looked at us over his shoulder,
and said, "That's what you do, boys – you cut out the cancer!" That was me, 17
years of age, and you're asking me if I was scared of him. But you learned, over
time, that you always wanted to play for him. His training and his sessions were
fabulous. If you were having a decent time and playing fairly well, a two-hour
session would pass like it was ten minutes.'

Fear or no fear, the Turnbull revolution was gaining a momentum upon
which it was impossible to apply brakes. Jens Petersen, who had arrived in Scotland a year earlier as part of a Scandinavian triumvirate (Jorgen Ravn and Leif
Mortensen were the others), would survive the cull and be acclaimed as a great
defender; Jinky Smith, the nutmeg specialist, was imported from Glasgow junior
side Benburb and sashayed effortlessly into the first team; Tam McMillan, from
Neilston Juniors and a team mate of Dixie Deans, was signed after performing
brilliantly in the public trial; Harry Melrose was shipped in from Dunfermline
to become the fulcrum of midfield. He cost £4,000 (Turnbull should have had
the decency to wear Zorro's mask when he made the signing); Frank Munro,
a drinker adjudged to be indolent and beyond redemption by Dundee United,
was another grand theft, at £10,000. 'Within a year, Eddie had transformed the
team,' says Taylor. 'It was like St Trinians morphing into Eton.' But, hey, top hats
were not compulsory here. 'We all agreed that it was a bit like being in the Army.
If you got on the same side of the track with him, there wasn't a problem. If you
didn't, the problems were huge.'

Munro's problem was his weight. Taylor reckons that Franny was carrying
approximately 2st of excess when he signed on. 'He'd disappear into the boiler
room, bin liners and gas ovens on. Eddie used to make sure he was running on

the spot. It actually worked. He wasn't naturally a good trainer was Franny, in the same way Joe Harper wasn't, so he had to go through quite a bit of the pain barrier. But he did it. Looking back, there's no doubt that Munro was one of the best-ever players at Pittodrie. Eddie played him in midfield. What a cultured player he was, though, playing out from the back. He would come through, hit great diagonal balls at times and at others he'd be in there at the back post with his head. I reckon if Eddie had kept Franny – I'm not saying he should have – he and Martin Buchan in central defence would have been the equal of Miller and McLeish.'

You suspected Turnbull might have gleaned his ruthlessness from a contract killer. When a player ceased to be able to, or couldn't, do his bidding, his interest in that person evaporated. Whyte remembers different occasions that illustrate the point perfectly. He was in the reserve team, while his best pal, McMillan, had established himself in the first team. 'We came in together one day. Turnbull was standing at the radiator. "Haw there, Tommy son," he said. "How's it gaun?" He looked at me and nodded. "Mornin'." That was it. I got a f***ing growl. But the positions were reversed a couple of months later. Tommy had been injured and I was in the first team. "How's it gaun, Chalky Boy?" he says. A curt nod to Tommy and "mornin". He didn't take him on. When I got my Achilles ruptured some time later, Eddie was staying in Rosemount, only walking distance to Aberdeen infirmary. He never f***ing bothered coming to see us. Oh, aye, there were two sides to Eddie Turnbull. He only wanted to know you when you were playing. If not, he didnae bother his heid. I suppose it was an extreme form of professionalism.'

Turnbull, who ultimately favoured a 4-3-3 formation, believed in extremities. You'll remember the picture Shewan painted of torture on the sands of Balmedie, plus his recollection of 'The Swivel'. There was also the pressing game. You know, it's the fashionable one employed from Jurgen Klopp to Maurice Pochettino, but, until recently, often absent from the current Aberdeen team's game plan. Turnbull believed that as soon as the ball was cleared, the back four had to push up to the halfway line, with the midfield players supporting the forwards. Lazy players didn't want to run out and consequently were caught offside. 'We got tarred with playing offside tactics,' says Whyte. 'That was completely wrong. We went up as a unit and back as a unit. He was incredibly visionary. I can remember we were playing Morton at Cappielow and we'd lost the first leg, 3-1. In the return, it was 0-0 at half-time, so we're still 3-1 down. Ernie Winchester was playing against John Madsen, though Hugh Strachan had picked up Ernie in the first half, with Madsen sweeping just behind. Eddie says at half-time, "Right, Ernie, second half, go up to Madsen and stand on his f***in' toes." We're looking at him boss-eyed: our striker marking the sweeper. What next? Eddie is on a roll. "I'm telling ye: f***in' stand on his toes and you'll see what f***in' happens!" Sure enough, when it restarts, Ernie goes right on Madsen, who shouts to Strachan to go back a bit. Hughie tells Madsen to get back as well. But Ernie follows him. The two Morton guys get totally zonked. They didnae know what to do. Strachan wanted to pick Ernie up, Madsen wanted to be spare, but he couldn't because he had someone standing on his toes. We won, 3-0. That was genius. What would Chris Sutton have been saying if he'd been commentating?'

In 1966-67 – Turnbull's first full season – the worth of the new management began to pay dividends and Aberdeen finished fourth in the league. There were still sceptics on the terracing and their numbers often failed to rise above four figures, but their scepticism didn't seem to apply to the Scottish Cup. Dundee were annihilated, 5-0, at Dens Park, with 23,000 in attendance; St Johnstone suffered a similar humiliation in round two, in front of 22,800 at Pittodrie; Hibs were next at Easter Road. Just over 37,000 (I was one of them) watched the Dons equalise through Jinky Smith in the last minute and force a replay. But what came next defies belief.

The relentlessly negative atmosphere on the P&J's sports desk is weighing me down. I cannot wait to get away and test myself in less parochial climes. But tonight I'm emancipated from all the cynicism. I've excused myself from my fiancee and thrown a couple of pints down my throat in a pub in Belmont Road, Kittybrewster, on my way to the match. Fortified, while I march on down Elmbank Terrace and Froghall Terrace, I consider for a moment my lady. She is not exactly enamoured of this decision to watch Aberdeen play a quarter-final replay. I've absconded quite a bit recently, having visited Dundee seven weeks ago and Hibs only last Saturday. But, thoughtless brat that I am, I mustn't give this another thought: romance cannot separate me from my first love.

As it happens, a big crowd is expected and the expectation is underpinned by the fact that the roads are crammed with humanity. Indeed, the famous Merkland Road is packed solid and the fans are moving at a pace that would humiliate a hedgehog. I'm delighted that I decided to stick at only a couple of pints and leave the pub at 5.30. If I'm lucky I'm just about going to get into the ground. When I do, I'm in the unaccustomed territory of the Merkland Road end. It's difficult to breathe, let alone move. I'm one of an incredible 44,000. There are fans on the gasometer, fans up above us on top of our stand, and kids on the track at the Beach End. You imagine Turnbull is more than anxious to beat his old team. But there is a slight problem: Jinky Smith, who scored the equaliser in the first match, is declared unfit. A collective groan sweeps the ground. Ernie Winchester is his replacement. Another collective groan. Ernie is a local boy and this species can rarely claim pin-up status with the fans. But Ernie decides that this is the night to overturn convention. He scores twice as he runs over the top of John Madsen. Jim Storrie, an import from Leeds United, scores the other. The place is thrumming with a crescendo of sound. This is almost better than sex.

According to Taylor, that Wednesday evening was a seminal one in the history of Aberdeen FC. 'That was to me the start of what things could be like. It was a throwback to the fifties, with the fathers talking about when Aberdeen were a right, proper side, winning leagues and league cups. (Back then) there had been a midweek game against Hearts when there were something like 48,000 present, but this was a wonderful night and just showed the potential the Dons had. You're like me – how many years were they in the doldrums? Ten. It was horrible. Aberdeen had fallen off the edge of a cliff –and landed in abject disarray. Eddie gets a hold of it and suddenly the Hibs result gave everybody belief.'

The Cup run, further enhanced with a 1-0 victory over Dundee United in the semi-final, came to a logical conclusion against Celtic in the final. Can it be possible to describe a 2-0 defeat as logical? It can. Turnbull fell ill on the Friday and couldn't travel down to Gleneagles with the team. Chairman Dick Donald drove him there in his car. The players didn't even see the manager, as he was whisked up to his hotel bedroom. But the next day, trainer Davie Shaw motioned the players up to the manager's room. Whyte takes up the story. 'You could see he was really ill and had done really well to even be there. Honestly, he was yellow. Even during the week, he'd been using a seat in the dug-out. Anyway, the team talk in that bedroom went on a wee bit. Consequently, because of this and crowd congestion (there were 126,000 there), we missed the police escort and didn't get off the bus at Hampden until twenty past two. Then you got your two comps and had to go back outside to hand them over to friends. We went on to the park to see whether it should be long or short studs, but never had a chance to have a warm-up, or nothing. Hey, I'm not saying we'd have beaten them, but we could have put in a better performance. We just never got going that day.'

No-one could criticise the performances of the Washington Whips a few weeks later. They lost to Wolves in the final, going down, 6-5, as previously stated. Jinky Smith had been sent off after 30 minutes of that match and an own goal from Ally Shewan gave the English their victory. What wasn't previously stated was the consolation that followed the Los Angeles defeat: the players were taken to Disneyland. Turnbull, who had missed the early stages of the tournament, was there together with coaches and directors. The ensemble was met by a gorgeous PR girl, complete with tartan mini skirt. This Miss World – without official portfolio, of course – was leading a conducted tour of all the different attractions. But she herself was the greatest attraction. She stood on a little plinth and asked if there were any questions the visitors wanted to ask.

Taylor recalls, 'Martin Buchan, who's standing next to me, mumbles, "Aye, what are you doing tonight?" Wee Jimmy Wilson tags on to that and asks Martin what he said. Jim Storrie, who was a really good guy and Jimmy's room mate, urges, "Go on, Martin, ask her." Martin starts panicking. Eddie Turnbull (now restored to some semblance of health after Gleneagles) joins in, "Go on Martin. Ask her." Martin responds immediately. "You f*** off!"

'Now, I'm standing next to Martin and I can't believe he's said this. I'm cute enough to think that he's going to play for Scotland 40 times and play for either Manchester United or Liverpool. I'm just a journeyman, so I step away from him. Now, Martin's standing on his own. Eddie turns round and says, "What was that you said to me?" Martin's sick. "Sorry, sorry, b-b-boss. I just panicked!" Jimmy Wilson puts a lid on it. "You know, that's the strangest way a player has ever asked for a free transfer."'

Lunch was announced and Buchan, worrying about his injudicious collision with Turnbull, could not even countenance food. Taylor admits it was difficult to provide his friend with any comfort. Eventually, after much deliberation, Buchan summoned courage, went back to his boss and offered profuse apologies. 'Eddie, to be fair, told him it was a lesson he should absorb. He also told him to keep his cool. There was no hint of him getting fined, or anything like that. But I suspect Eddie laughed about it himself.'

Buchan, in fact, was one of the Turnbull favourites. But there were others: Joe Harper, who was plundered from Morton for £40,000 in 1969, Munro, who signed for Wolves in 1968, Bobby Clark and Jinky Smith. But his allegiance to Smith began to fray around the edges when a newspaper story declared that the player was about to join Celtic. Smith confided to Whyte that Jock Stein had told him to have his passport in order because Celtic were going on a trip at the end of the season. Turnbull's message to him was unequivocal. 'If you think I'm f***in' sellin' you to go there and f***in' take the pish out of us, you've got another f***in' think coming.' Whyte remembers, 'He wouldn't let him go and Jinky was spewin' because he was Celtic daft. Jinky was going with builder Peter Cameron's daughter at the time. Peter was a big horse man and so was Jock: they met up at the races, and the story I heard was that Cameron told Jock no' tae touch Jinky because he was a big gambler. But it was Turnbull who kyboshed the move. Turnbull said if he was gaun anywhere, it would be south. Not long afterwards, he went to Newcastle. There was no fall-out with his manager, though. Jinky was so laid back he wouldn't have fallen out with anyone.'

Turnbull, on the other hand, could spontaneously combust with anyone, favourite or not. When Storrie arrived from Leeds, he appeared to be the shining light of the manager's life. Whyte again. 'See that Storrie – he's a great talker, just what we need. He's a good influence.' About three months later, he revised his thinking. Storrie, apparently, in fulfilling his role as a great articulator, had been mentioning Don Revie's name too often for Turnbull's liking. It was one extreme to the other. 'See that Storrie – he's a c***! He's too much to say for hiself.'

The idolatry of Joe Harper was an enduring one, however. Turnbull eventually signed him twice, once for Aberdeen, the second time for Hibs. But Joey, being Joey, sometimes made idolatry difficult. Whyte recalls: 'Joey paid his way and as long as you did that, you were okay. He cost them a few bob but, by Christ, he was worth it at the end of the day. He and Cup-Tie McKay had a flat in King Street. The manager said there was no way they were staying together, so that particular arrangement was brought to an abrupt end.' No doubt he had spotted the white sheet that hung on a wall, onto which the pornographic films were shown. 'It was supposed to be a white sheet, but it had spunk marks all over it. Turnbull blamed McKay for it. It wasn't Wee Joe's fault – it was McKay's.'

The infamous story with the sand lorry, co-starring Ernie McGarr and Joe Harper, has been repeated on a 'Gone with the Wind' basis and thus doesn't need repeating here, but another Whyte tale involving strong liquor does. 'Another time, Wee Joe got breathalysed, after the opening of Bill Cruickshank's tie shop in Rosemount. I was newly married and didn't bother going. But they ended up at the Palace Ballroom. I went into training on the Thursday morning. Normally, it was a relatively easy shift. You knew if you'd had a few drinks, you could handle it. We went to Linksfield, but Turnbull says, "Right, first team squad back to the park." At that time they had a wee gym at the corner under the Beach End. When we get back, he says, "Right, I'll f***in' breathalyse you!" We're all looking about, wondering what's going on. He told us he'd had the Chief of Police on to him early in the morning. So now we were going to be circuited. Normally, we did it about three times and it was a case of breathing out of your arse. So we've done it three times. "Again!" he cries. That was four times. "Again!" That was five and, by this time, we're on oor hauns and knees. Then he took us on what was know as Doggies, up and down the trackside. "That'll teach ye," he roars. "It'll no' f***in' happen again!"'

So Saturday arrived, but the result scarcely put Turnbull in a more equitable mood. The boys could only draw. The inquisition began. The Scots version of Torquemada was in masterly form. Martin Buchan, according to Whyte, could be quite outspoken in his own way. He tried to explain to his boss that the players were fatigued, but he framed it in a way that Turnbull would perhaps appreciate. 'We were too f***ing tired – we were knackered after Thursday!'

Turnbull was devoid of sympathy. "Tired?" he echoed. "I'll f***in' tire you." At that moment, Buchan realised he had said the wrong thing. Now, a couple of directors used to come in the dressing room after games. Not this day. Teddy Scott was ordered to hold the door. 'There was an investigation into everything then. He was an awful man for that.'

> *Christmas is a time for good cheer, or so say its advocates. Except, in the year of 1969, I cannot find any cause for celebration. I have left the P&J, served a year on the subbing desk of the* Scottish Daily Express, *in Glasgow, and am now deputy editor for the* Crawley Advertiser *(circulation nudging a mammoth 4,000). I wanted to be nearer the hallowed ground of Fleet Street and this has been achieved. I perform casual shifts for both the* Daily Mail *and* The Observer *and indeed am earning enough money to afford a Mk 2 3.4 litre Jaguar and live in a Tudor-style cottage in Sussex. Shortly, I will be joining the sports desk of the* Daily Mail *on a permanent basis. Significantly, my engagement has ended.*

> *I receive a call from my mother advising me to come home. Quickly. My father is dying. I fly to Aberdeen and arrive in time to see him being prepared for hospital. Cancer has devastated him and now he is an emaciated shadow of a once formidable man. The ambulance arrives. I hear the pitiful cries of my father as he is transferred from the bed with which he's familiar and onto an impersonal stretcher. Me? I'm hiding in the kitchen, my back pressed up against the wall, sobbing gently but, more significantly, filing my credentials as a coward. Mum receives a bulletin from Foresterhill. It is scarcely an optimistic one. I imagine they will operate on Dad and wait to see if miracles still happen.*

> *A day later I visit the hospital. He is sitting up in bed after surgery and looks fractionally better, but there's a look in his eye which suggests this is only a temporary situation. It's Saturday, 20 December. Aberdeen are playing Rangers on this day. I'm not at my best in hospitals, but this is a craven excuse. I tell my father that I'm going now, that I have a football match to attend because it's my job. Then I must fly back south. There is a look of reproof on the face of the man who took me, aged four, to my first football match. 'Ah, well he's forgiven,' he whispers to my mum. I have absolution, or pretend I have. I leave for Pittodrie and, when I get there, studiously ignore proceedings. I am totally uninterested in the fate of my favourite football team today, Eddie Turnbull or no Eddie Turnbull. I go into the bar under the Pittodrie grandstand and begin to drink my way towards a signpost marked 'oblivion'. So why have I come? For the football? Not a chance. I'm here because I couldn't bear to witness the death throes of the man who gave me life. Aberdeen, in the event, lose, by three goals to two. I return to Sussex. My father dies three days later. The events of that afternoon haunt me to this day.*

The very next December was to demonstrate that Turnbull was a man whose word was inviolable. Aberdeen were due to play Celtic in Glasgow. They were a point behind the leaders, but a win would see them go top. Harper, inevitably, scored. So Buchan, as captain, was urged by his team mates to go and ask the manager the bonus for such a marquee victory. He was informed it would be the same as usual. Buchan, remembering, no doubt, the Disneyland affair, was respectful, but claimed, quietly, that the boys would be disappointed. Turnbull reminded him that if they could not charge themselves up for a game at Parkhead, knowing the implications of a good result, then they would never be up for it. But he added if they won their next fixture, then they would receive double the bonus. This they did. Mind you, this didn't win the league for Aberdeen. They failed by two points to best Celtic. Of course, they had a 3-1 Scottish Cup final victory over the Glaswegians to reflect on the previous year. This was the four-goal year of Cup-Tie McKay. How best to describe Derek McKay? The visceral game of football suggests he came from nowhere (he played 12 times for Dundee in three years), spent an ostensibly unproductive two years with Aberdeen, aside from that Cup run, and then disappeared into that same vacuum. I met him at a party in Skene Square some years later: he was a good-looking guy and utterly delightful company. I suppose you could say he was just part of a Hollywood script. He was an extra who, for one film franchise, was thrust into the leading role, and then went back to being an extra. He died of a heart attack in 2008 while he was holidaying in Thailand.

Yes, Turnbull would rant and he would rave, but these were necessarily abbreviated forms of expression. For all his bombast and profanity, he realised that if he forfeited his composure on a regular basis, he would lose the respect of his players. Taylor was with him for five years and can remember his manager becoming utterly manic on only two occasions. On the first occasion, Aberdeen were favourites to reach the quarter finals of the League Cup. All they required was a point at home against Clyde. Instead, they lost, 2-0. It was an extremely hot day, so when Turnbull came in to the dressing room after the game, he sat down and prepared for a fire and fury session. It ended with a memorably short but ominous speech. Taylor recalls it now: '"There are players here who are getting above their stations in life." At that point we had Under 23 internationalists in our side, and there were teams looking at them. Now, Eddie didn't mind players having a drink – in fact, he loved a drink himself – but then he said, "Some of you Bacardi Boys will not be playing next week!"

'Well, would you believe that when the team sheet next went up, the only missing player was Martin Buchan – and he didn't even drink. Martin was outraged. "He (Turnbull) thinks I'm a Bacardi Boy!" He asked for a transfer. The matter was soon resolved when Martin was called into Eddie's office. They talked the thing through and Martin withdrew his request. But, no question,

Eddie lost it that day. The only other time it happened was the 70-71 season when we needed to take four points from the last three games to win the league. We blew it. Falkirk beat us, 1-0, in the last game, and thus Celtic were champions. Eddie came in and had a right go at us and accused us of completely bottling it. I do admire Harper for his response: "Ah, well, that goes for you as well, boss. You keep saying we're all in this together, so, if we are, you bottled it as well." Eddie went over to Harper, eyeballed him and said, "I took you from a tuppence halfpenny club (Morton) and I'll put you back there!" That was only twice in five years that Eddie gave it the old Fergie hairdryer treatment. Reputed hard man that he was, he wasn't so daft.'

No, stupidity didn't figure in the complex make-up of Turnbull. Only months after the initial Scottish Cup final reverse to Celtic, the team was breaking up: Munro, Smith and Tommy Craig had departed for England's green and pleasant land. Turnbull determined himself to bring pace and goals to the attack. Jim Forrest, once a victim of Rangers' Cup humiliation at Berwick, had not settled at Preston. He was given the No. 9 shirt by the Dons. Harper came in the next year. Soon, Turnbull was learning how to deal with ego, but emanating from a most unexpected quarter. Taylor recalls, 'Forrest was the fastest ten yards you've ever seen and a goal machine. Now, I don't think I ever had a conversation with Jim in all the time he was at Aberdeen. He was pretty quiet but a good guy. I liked him. But then along came Joe. If there ever was a strong personality in a football team, it was Harper. I got on great with him. So, suddenly, there was Harper and Forrest... and ego. Nothing wrong with having an ego, especially in the area they played. But there was a problem. Forrest was playing wide right in a 4-3-3.

'Eddie told me this latterly. Forrest knocks on his door and says he needs to see him. Eddie steadies himself for trouble. "I just want to clarify something, boss. I was bought as your No. 9..." Eddie's thinking this is going to be difficult, but then he twigs that Forrest isn't arguing about playing centre forward, he's more concerned about wearing the No.9 shirt.' The problem is solved by sweet talk. 'Any time after that, when they played together, Harper wore the No.10 on his back. It was Forrest (No.9) wide right, Harper (no.10) central, Arthur Graham (no.11) wide left. Again, you're talking wingers with real pace. Forrest finished up getting a cap for Scotland, against Belgium, I think, at outside right. He never complained again.' For the record, he scored 62 goals in 186 matches during his time at Pittodrie.

Tough enough to at least contemplate running through brick walls, and arguably dafter than a brush ('The Brush' became his nickname), Davie Robb also earned Scotland recognition under Turnbull's tutelage. He was also proficient in arousing his manager's vitriol. Turnbull was missing from Pittodrie on this particular day, and training was taken by Jimmy Bonthrone, his deputy. With the top cat away, an opportunistic representative of German sports manufacturers Hummel seized the moment to visit. He offered a free pair of white boots to any player who would promise to wear them. The next day, the players decided they would wear them in training and therefore break them in. Turnbull arrived. 'What the f***'s this?' he shouted. 'White boots? Aye, that'll be right. Get them in the f***in' bin!'

Whyte remembers, 'Enter Jimmy McGregor, Ally Shewan's pal in Aberdeen Journals. He got some black printer's ink and gave it to Davie. Davie was adamant about Turnbull's directive. "F*** him! I'm wearing these Hummel boots." So away he goes and paints the boots black. We had red socks at the time, with white feet. At the end of any game, you put your boots together, your socks, etc. They were all laid out this time when Teddy Scott came to pick them up. So Davie's sitting there. He's managed to hide his socks, but his soles of his feet were black. Turnbull spots the anomaly. "You, white boots? With your skill? You think you're f***in' di Stefano or somethin'? There's no way you'll be wearin' them again!" Davie thought he'd have one over Turnbull, but not so. The boss caught him.'

Taylor's recollection was there were only two major Turnbull apoplexies. Whyte, however, remembers other explosions, but these were confined to directors and a city dignitary, and were initiated strictly on humanitarian grounds. By 1970, Whyte, in his middle twenties and now recovered from his Achilles rupture, was either featuring as substitute or playing in the reserves. He explained to his manager that he wanted to play and that this present role was wholly unsuitable. He explained that Kilmarnock were interested in him. Turnbull told him to leave the matter with him. The upshot was dramatic. 'F***in' directors – they're wantin' money for you!' Those directors, however, ran into Turnbull's defiant gene. He presented the case like an eloquent defence barrister. He pointed out that Whyte had given the club years of loyal service and had been through a hideous injury. He urged them, out of loyalty and fairness, to let him go for nothing and thereby pick up a good signing-on fee from Kilmarnock. The directors relented. But Turnbull wasn't finished. He told the departing player, '"If anyone approaches you and if there's anything you want to know, give me a shout and I'll help you." And then he said as long as he was at the club, I could go there and train.'

Whyte went on to Kilmarnock and played 104 times for them in five seasons. 'Now, the complete opposite happened with wee Jimmy Wilson. He was a wee buzz bomb and a flying machine, tae. He was infectious and was always guaranteed to keep you going. He'd a great attitude and helped all the young guys at the time. Harry Melrose was also a motivator and I looked up to them.

Turnbull encouraged them to help us. Eddie loved Wee Harry and said he was the best signing he ever made. He was a great worker, even though he was getting on a bit. Turnbull used to tell him to ease off a wee bit, but Harry would say he was fine. A good liver? He was whisky daft. Wee Harry and Wee Jimmy had flats up at Cairnfield. We used to go up to their places. I'd give them 30 bob as my contribution, so Harry and his wife would go to the supermarket and get the drink in. But Turnbull liked Jimmy as well. Certainly at the beginning. Unfortunately, their relationship soured a wee bit in the later stages.' More than wee bit, it seems. It's alleged that Turnbull told him, 'You get tae f*** and don't put your nose back in here!'

Wilson, having in Turnbull's eyes overstepped the mark, left for Motherwell (I should report that the feud did not evolve into one of those awful lifetime affairs: the pair later met up at golf days for former Aberdeen players and resolved their differences).

But Whyte had previously seen the loyal side of the man who stood by those he valued. The 1970 Scottish Cup victory spawned a civic reception, at the Beach Ballroom. Watches were presented to the 12 members of the team, plus the manager, Jimmy Bonthrone and the physiotherapist. 'The four who weren't stripped that day, Winkle (Taylor), me, Tommy Wilson and Jimmy Hamilton, were left sitting on our arses. Turnbull went mental – at the Provost! "Well, if I'd known you were going to embarrass these f***in' boys here, and no' gie them a watch, I'd never have f***in' come." The annoying thing was that Hammy played every round until the semi. If there had been any sentiment in fitba, he should have been sub that day. He, Winkle and Wilson had all played their parts. But that was Turnbull, looking after you.'

The Turnbull departure came shortly after the Cup success. Typically, it was of the short and sharp variety, with very little emotion attached. He arrived at the pre-season training in Persley Den and sat the lads down. 'I've been offered the job at Hibernian and decided to take it. It's been a pleasure to work with you. Whoever takes over here is inheriting a great bunch of boys and a great club.' It cannot be said there was a rush on Kleenex that day, but there was an instant division, one half of the players lamenting a manager who had led them towards a possible Garden of Eden, the other half feeling that life was suddenly going to be far less strenuous, not so much physically as mentally. Edward Turnbull kept the brain cells activated.

The guy who would actually replace Turnbull was Jimmy Bonthrone, who was put in charge of the pre-season tour and was handed the keys to the strong box on his return. Now, admittedly Bonthrone's contribution has been grossly overlooked in this chapter. He had joined the revolution in 1969, after managing East Fife.

Taylor remembers, 'You know, Turnbull smiled very seldom. But the thing was he didn't want to get too close to you. Sooner or later, he'd have to get rid of you. Consequently, we didn't really know him. But I notice there was a big difference in him when Jimmy B arrived. Eddie flourished when he got hold of Jimmy. There was someone to bounce ideas off, someone he respected. Jimmy was the best No. 2 a man could ever have. He was an absolutely fabulous man. He was the shock absorber between the players and Eddie. So they played the good cop, bad cop game and played it very well. But Jimmy was a naturally good cop and it (his management) didn't quite work out.'

In comparison, Turnbull's nine-year stewardship of his old club worked out quite magnificently, certainly in its early incarnation. Turnbull's Tornadoes, as they were known, took Hibs to heights they'd almost forgotten existed but they overcame their vertiginous fears. It all ended, sadly, in 1980, after chairman Tom Hart had decided that George Best, by this time an alcoholic and a distance past his best, would be good for football and Easter Road, in particular. Best, indeed, drew in the crowds initially, but his most committed and consistent form was reserved for the hostelries of Edinburgh. He certainly was not good for Turnbull and, ultimately, he was confronted by something he had never known before in his managerial career: his P45. He retired to daydream about an illustrious past and, criminally, the old band of incompetents at the SFA failed to harness the experience and genius that was open to them.

Turnbull's daughter, Valerie who, I'm informed, is very much in her father's image, once told Taylor that if her father had had his time over again, he wouldn't have left Aberdeen: the Hibs side was a cracker – his club and whatever – but the real quality had been at Aberdeen. 'What a compliment!' he says now. 'The thing is Aberdeen had been a real force in Scottish football but had lost its way completely. He put it back on track. Now that's always a great thing. He laid the foundations and I still think he laid them for Ferguson.

'Just think, if they'd made a bad appointment instead of Eddie, Aberdeen could have become a backwoods club. But they were lucky enough to get him. I remember Teddy Scott saying that he made him really waken up and get the values of what needed to be done. And Teddy became a legend at Aberdeen. So, really, it all started with him. It's a real irony that Ferguson and Turnbull couldn't get on with one another, considering their disciplines and their tactical nous.' Turnbull, in fact, had never met Ferguson, but he told me in a radio interview later that he had no wish to. 'Listen, we (Hibs) were playing Falkirk and he broke Alex Cropley's ankle. It was a cowardly action. I don't have any time for him and never will have.'

Taylor again: 'Fergie was far better with the Press; he was just that bit smarter and certainly appreciated that you needed the press on your side as well. Eddie didnae miss under those circumstances. In later life, I got to know him well and what amazed me about him – he really liked me – was his all-round knowledge, including politics. I remember him, also, talking about his time on the Atlantic convoys during World War II. He didn't know whether he was going to get blown out of the Atlantic Ocean at any minute. It must make you different.'

Turnbull was different all right. As he aged, he mellowed, but a man could still cut himself on the sharpness of his observations, not to mention his memory. Some years ago, he was invited up to watch Barcelona train at St Andrews. He had someone drive him to the Fife town, where he was welcomed by a young coach called Pep Guardiola. He positively raved about Guardiola and what he described as a most magnificent set of footballers. 'That was before Barcelona became the name they are now,' says Taylor. 'Eddie was smitten. Before this, I can remember saying to him, "Tell you what, boss, I don't know if you watch much telly, but I'll give you a name: this boy's going to be another Pele." He asked for a name. I said, "He plays for Barcelona and his name's Lionel Messi." About two years later, he says to me, "You're no' so daft, eh? You were right about Lionel Messi. Well done, you." Well, I had a good teacher, hadn't I? You know, from being a young kid absolutely terrified of Eddie, 45 years later he was like a friend. And yet, I never called him Eddie in my life. Just "boss". He said once that he wouldn't have a problem if I called him by his first name. I responded, "We just call you boss because that's what you are – the boss. It sits on our shoulders a lot better." The man was from a different class.'

*John 'Tubby' Ogston died, age 78, on 16 August, 2017.

CHAPTER 4

Willie Boy Was Here

PITTODRIE has surely witnessed countless acts of insubordination in its 114-year history – most of them, mercifully as far as the host club is concerned, conducted in camera. Few have equalled that which occurred on 13 September 1975, however. The blood brothers of tact and diplomacy were absent when William David Young bade a very public farewell to Scotland, Aberdeen and, crucially, manager Jimmy Bonthrone. A league match against Dundee United had not exactly been going according to Young's plan (Aberdeen eventually lost 3-1). It seemed that his mind was somewhere else, certainly not within touching distance of the game's pulse. Bonthrone employed the half-time break to aim an uncharacteristic volley of vitriol at the centre half. Chastised if not comprehensively chastened, the centre half re-entered the fray in the second half, without, apparently, any noticeable quantity of conviction. In his defence, perhaps he was still up to his eyeballs in another form of grievance: a couple of weeks before this, he had been banned sine die by Scotland, along with four others (Billy Bremner, Pat McCluskey, Joe Harper and team mate Arthur Graham), after a nightclub incident in Denmark. He had lost the Aberdeen captaincy as a result.

Anyway, by this juncture, Bonthrone decided that Young had to be sacrificed, and ordered Duncan Davidson to prepare himself for action. As he was finishing his warming-up shuttles up and down the track, the young striker swallowed hard, no doubt because he guessed who was coming off. It wasn't difficult to predict the consequences of such a decision. There are some men in this life who possess the intimidation factor. Young's was a ten out of ten in this department. Someone from Pittodrie once attested to those aggressive qualities. 'When he fights, he's a windmill in a storm.' Physiotherapist Ronnie Coutts, well aware of the man's volatility and perhaps even the unconventional fighting style, was in charge of the number plates. He looked at Bonthrone as if to suggest he should rethink the situation.

But, on this day, Bonthrone was sure that this decision was the correct one. Coutts, in some trepidation, held up the No. 5. At the time, Aberdeen had just secured a corner at the Beach End. Young was already up in the penalty box, ready to receive the corner kick. He turned round just as the 5,500 crowd digested the ramifications of the number on the board. Their contribution to proceedings was the sound of astonishment. Young, not to be outdone in the drama stakes, stood rigid and glared right across at the dug-out. It wasn't so much a scowl as a declaration of war. Even those without a sense of smell might have predicted the manure was about to be distributed every which way. Striding towards Bonthrone, his de facto tormentor-in-chief, Young divested himself of his shirt, threw it at the dug-out, and, bare-chested, marched down the touch-line and disappeared down the tunnel. Whereupon, he attempted to remove the dressing room door from its hinges with a kick that possibly had its origins in a Bruce Lee movie. He was never seen at the old stadium again. His record of 118 games for Aberdeen had ended. He described the indignity of it all to Aidan Smith, of The Scotsman, in 2014. It should be noted that this wasn't so much a mea culpa as a self-justification.

'This was right after Copenhagen and Jimmy had already stripped me of the captaincy. Then he hauled me off as the second half began rather than in the dressing-room to make an exhibition of me. I never thought he was up to the job. He was too soft and let players talk back to him, me included. Because he was bald we called him "Coconut Heid". I gave him a tough time but I was frustrated because he wasn't taking Aberdeen forward. I apologised for throwing my strip at him but he said he didn't want anything more to do with me. He resigned shortly after and that was me, too. Apparently the dressing-room was renovated later but the door was kept as it was, all bashed in, as a memento.'

Davidson, who is about to help me reconstruct the sound and the fury of those days in the seventies, recalls, perhaps thankfully, that Young had disappeared by the time the team entered the dressing room at full time. 'I think it was the next day we were going to a 21st birthday party in the Lang Stracht, and Willie was there. Of course, there was no problem between him and me.' Did he say anything at the party? 'Not directly, but he did admit that something was going to happen out of this. And it did. I do believe that the next day he was on a plane to London and signed for Tottenham for £100,000. But, as I remember it, I think something had happened between him and the club (before this), because his mind was nowhere near that game.'

Bonthrone left Pittodrie less than a month later, but his departure, unlike that of Young, was allegedly undemonstrative: there is no evidence of him stamping his feet, kicking the nearest feline form, or launching a frenzied attack on his office door. Indications are he simply informed Dick Donald, the then chairman, that his managerial journey was over as he'd taken the club as far as he could. Jimmy was a most pleasant man, one whom your mother would have been pleased to invite for afternoon tea and scones. Unlike many of his contemporaries, you asked him a question and he responded with the truth, as he saw it. I remember quizzing him about Willie Miller, whose goal-scoring exploits on loan with Peterhead were suggesting he was a realistic proposition for striking stardom. Jimmy thought for a moment, then replied, 'You know, I don't know if Willie will make it as a forward. He cannae kick the ball properly; he sorts of sclaffs it…'

The 13th of September had been a dramatic departure from Bonthrone's modus operandi. Normally, he was neither ruthless nor antagonistic and thus lacked two essential prerequisites for survival in the maelstrom that is football management. No, here was a fair man who had been ideally suited to act as a buffer state between the players and Turnbull. On his own, he was vulnerable in this cruel, elemental existence. So players, like Young, were tempted to exploit that vulnerability. But this is no time for hypocrisy. Young was not alone in this. Now, we all have skeletons clanking around in some corner cupboard or cellar, and I reckon I have amassed enough to warrant the opening of a bone factory. Jimmy Bonthrone is a statistic of that factory. The next event I'm about to describe, which occurred some months before the Young incident, should have remained a secret, if only a guilty one. I can only imagine his embarrassment when it occurred. It has become my embarrassment. After all, he was the guy who had the unenviable pressure of succeeding a genius. He didn't need, or deserve, my intervention and what was presented to him in big, bold capitals one morning on 12 February 1975. And, consider this: would I have done the same had Turnbull been in charge? That is what would be considered a rhetorical question. Of course I wouldn't.

Thus, the narrative rewinds and pit stops at troubled times for not only Aberdeen FC but me. This was when my relationship with the club became very personal. By then, I had acquired Fleet Street status and was an employee of Rupert Murdoch's *Sun*. The *Daily Mail*? I had scarcely achieved a rhythm in my job as a stone sub-editor at that newspaper when it merged with the *Daily Sketch* and I was presented with a redundancy letter. However, it all eventually played out to my advantage: after a couple of years working as a sub-editor in the London office, I was now the football writer of the newly-launched Scottish edition of what we know as the '*Current Bun*'. I had a London salary, expenses that almost equalled that handsome stipend, and a Cockney-style swagger. My dalliance with first fame, together with a reservoir of alcohol, was beginning to dictate the direction that my life was taking. If ever a young man was headed for a fall of seismic proportions, then it was yours truly. A couple of nights before Scotland drew 1-1 in the 1975 European Championship qualifier with Spain in Valencia, I disgraced myself at an official reception and finished up sleeping in an SFA selector's bed (there is a token reference to this in the second chapter).

I arrived late, after drinking copiously at another hotel, and had to be carried to my room by the Scotland backroom staff.

Unfortunately, they deposited me in the wrong room. Anyway, the hapless selector, locked into a situation not dissimilar to the tale of Goldilocks and the Three Bears, sent for a pass key and then medical assistance. The Scotland doctor, I was told later, initially stared dolefully at this immoveable, bed-beleaguered object and failed to locate a pulse. Further investigation, thankfully, confirmed that I was still alive. Scotland's football rulers, outraged at my behaviour, sent a letter of admonition to my employers. A yellow card was flashed before my eyes. An inevitable red card was about to arrive in May of that year but, first, there was time for another fiasco.

On 10 February I attend a Scottish Cup third-round replay at Ibrox: Rangers versus Aberdeen. The team have no great expectations: the Turnbull era is simply a distant, if beautiful, memory. Sure, there's youthful promise in the team, but the league form is erratic. I arrive at Ibrox, my throat already well lubricated, with a half bottle of whisky in my pocket. I'm not normally a whisky drinker, but tonight is destined to jettison normality. Goals by Arthur Graham and Duncan Davidson give the Dons an unexpected 2-1 victory and this embryonic big shot an opportunity to antagonise the nostrils of the Glasgwegian press. Here, in our eerie on top of the old main stand, I'm celebrating a major upset of the odds. I'm a vaudeville act rather than a football scribe, singing, dancing and ad libbing my match report to a long-suffering copy taker. But this is only the beginning of the night's fol de rols.

I'm staying at the North British Hotel, George Square. When I arrive at the establishment, I'm surprised but delighted to find myself in the company of the victorious Dons, a few of whom I already know. They are also staying the night, but more importantly, debating as to which nightclub they should choose to launch their celebration. I warn them of the dangers of Glasgow nightlife, particularly when Rangers have had their backsides roasted. I urge them to stay within the relatively safe confines of the hotel. There's all we need here; my expenses take care of a few crates of beer. Is there a bottle opener in the house? Who needs a bottle opener when you have Willie Young and teeth that are impervious to pain? At around 3a.m., with spirits fairly high in the optic, we are debating the players' fitness levels and, crazily, I'm calling them into question. I'm a template for the body beautiful, of course: I smoke up to 60 cigarettes a day, and bend my elbow almost as often as a violinist playing the William Tell Overture. To settle this nonsensical argument, we decide that I will take on their chosen nominee in a race around a dark and deserted George Square. I am to be given approximately half a lap of a start, owing to my 31 years and sybaritic lifestyle. Ominously, however, I am to face the fleetest of feet in the Aberdeen FC business: Duncan Davidson, the youngster who scored the winning goal at Ibrox. Sadly, for me, Duncan reinforces his reputation as a flying machine, catching me a couple of yards before the line and somewhat dismantling my scurrilous accusation about their general fitness. The rest of the squad is positioned at the finishing line, absorbing my humiliation. I note that Willie Miller is looking inordinately pleased with himself. We filter back to the hotel for a nightcap at 3.15.

Now, all this nonsense might have been acceptable had it stopped right there. But, unfortunately, when the drink is in, the wit inevitably seeks another location. It did not stop there and I probably staggered up to bed a couple of hours later. When I wakened, it felt as if my head had been sabotaged. More drink was required before I even contemplated going into the office. More drink was taken and an idea infiltrated that drink-sodden mind: wouldn't it be novel to write about the night's experience, particularly the segment involving George Square? That would set it apart from the conventional follow-up. Soon, I was back in the office pumping out what would be the next day's sensation. I recounted the night's adventures in excruciating detail, not stopping to consider what the implications might mean for the club, or indeed its venerable manager, Jimmy Bonthrone. I talked to him some time afterwards and it was apparent that the 'Exclusive' had hit him in the solar plexus. I apologised profusely, insisting that the devil drink had been partly, if not wholly, to blame. But the fact was that the embarrassing story about a player running around George Square in the wee, small hours, with his team mates cheering him on, could neither be forgotten nor rebutted.

Is Willie Young experiencing any regret concerning his last act of defiance at Aberdeen? I had hoped to catch up with him and include his reminisces in this book. We know each other of old, the friendship having been formed when I visited his house for an interview after I arrived back in Scotland in 1974. Indeed, he attended my wedding in the August of 1975, some months after I had been sacked by *The Sun*. We met again some years later on a lively Arsenal trip to Athens, when I was working for the *Daily Star* and the Gunners were about to visit the breakers' yard. Just a few months ago, we came together on Facebook and exchanged views on both the Dons and, of course, Arsenal. I also received warm birthday wishes and the hope that I would have a prolonged life into my nineties. But, curiously, my request for his help in my literary escapades is ignored. I wonder if this reluctance is conscience-based. Perhaps, having digested what he said in that *Scotsman* interview, he, too, is experiencing the rough edges of embarrassment.

As for Bonthrone, he had just recovered from this particular indignity, when he, too, was left combing the wastelands of unemployment. But any person purporting to be discerning should not dismiss his tenure out of hand. His league placings – second, fourth, fourth, fifth – were almost respectable, if in no way an enhancement on the Turnbull template. Time would state that he was by no means the worst manager Aberdeen FC would ever have. In the season he left, the Dons narrowly escaped being relegated, but by then it had become the responsibility of Ally McLeod, rather than the man he replaced. Bonthrone's strength, aside from distributing calm over troubled waters created by Turnbull, was in identifying good footballers. Three come to mind: he signed a rock at the back, Eddie Thomson, from Hearts. He brought in the energy, goals threat and longevity of Drew Jarvie, who put in 386 appearances and 131 goals in ten seasons with the Dons. Then, ostensibly out of nowhere, he plucked the legendary Hungarian Zoltan Varga, who played only 26 times but left an indelible impression in the psyches of the fans. Varga, as you will learn, certainly left an imprint on my mind.

My 1975 George Square nemesis, Davidson, and I catch up one Friday afternoon in the Dutch Mill hotel, Queens Road, which is a traditional meeting place and drinking hub for Dons fans. Today, the man who once showed me an immaculate pairs of heels is a successful businessman. If he was the fastest footballer at Pittodrie back in the mid seventies, his playing record tells you he wasn't the most accomplished. Yet his 112 first-team appearances in eight years, allied to 27 goals, plus the fact that he survived four managers, supplies evidence that he was a most valued member of staff. He later played for Tulsa Roughnecks, Toronto Blizzard, See-Bee (Hong Kong) and Manchester City. He is ex-chairman of the Aberdeen former players' association, and therefore a valuable conduit to my research.

The subject of a nocturnal escapade in George Square is soon on the agenda for discussion. I wonder whether there had been any repercussions, particularly the next morning when the headlines hit. It seems not. 'I never knew of this conversation about our players not being 100 per cent fit,' he says. 'I'm pretty sure it was either Bumper, Willie Young or Willie Miller who first suggested a race. I didn't know I was to be the guinea pig. All I remember is going out and running in complete darkness. Aye, and winning. I also remember going back up in the train to Aberdeen the next afternoon. We went into Ma Cameron's for a few pints. We ended there until tea time. Then I just got the bus home. Repercussions? There were none. Maybe the result softened the blow a wee bit.'

Our conversation soon settles around Varga and I find myself recounting memories of an unconventional Saturday morning interview with the Hungarian, in 1972. The player and I had arranged to rendezvous at the Caledonian hotel at 10a.m. Can anyone imagine being able to interview a current player on match day? Anyway, Varga, who had been signed from Hertha Berlin after being caught up in a bribes scandal, arrived at the appointed hour. I was already in situ, but by then my nerve ends were tauter than Jerry Lee Lewis's piano strings.

Half an hour earlier, I had left my mother's house in Hilton Drive in an altogether different frame of mind. Jauntily, I vaulted over the low wall and galloped across the road to catch the No 17 bus into town. I went upstairs, lit a Benson and Hedges filter, and considered that life could not be improved upon. An interview with a foreign star was feeding both my ego and ambition. At the time, I was a sub-editor desperate to become a writer. This interview, conducted whilst on holiday in Aberdeen, would undoubtedly promote my cause. But there is, of course, a terrible fragility about emotions: these can never be confused with consistency. So, suddenly, when I heard the conductor asking for fares, my self-satisfied world began to disintegrate around my ears. I discovered that I had left my wallet at home and that I had about three shillings in my pocket. And three bob, even back in 1972, was scarcely going to buy you two cups of Lipton's in a four-star hotel. I mean, we were not meeting in some greasy spoon, for f***'s sake. I could scarcely ask Varga to pick up the bill, could I? Consider the embarrassment attached to that. And yet I daren't go back to my mother's house. If I did, the man would be entitled to curse my wayward time keeping and walk away. I'd miss the interview. The alternative, however, was equally untenable. But there was little option but to proceed and sweat it out. So sweat it out I did.

And by the time Varga appeared, I was in danger of surrendering to the floodwaters: the Hungarian had only turned up with his little boy in tow! All sorts of horrors were now careering along the corridors of my mind. I could hear myself asking. 'So what would you and your son like to drink, Zoltan?' And I could hear the response: 'Well, he'll take a knicker-bocker glory, please!' And that, all on its own, would knock my f***ing few shillings right out of the ballpark down into Union Terrace Gardens. Would I end up washing dishes in the Caley kitchen? But, hey, this was a day when I must have secured a credit line from The Man Upstairs. The little boy, bless him, politely refused the offer of a Coke, a bag of crisps, or indeed any light refreshment. Zoltan, in turn, contented himself with a coffee. I didn't even bother ordering anything for myself, just in case it was exorbitantly priced. I had been let off a hook that threatened to impale me. As it happened, I completed my interview – of which, thanks to the floodwaters, I remember almost nothing – and inserted a small but significant feather in my journalistic cap. Oh, and there was just about enough left in my trouser pocket for the smallest of tips to the waiter. I received one of those boss-eyed looks from him, as if to say, 'You tight bastard!' Oh, if he'd only known the hell I'd experienced that day. Whatever, I was obliged to walk home and collect more funds before I did anything else.

Davidson's recollections of the Hungarian are far more detailed and subtle than mine. 'It was completely different to see a continental player coming into the club,' he recalls. 'Different, too, in how he went about his training and practice sessions. First of all, he was two-footed and you would have found it difficult to say which his better foot was. He was a bit like Bobby Charlton. He was slight but his ability was outstanding. But, probably the biggest thing was when we had finished training and we'd go back to Pittodrie, Zoltan hadn't finished. He would then get half a dozen balls, go out onto the park and practise corners, either side, either foot. He'd curl them into the corner of the net. So, what we as young players saw was that your training didn't finish at 12 o'clock. We began to do the same.

'I remember one practice game we had down at Woodside, Zoltan said he was injured with a bad knee. But you would never have known if this was correct or not. So this day he said he'd play in the reserve team. We were all there – Willie Miller, Ian Hair, and Joe Smith. He said as his left knee was sore, he'd only kick with his right foot. This he duly did. We won that match. You know, there was obviously this story about him being involved in bribery, which he always denied. But he was a quiet guy and he learned to speak English. He stayed out in Milltimber, where we live now. He was a neighbour of Bobby Clark's, so Bobby kinda took him under his wing. I remember he was a very keen photographer and always had a camera with him.

'Come a Saturday, when he played, the crowd had never seen anything like him, well for a number of years, anyway. But then he just seemed to disappear. All of a sudden. And, of course, when that happened, he went to Ajax to replace Johan Cruyff, who had gone to Barcelona. Someone once asked Zoltan if he could take any player from Aberdeen to Ajax, who would it have been. It was Arthur Graham. He really rated Arthur.'

But others rated Varga. Billy Bremner was one. Davidson remembers, 'We often tell the story about just before the 1974 World Cup. Zoltan was down at Largs and they put together a team from the players doing their coaching courses against Scotland. The story goes that Billy Bremner knew all about him because Leeds had played Ferencvaros some time before. So there they were at Largs, with Bremner running around trying to kick him the whole game. Bremner said he was one of the best midfielders he'd ever faced.'

Varga's career at Ajax was even more temporary than it had been at Pittodrie. He played only 12 times for them before he found a more permanent billet at Borussia Dortmund. Even then, it lasted only two years. He died on 9 April 2010 whilst playing in a veterans' five-a-side. He was 65. 'So sad,' says Davidson. 'It wasn't as if he just came, sat in the dressing room and never took anyone on. His English wasn't great, but he tried to communicate. This was just a staging post for him. He could have come and played the superstar, but he was something else as a human being. He was very humble.'

I think back to that meeting in the Caley. You wouldn't wish to share an evening with some of the embryonic superstars I have met. Yet here was a shy and pleasant man who spoke in faltering English but was wholly familiar with good breeding. And that had been passed on to a little boy who sat quietly and respectfully beside him; this was a little boy who turned the Oliver Twist theme on its head. He made my day by not asking for more.

* *

IF BONTHRONE WENT WITHOUT a murmur, it would have been appropriate if a brass band had heralded the arrival of the next manager at Pittodrie. Ally McLeod, as subtle as a Glasgow Kiss, was not a man known for dodging radar guns; he was more likely to be operating the technology! During my short tenure at the *Scottish Sun*, he and a couple of my sporting colleagues would meet for lunch in the Glasgow Press Club. He was manager of part-time Ayr United back then. Martin Frizzell, of the *News of the World*, told me those lunch-time sessions were memorable. I found him no less entertaining when I asked for his expectations concerning a league match. 'We'll contain then in the first half, then rattle down the hill in the second and stick five goals past them!' Can you imagine today's masters of managerial diplomacy saying something as provocative as that? Davidson remembers the McLeod tenure in terms of a whirlwind – one that whistled right through the club and up into the town, without leaving a trail of devastation. 'He obviously made a big effort with the fans. There was always a story (in the newspapers) and if there wasn't, he would manufacture one. He got interest going again. He was never the most tactically aware, but the enthusiasm couldn't be criticised. And he got players to play. He made a huge difference in the short time he was here.'

McLeod imported three influential players: Stuart Kennedy, from Falkirk, and Dom Sullivan, from Clyde. Joe Harper, meanwhile, was brought back from Hibs. There again, there was the 'sitting tenant', Jocky Scott, a striker who had arrived from Dundee to give Bonthrone scoring hope. All those players bought into McLeod's ideas, no matter how unconventional or zany they were. We return to the tactics theme. There was a manoeuvre that developed straight from kick-off when the ball was returned to Joe Smith, who would hit it diagonally down the left touchline: three players would charge down the line to confront and hopefully confound an apprehensive full back. Davidson laughs. 'No one has ever figured that one out. It was never explained. Not even by Ally. He just told us to do it. So you did it. There sometimes used to be more than three players when the ball was lumped down there. I suppose it was to get into the opponents' half early and put pressure on them.'

Aesthetically, the move delivered little satisfaction to the purists, but it did work some of the time, according to Scott. 'Sometimes you were getting a corner kick in the first 30 seconds, so you're putting pressure on the opposition right away. It wasn't a bad move because nine times out of ten, the right back, with three players bearing down on him, was not going to make a pass or try to be clever. The best he was going to do was head it back up the park again. It certainly let them see that you were going to be positive.'

McLeod was a huge admirer of Jinky Smith's brother, Joe. 'He was played just in front of the back four,' Davidson recalls. 'When the back four got the ball, it was a case of give it to Joe. This didnae please Willie Miller. Willie's view was if he had the ball, why pass it five yards to Smith when he could pass it 20 yards to midfield? Still, everything reverberated around Joe at that time.' Miller, it should be added, was just beginning to emphasise his importance to the team at the back and not, as Bonthrone had predicted, the front line.

Anyway, the reverberations were largely positive. Away back in his youth, probably when he was at Chelsea under Tommy Docherty, Scott had discovered a champion in his fellow Aberdonian, Denis Law. Consequently, he wore his shirt outside his shorts and had a habit of raising one arm when he scored. He liked to be different, something that curiously had never been encouraged by Bonthrone at Pittodrie. 'Wear your shirt inside your shorts, sir,' he was advised. Scott also thrived on appearing to be lugubrious, although the mournful look had no associations with the strictures. But, if you looked hard enough, you could just about discern happiness bubbling away inside him. 'It was fun going into work in those days,' he says. 'Ally was a motivator and a lovely man. He came away with different ways of getting you to work hard, but it was enjoyable. So you were working hard without realising that you were doing so. We'd have eight-a-side games in the car park. During them, Ally would throw in various conditions. When you passed the ball, for instance, you had to run full-paced for 20 yards. At other times, if you passed the ball, you had to do an overlap on the boy who'd received it. By that time, he was running with the ball, so when you got to him, you were knackered. As players, we were going, "What's this all about?" But, as I said, it was enjoyable. All the boys took it on board and worked away. We got results and when you got results, you didn't question how things worked during the week.'

In any situation, however, there is always one militant willing to stand up and question the orders. Scott takes us back to those games in the car park. 'One team might be winning 10-6. So Ally would say, "The next goal is worth five." So it could be 15-6 or 11-10. This particular day he told us the next goal would be worth four. Bobby Clark was in one goal, which was two 8ft poles attached to wheels: there were nae nets. Bobby's team was winning, but someone from the opposition shot and it went in between the sticks, although very high. Bobby did his usual. "That's away!" he cries. Ally shouts "GOAL!" So that was Bobby's team losing. He had a go at the gaffer. He retrieves the ball. Ally tells him to get it back in play. There was a row of houses behind the car park. Bobby boots the ball away over the fence into the garden of one of the houses. "Well, that's what I think of your f***ing game," he says. And he walked off. That's just the way Ally got you. Even in training, he got you revved up.'

But McLeod's highly-tuned motor was liable to rev itself up away from the car park and, indeed, during games that mattered. Scott: 'Oh, aye, you'd see him in a temper. He'd ladle in at half time or full-time, whatever. He wisnae slow in giving you dog's abuse if you weren't pulling your weight. He had an awful habit of flicking his arm. One day, his f***ing watch fell aff. Everybody was trying no' to laugh while he was stoatin' about.'

But if there was a time for laughter, there was also a time for professional motivation. 'Once he had you wound up, he'd say that we had to make sure we were the better team. He never said anything derogatory about the opposition or their players. He would concentrate on his own team and how good you were. But, believe me, you'd go out on that pitch and believe you were the best team going. You were convinced that you'd run over the top of the opposition that day.'

But there was a period in Mcleod's first season when Aberdeen would have found the greatest difficulty in negotiating a bump in the road, never mind run over the top of people. In March and April of 1976, they suffered five straight defeats and then contrived to draw the next three games, giving them three points out of 16. This was exactly the sort of form that had teams relegated. And now the R word was being bandied about, albeit in whispered terms, in the dressing room. Worse still, there were legitimate fears that the team might have to go part-time. Davidson spells out those fears. 'I think by then teams had begun to realise how we played. So then you got into a run of losing games. You kept thinking that it would come together, but it got to the stage where it looked pretty serious. Coming to that last game of the season, against Hibs and Eddie Turnbull, you were beginning to think that we would no longer be full-time players if we went down. I remember we were sitting in the bath one day and George Murray, the coach, said, "People's jobs are going to be at stake here." I mean, never before would you have associated Aberdeen with part-time football.' Somehow the Dons left the nightmare scenario in their slipstream. Two victories within four days allowed them to breathe again without the assistance of an artificial aid. They beat St Johnstone away, 2-0, then Hibs 3-0 at home. Goals in the final game came by courtesy of Jarvie, Smith and Robb.

McLeod, still smarting over the indignity of a possible relegation, laid his marker down with a vengeance the very next season, winning the League Cup and finishing a creditable third in the league. Scott's contribution to the cup competition was considerable, scoring three times against Rangers in the semi-final. 'All with the right foot,' he reminds you. But it's time to turn the spotlight on one of Scott's henchmen.

Davie Robb – you'll remember his football stockings were once covered in printers' ink – failed to respond to a request to be interviewed for this book. It was my loss. I remember talking to him in his office at Holborn Junction: he was splendid company. But the man who scored the winner against Celtic in that League Cup victory rarely features when people talk about their favourite players. There were times when he looked like a thoroughbred footballer; there were others when it looked as if he should be driving a tractor. He was highly regarded within the confines of Pittodrie, however. 'I remember speaking to Pat Stanton,' says Davidson, 'and he described him as his most difficult opponent. Billy McNeill said that as well. He was a great guy to have around a dressing room, and a funny guy in his own way. But he was one who would do the opposite to everyone else. Once, we went on a pre-season tour to Germany and were staying in a little village where both Puma and Adidas had factories. We were to be shown round the Adidas factory and museum; we all thought this was good because maybe we'd get a tracksuit out of it. So we all went. Not Davie. He organised it to go to the Puma factory on his own. And, boy, did he have a windfall! He came back with tracksuits and hold-alls.'

Life, then, was special rather than tolerable under Ally McLeod. Strangely, however, one man refused to buy into the bonhomie and banter: the ever faithful Teddy Scott. 'It was a strange thing,' Davidson recalls. 'Teddy was there forever, but he and Ally never got on. There seemed to be something that just didn't work between them. Maybe it was because Ally was solely concentrated on the first team, whereas Teddy was with the reserves and the young players trying to push them through. But the antipathy was noticeable. The training staff all used to change in what was called Teddy's room. But Teddy finished up changing in the dressing room with the players. Yes, there seemed to be an uneasy relationship. This, of course, completely changed when Billy McNeill came in and then Alex Ferguson. Teddy was really close to both of them. He also had an awful lot of time for Turnbull, because Turnbull probably incorporated him into everything. And he could see the benefit of young players. Teddy was never slow to say to the manager, whoever that might be, "He's ready. Give him a chance." You know, he was a nice man but he could also be quite hard as well. He was always there, though, to give you a bit of advice. If you weren't training properly, or if you were doing things wrong, he would tell you to your face. And he'd also bring it up in front of the manager. Probably his best gift was with players coming from the South of Scotland. He would make sure they were looked after as well as possible and would understand the difficulties of them being away from their families. What a survivor he was.'

The domestic exploits of McLeod captured the attention of the predatory SFA, who were ready to jettison Willie Ormond for someone they believed to be a more charismatic figure. They wooed McLeod, but the courtship was supposed to be a secret. In May of 1977, Aberdeen flew to what was Yugoslavia for a friendly. When they arrived in Dubrovnik, McLeod told his players that he had taken the international job but would not be making it public until after the trip had ended. I ask Davidson who was first into the telephone box. Cue uproarious laughter. He doesn't answer the question but offers, 'We played a game and then stayed another two or three days in what was a nice end of season break. We were all sorry to see him go because he'd done a lot at the club and was going to better himself.'

But, if McLeod was intent on improving his station in life, Aberdeen FC were determined not to be shunted into the sidings. Another major name was about to be plundered from the lower divisions: Billy McNeill. The Dons' trajectory was heading inexorably upward. But, before we attempt to deal with life at altitude, we must revisit the matter of essential players and address the hugely important factor of Stuart Kennedy.

CHAPTER 5

A Template for Arsenal

Aberdeen may have found a way to combat the curse of relegation. I've already experienced an even more serious form of demotion and failed to react with similar fortitude. Another drunken rampage by yours truly warrants a summons from News International's *head office and the additional supplement of a swift and brutal denouement on arrival in London. I am 30 years of age. My colleagues withdraw their labour in support of me, but their laudable efforts are countered with implacability from the suits in Rupert Murdoch's squad. And so my rented home in Stirling turns into a bleak house. I have no job, no prospects and, critically, very little money. What do I do? I opt for the crazy option and propose marriage to my girlfriend, Margaret. She has three children, two of whom live with us. She's crazy, too. She accepts the proposal. We quit the rented house and move in with my mother in nearby Cambusbarron.*

After staring at the ceiling, or alternatively the wall, for some months, I decide that depression doesn't suit me. I begin working on the oil barges at Leith docks. It's a 20th century acknowledgment to the slave trade: 12 hours a day, seven days a week, £1 an hour. There are characters here that even Dickens could not have invented. On Saturdays and Sundays, an exasperated foreman called Peter turns a blind eye and we are allowed to break off early – in late afternoon. There is no sunshine over this part of Leith. Slavery sucks. Every man deserves one complete day off. I search for something more suitable. I start selling penny insurances in deprived areas of Stirling. In many ways I'm part of the deprivation, for I'm on just over 20 quid a week. This also sucks, but at least I'm not coming home at night smelling of oil and seawater. My wife Margaret not only looks like a model, she doubles as a saint. I appreciate such sanctity: she works in a lawyer's office, cleans the house till it sparkles, and looks after the boys. She mollycoddles me in her spare time. I should be the one doing the pampering: there's a baby on the way. When the child is born, we leave the safe haven of my mother's house and rent a small tenement flat in the town, two floors up. I supplement my wages by writing a page of sport for Reveille. *But this golden egg is shattered when I attend a soiree and punch a fellow journalist for dancing suggestively with my wife. I lose my union card and my job with*

Reveille. *I'm now a reluctant resident, sitting at the bottom of life's ladder, and I've formed an attachment with desperation. My life once flowed like poetry. Nothing rhymes any longer. My love affair with Aberdeen FC has been necessarily suspended. I don't have enough money to go to football any more.*

One day, however, I find some and travel the short distance to Alloa to witness the Dons and the local worthies in Scottish Cup action. We triumph 4-0 and, with a few pints of lager under my belt, I take part in the celebrations on the pitch. Chris Anderson, the director around whom many of Aberdeen's dreams will be built, is on the pitch as well. But he's there to trying to clear it and restore respectability to the good name of Aberdeen FC. He admonishes me. There is enough about me to experience a sense of shame.

SOME events in football are quite unable to correlate with logic. How, for instance, does one explain the dichotomy of Aberdeen flirting with relegation in 1975-76 and then winning the Scottish League Cup the next season and indeed going on to finish third in the league? It couldn't solely be the vigorous input of Ally McLeod, could it? The answer is supplied, to my way of thinking, by making the short journey from my home in Glasgow to Stirlingshire, and focusing on one of those influential signings mentioned in the previous chapter. There, I meet a man whose name has formed a liaison with legend. Stuart Kennedy is such a livewire that there is a danger of static electricity when he shakes my hand at the door of his beautiful home in Grangemouth. At the time of my visit, he is 63 years of age and yet there is no evidence of a companion with a beard and a sickle. Kennedy's sheer vibrancy, I imagine, keeps Father Time at a respectful distance. After introducing me to his son and his wife, we sit down at the breakfast bar, but sitting is scarcely an attractive option for my host. At times, he favours vacating his bar stool and illustrating his unconventional, somewhat immodest, arrival at Pittodrie.

But, hey, you can forgive Kennedy for representing himself in any way he chooses. Just concentrate on the fact that he bequeathed to Aberdeen seven years of indomitable spirit, including 333 league appearances. And when he succumbed to an abominable knee injury that stopped his career in its tracks, he did what possibly no player has ever done before. We shall return to this incredible decision in the next chapter in more detail.

We're back, meanwhile, at the summer of 1976. Kennedy was a part-timer with Falkirk who had signed with Aberdeen for a £20,000-plus fee. (It stipulates £40,000 on *afcheritage.org* but I'll take Kennedy's word for it). He had been warned by a friend who played for St Johnstone that by joining the Dons, he would be regressing rather than progressing. The forecast was uncanny in its prescience, as far as the newcomer was concerned. 'Myself and Dom Sullivan, part-time frae Clyde: this was our first pre-season. Were we able for this? Well, that theory was soon forgotten. We started training and I was on a different planet, fitness-wise. I was a dedicated athlete who lived properly, who never drank and who was obsessed by fitness. I was a cross country runner – that was my game. I was also quick. I was 60 yards ahead of the others, but that was their problem. And I'm no' showin' ma full hand here. I'm being polite. Big-style polite.'

The consensus between Kennedy and Sullivan was that Jimmy Bonthrone had been too easy on them. They felt it needed someone to come along and expose them. 'Myself and Sullivan certainly did that. We were in a different league from the rest of the players, fitness-wise.' So the exposure assumed an embarrassing and sometimes acrimonious shape. Kennedy noted that there was a powerful clique that organised the dressing room. He recalls it comprised Jocky Scott, Joe Harper, Davie Robb, Drew Jarvie, Billy Williamson and Arthur Graham. 'They were the group that ran the show and no' in a good way. Too many players had chosen the soft option. There needed to be a wake-up call. And I'm thinkin' to myself: "I'm sortin' this out. Good or bad." Hey, the others didn't react very well, but there was a problem for them in that I'd served my time as an engineer in the shipyards. Their acting no' very well was play-school stuff for me. I knew the bitchin' that goes on with Joe; I knew the actions in the background. "Oh, the new boy is tryin' tae impress. He'll eventually crack up and come back to the pack." I heard all these snippets in the background. I'm thinkin', "What a shame for these boys, eh? They think they're gonna rattle me with that?" I came into the dressing room one day and made an announcement. "Hey, I've no' been showin' ma full hand here. I'm gonna start trainin' properly for your cheek." And that's what I did. I exposed them.'

The exposure had dramatic consequences. There was one race across the sand dunes of Balmedie in which Kennedy felt he was being hampered by one of his colleagues – George Campbell. He appeared to be ignoring Kennedy's pleas to let him past. Kennedy's main opponent in these events, Sullivan, was catching him, so this was not the occasion for gentlemanly conduct. 'It was like a Grand Prix situation, so I just manhandled him to the ground, trampled across him and ran on. At the end, George reported me to Teddy Scott.'

This occurred on a Saturday morning. Kennedy went back home for the weekend and returned to Aberdeen on the Monday. He was told that McLeod wanted a word with him. Within himself, he suspected the 'sweetie wives' of the dressing room had exacted their revenge over him and that he was in line for a reprimand. He resolved within himself that if he was not happy with the result of this conversation, he'd get back in his motor and return to Grangemouth, whereupon he'd sign for someone who appreciated his strict adherence to pre-season training. His conversation with McLeod appeared to begin negatively. 'You've been involved in a few incidents, son.' Kennedy agreed readily, but asked, 'So, what's the problem?' There was, in fact, an accolade rather than a problem. 'I paid £23,000 for you and I thought I knew what I was buying. But I'd have paid four times that for you!'

A jubilant Kennedy returned to the dressing room and announced to his team mates that he had been offered a new contract. 'Then I went aboot ma business.' Such pragmatism seemed to have a revitalising effect on those players who had been savouring the sweet life. The yawning gaps in fitness between the residents and the newcomers began to close, in Kennedy's opinion. People began to pay attention to professionalism. There was additional and inevitable drama with Harper, however. 'Hey, Joe was the king. He was the greatest goal scorer that I've ever seen playin' for Aberdeen – nae question about that. So he's the top scorer and no' an easy guy to take on. But I'm no' goin' away. Anyone watching the Tour de France knows there's a guy who gets a yellow jersey every day. Well, that was my property. It doesn't matter what your daen, I'm in the frame. Maybe Joe was thinking that I was a wee boy coming in frae Falkirk. I did actually say to myself that I'd wait two or three months before I said somethin'. But then, no, I fast forwarded the situation. Joe's quite verbal and quite a clever wee guy. So we had a couple of scuffles at training and even although I'm givin' away a few stone, we always managed a draw. You got 20 or 30 seconds and then they stop it. If you're goin' to clash at trainin', I stick up for what I believe in.'

The competitive edge, once honed to perfection by Eddie Turnbull, re-emerged and the dividends were there for all to see. Aberdeen topped the league at one point and were simply irresistible in the League Cup. In the semi-final, Kennedy remembers they somehow managed to improve on standards and whipped Rangers, 5-1. 'It was a demolition job,' he says. 'People had hardly seen better football from an Aberdeen team. I played in a lot of games, but that was something special. The standard, with the one-twos, well, it was like Arsenal. I think that must have been the template Arsene Wenger used. It was everything about how football should be played. And then we beat Celtic, 2-1, in extra time to win the trophy.'

By this time, when Kennedy surveyed his immediate surroundings, he was enthused by the commitment displayed by his colleagues. He was further cheered by the influx of youth at the club. He witnessed the emergence into the sunlight of players like John McMaster, Andy Watson and Alex McLeish. He shared digs in Crown Street with the latter; he hadn't even seen him play, but he was convinced that here was a talent. 'I told him that. He was big and gangly, but I says, "You're a player, big man." He carried himself well at training. He was vocal, maybe too vocal for his pay grade, because he wasn't qualified to hand out stick to certain people. But he won my protection on that. I gave the big man a lot of political asylum, call it diplomatic immunity. 'Cos I knew – whit a player he's gonna be. And he was.'

If Kennedy could enthuse over the arrival of Alex McLeish, he would mourn the exit of Ally McLeod. But you imagine there was the compensatory factor of Billy McNeill and an introduction that no-one could have envisaged.

The earth seemed to move up in the Granite City in the season 1977-78, and it was the sound of McNeill hitting the ground running. He had been manager of Clyde for only a year when the temptation of Aberdeen became irresistible. McLeod had left his fellow Glaswegian a UEFA Cup place, but a double header against FC Molenbeek left the Dons free to concentrate on domestic competitions. There was a major improvement thereafter, however. McNeill took them to second place to Rangers in the league and to the final of the League Cup, where they lost 2-1 to the same team. 'We beat them three times in the league and were the better team. We just didnae have Cup final players at that time.' Goals at this time were not a problem, with Harper, Jarvie and newcomer Steve Archibald sharing in the considerable bounty.

So, whatever happened to Jocky Scott? His career at Pittodrie probably peaked when he scored three goals against Rangers in the semi-final of the 1976 League Cup, but now he had to convince another manager of his worth. And it seemed the manager was not keen on being convinced. 'A couple of weeks after Billy took over, Billy admitted to me that he'd approached Dundee about Gordon Strachan and that they'd asked about me in a possible swap deal,' Scott recalls. 'I told him I wisnae interested and I don't think he was too happy about that. I did play for the first team under Billy, but it wasn't as regular as it had been with Ally or Jimmy. Billy admitted later that his initial thought about me was that I was a lazy bandit, a bandit who didnae have the right attitude. He also admitted later that he'd been wrong; he saw me working in training and how I performed in reserve games. But by that time, he'd made up his mind that he didnae want me. I eventually went back to Dundee, and Gordon moved to Aberdeen.'

Scott, the lover of all things Denis Law, was described by commentator Archie McPherson as one of the most enigmatic players in Scotland. How does he feel about that now, all these years later? 'If I knew what that meant, I could reply to it,' he smiles. 'I think Billy got his perception of me being inconsistent through being a player himself. And if it was his perception, I could fully understand it. Throughout my career, with Dundee and Aberdeen, I would play well against Rangers, but not so well against Celtic. Of course, at that time, Celtic were the top team. It had nothing to do with feeling inferior. I never went out there thinking this was going to be difficult. But, against Rangers, I couldn't stop scoring goals. Against Celtic, I couldn't score. In fact, I think I scored less than five against them with the two teams. Whereas, I was into double figures against Rangers.

'Mind you, I was never played as a striker who was the one furthest up the pitch. I got a bit of licence to go where I wanted, providing I was doing the business. I wasn't a Wee Joe Harper. Every time you attacked, you knew you'd find him in the penalty box. Wee Joe was never out of there, unless he was taking a free kick. But, enigmatic? To be honest, I've been called a lot of things and it's water off a duck's back. When you're involved in the game, people form opinions of you, and you're either a good player or you're crap. There's no in between when you play football. You know, people write things about you and they say things on radio or television. If I had worried about it, I probably wouldnae have lasted the time I did. Fans say that they pay their money and are entitled to shout. Fine. I wisnae allowed to shout back at them – although I did a few times.'

I ask him if he is being flippant. He tells me not. 'Oh, aye. I told them where to go. It was only when I went into coaching that I realised why I had been getting the abuse in some games. You started working with players and realised their potential. When they're no' doing it, you put your opinion across and start trying to motivate them and telling them to get their fingers out. It wasn't till then that it dawned on me that was possibly why the fans started abusing me – I wasn't performing the way they thought I should be and the way that I'd been in previous games. So, from that point of view, maybe I shouldn't have shouted back at them.'

But if the McNeill-Scott dynamic scarcely warranted the description of a mutual appreciation society, the relationship Kennedy shared with his new gaffer had even darker influences. Initially, anyway. 'At first, Billy wisnae my favourite manager. Me and him clashed and clashed very badly. I'm very vocal, but only for malingerers. If you're no' touchin' cones and no touchin' markers, I'm gonna expose ye. So Big Billy would say that this was a great run by somebody. He, remember, was looking from a front elevation. The guy's two or three yards short. So I would say, "Was that a great run? He never touched a marker yet! See if I don't touch them, you tell me." Billy didnae like that. Why? He was the first guy to hold the European Cup. When he came into the dressing room, his chest came in ten minute afore his body. He just had this thing that he was Billy McNeill. Me – I'm a hard-working player who wants to know that someone is not going to jeopardise my bonus. Now, the young boys were watching all this. I'm sayin', "Do you want them to learn properly? If so, don't copy him – copy me and him over there." So, aye, we clashed regularly.'

It was in Seaton Park that their problems with one another threatened to multiply. Instead, it was the turning point, where they began to share respect and an understanding of each other. Kennedy says he had never complained about training either at Falkirk or under McLeod. But now in the playing fields down by the River Don, he was ready to sign a complaints form. 'I go from byline to byline. I'm no' a centre half, headin' the ball now and again. I need to be properly fit. I felt we were getting too much of a slog. You needed to be tapering down. The season's about a fortnight away and I need to feel sharpness in my legs. But I wisnae feeling that. Billy gave us this drill called "The Train."'

This was a series of punishing running exercises which gave the Lisbon Lions their fitness and ability to outrun teams. Kennedy made a comment that penetrated deep into lead-balloon territory. 'Oh, no "The Train" again... ' McNeill responded heatedly, saying that if it was good enough for Celtic, it was good enough for Aberdeen. Kennedy's wits were as quick as his feet. 'Was that the team that we beat in the League Cup final last year? Hey, Tommy Burns, it didnae work for him. Then they played Paul Wilson against me. That didnae work, either. And, guess what, in extra time, they put Bobby Lennox, the buzz bomb, on. He never caused me any bother, either. So dinnae worry about ma fitness.'

McNeill's response was to shout of the names of the teams for the relay. 'He announces Joe Harper's name. I'm sayin' to myself that I hope I'm no' in his team. Willie Garner is next. Hey, milk could turn quicker than him. The third person is Joe Smith; now, he hardly ever leaves the centre circle. Then it's "KENNEDY!" I tell him I've got a first name. It's obvious he wants me to be last. Childish. Now, I don't want to be last and running 4 x 100 yards is no' Wee Joe's distance. But at the baton changing, he's goin' to be hustlin' and upsetting people. So we finish not last but second last. I'm shoutin', "I'm Spartacus!" We were reported to the manager for cheatin'; I says, aye, there were two cheats: Joe Harper for obstruction. And me running 120 yards instead of 100. I want this in the Green Final that I was an effin' cheat. As it happened, I had a friend in Billy's assistant, John Clark. He was a big fan of me and I think he probably said to Billy that I couldn't be a bad influence.

'Anyway, we played Arbroath in a pre-season friendly. Billy says I'll need to pay particular attention to their left winger, Tommy Yule. Said he faced him a couple of years back when he was still playing and that he was quite a tricky player and had given the Celtic defence problems. I said that I had mair problems with dandruff than he'd gie me. I proceeded tae stick him in ma back pocket. In fairness, at half-time, Billy came up tae me and said, "Point taken." I thought, "That'll dae me." All the conflict was contained in pre-season. Look, he was a young manager and maybe his man management was no' the greatest at the time. But I'll gie him this: he bought (Steve) Archibald and (Gordon) Strachan, two of Aberdeen's greatest ever signings. And what a record he had in only one year. I certainly never had any problem with him after that. He was always polite tae me and vice versa.'

Duncan Davidson, in contrast, enjoyed a far closer and amicable relationship with his new manager. That season of 1978, the latter scored eight goals in the league, and four in cup competitions. In spite of the managerial upheaval, things were looking good: there was presence in the manager's office, pace in the team, results on the field (they went 23 games unbeaten) and, critically, peace in the dressing room. John Clark had brought his soothing oil along with him. Teddy Scott had resurrected himself after his disputes with McLeod and now was much more involved. There was time for impromptu comedy, even when they were attempting to chase down the eventual league winners.

The Dons went to Ibrox in early March and put three past them, without reply. That afternoon McNeill, no doubt recollecting his fabulous playing history with Celtic, walked out of the double doors at Ibrox, his magnificent chest as ever thrust those famous several inches in front of him. Davidson, a couple of steps behind, watched his manager being harangued by a gray-haired lady. 'She was an old granny and must have been 80,' he remembers. 'She was giving McNeill dog's abuse. I turned to tell her to go easy – and she's whacked me in the face with her handbag!

'Stevie Archibald scored twice in that game, with Wee Joe grabbing the other. And that's what got us going for the rest of the season. We were catching Rangers all the time. I think they had to go to Tannadice twice and we thought they were bound to drop points. But they won them both. Still, Big Billy had one of the best records of any Aberdeen manager – about 60 per cent winning rate. It was all about attacking football. It was a case of, "Get in among them and get the crowd on your side early on." I enjoyed my time under McNeill.'

Celtic, embarrassed that they had finished only fifth in a ten-horse Premier Division race, were consorting with the unfamiliar figure of mediocrity. Their board of directors determined that this relationship had to end quickly. So they invited their legendary manager, Jock Stein, to stand down and offered him a post as manager of their pools company. The derisory offer was speedily and justifiably declined. The Glasgow club had better fortune with their next invitation, however. They looked at and lusted after McNeill, the man who held the European Cup aloft in Lisbon back in 1967. The temptation for McNeill was too great, but anyone believing this was a straightforward decision is deluding himself. I had always suspected that he left Aberdeen reluctantly and I received confirmation of this one day a few years later when he was established as Celtic manager. He told me, 'We had played Stenhousemuir in a pre-season friendly and if you hadn't known which shirts the teams wore, you wouldn't have been able to identify Celtic. It was that bad. I came back up the road that night and I stopped in a lay-by before entering the city. As the dawn came up, I placed my head in my hands. "What the hell have I done?" I asked myself.'

CHAPTER 6

The Blast Furnace

Soon, the Cooneys are moving to a co-ownership house on the outskirts of Stirling to accommodate this family of five. God alone knows how we are going to afford it. The impecuniosity that keeps me apart from my beloved Dons is tormenting me. Is there to be no reprieve from its strictures? It appears not. There's time for another major reverse in finances before we quit our tenement flat. My mother gives us her old Austin 1100, but it's in good condition and is low mileage. It's parked innocently outside when some moron decides to write it off. The insurance company, after much deliberation, delivers a cheque with a pittance attached. Something is certain: I must get back to doing what I do, or my life is going to be over before I know it. The manager of my insurance firm is talking about buying a fleet of Morris Marinas. That's his fantasy. My reality is that the guy from the head office has just visited Stirling and described myself and another insurance inspector as 'peanut producers.' I don't even begin to take offence. My heart is not in this job: I would find it difficult to sell sun tan oil to a beach replete with red-heads!

Suddenly, the stricken man is talking to an unofficial branch of the Samaritans. I have written to David Emery, a former colleague on the Daily Mail. Now working as an executive in the Daily Express, he invites me down to Fleet Street for some casual shifts. A couple of days later, in this summer of 1978, the sports editor makes me a member of staff. I'm back in what is known as the mouse race. Not long after this, I hear that a guy called Alex Ferguson is also back in the respectable world in which we all wish to live. He's been sacked by St Mirren, but Aberdeen have tossed him a lifebelt and thus he's been plucked from the troubled waters of unemployment. The Dons have had three managers in just over three years; will he last? I doubt it. I once sat beside a colleague when he phoned Ferguson during his spell at East Stirling. The pattern of the subsequent conversation informed me he was a bolshie bugger. Bolshie buggers don't usually last, do they? Unless, of course, they have reservoirs of talent.

FRIENDSHIPS are constructed in many different ways and over myriad timescales. Some take weeks, months or even years to germinate. Others are instantaneous. The one designated for discussion was to become one of the most important liaisons in the history of Aberdeen FC. It was formed, without cere-mony, circa 1971 – almost a hundred miles from the Granite City. Stuart Ken-nedy, an apprentice engineer in a Grangemouth shipyard, was jogging from Grahamston Station towards Brockville, home of Falkirk FC. Alex Ferguson, a senior player, was also heading towards the old stadium, but he had the advan-tage of his own transport. He stopped the car and offered the young man a lift. The offer was declined because the player explained that the jog was essential to his part-time training schedule. Ferguson, already quietly impressed, point-ed out that it was raining. Kennedy's reply was succinct, even cheeky. 'I work in a shipyard and know all about f***in' rain.' But the brusque riposte only emphasised the synergy between them. He recalls, 'When I mentioned the word "shipyard" you'd have thought someone had given him a Playboy magazine!' Ferguson, you'll remember, also had worked in a Govan shipyard earlier in life.

This is the cue to fill in their personal histories at that time. Ferguson was still a playing as a striker and a pugnacious one at that, but he was also work-ing out strategies for the moment when age removed the serrated edge from his game. He wanted to understand that game and, being a diligent pupil, had taken all his SFA coaching badges. 'Those badges were comin' out of his ears,' Kennedy remembers. 'So, in some ways, he's all dressed up with no place to go.' There was a solution, however. Ferguson asked the manager, Willie Cun-ningham, whether he could watch the part-time training sessions and maybe project some of the ideas that were filtering into his head. Cunningham had no intention of declining such an offer. So Fergie attended his first evening session, auditioning for a future that probably lay beyond even his expansive dreams.

Kennedy's lot was perhaps no less complicated. He was a Falkirk player, but one pummelled by frustration. He was only 18 and yet yearned to be playing first-team football. But this pathway was blocked by a right back called Gregor Abel. Kennedy had the confidence and certainty of youth. 'Yeah, Gregor was the right back at the time, but it should have been me.' Kennedy had originally planned to sign for Stenhousemuir and a manager he virtually idolised. 'Alex Smith was the doyen even back then; he was a Mount Rushmore kind of guy.' But club loyalties – Kennedy was a staunch Falkirk fan – had won the day. He signed for the Bairns, but now he was beginning to suspect that those loyalties would undermine his career.

Ferguson was waiting when a bedraggled Kennedy arrived at Brockville. He had seen something in the young man that promised much for the future. Kennedy changed and embarked on what he described as a 'brutal run.' Fergie was further impressed and described his attitude in glowing terms. Kennedy was confused because he'd never been praised in such a way before. 'I'm thinking, "Hey, I run like this all the time." Now, Willie Cunningham was the manager, but he didn't even come to part-time training. The two coaches were Alan Cousins and Dunky McGill. Neither of these coaches had ever said anything about me being brilliant.' Another brutal session ensued. 'Fergie was right there. He told me again that I had a fantastic attitude to training. We get talking about work. I told him I took a propeller off that mornin', but I was really just a gofer. He seemed interested in me.'

That interest was maintained when the training session recognised the tradition of a five-a-side game. At one point, Kennedy played a ball into space for another player to run onto. The player remained static. The two coaches dismissed the pass as another bad ball. Fergie disagreed. 'That was the right ball, son.' Kennedy's ears rang with the sound of endorsement from the older man, and now he was willing to listen to some more advice. 'Later that night, Fergie says, "You're a first-team player, son. I'll get you in the first team." I told him that I would be going to Stenhousemuir with Alex Smith, where I'd get a two-year contract. I was going to ask for a free transfer and my career would get to where it was going. But Fergie's advice was not to be hasty. I'm wonderin' how he can get me into the first team. He told me that the manager was coming to a reserve game the next Thursday: I would be playin' and I had not to let him down. That was it. And from there it all happened: he got me into that first team.'

With Falkirk safe from relegation, there were two first-team games left that season. Kennedy fretted that Fergie's overt praise might go against him. 'Listen to this,' he advises, 'if you go to a manager and flourish a protégé under his nose, he's no' gaun to like it, is he? They (Falkirk) had Arbroath at home and, wait for it, Aberdeen away. What game do I get? Aberdeen away! They've hung me out to dry. As far as football was concerned, I was 18 gaun on two. But, see streetwise – I was 18 gaun on 50. So I go up there. I'm feeling comfortable. The seagulls are there. I like this place. Fergie is playin' and he offers to play no' so far forward, in a right-sided role, to keep an eye on me. I'm playin' against Arthur Graham. I'll fast forward to the scoreline – it's nothin' each. I stroll through the game. Fergie comes up and ruffles my hair – I dinnae like people touchin' my hair – and says, "What a defensive performance that was, son!" Arthur Graham tried to run me for pace. I'm f***in' 10.8 seconds (for 100 yards). Was I lucky there? I run him again and I feel I could have got away from him with a bag of cement under my arm! So that was my introduction to Alex Ferguson. I never looked back.' The same could be said about Ferguson.

In 1978, with Billy McNeill chastising himself for having stepped into turbulence, if not chaos, at Celtic, there was an unexpected vacancy in the manager's office at Aberdeen FC. A voluble and volatile character called Alex Ferguson was plucked from the dole queue and asked to maintain the excellent work of his immediate predecessors, McNeill and McLeod. Easier said than executed, of course. Can you imagine the criticism that would have been directed at him had he failed with what was a team just short of being validated as the finished article? Ferguson, making his way in his new profession, was still as raw as a side of Aberdeen Angus beef. He had initially discovered managerial traction at East Stirling, where he ignored the 'do not resuscitate' notice that was pinned to the front door of Fir Park. The patient was duly restored to reasonable health. He'd successfully taken on another infirmity at Love Street, Paisley, and, loudhailer in hand, toured the town selling the club to the fans like a firebrand politico. But disharmony can manifest itself when you least expect it. This fomented with a doubting chairman called Willie Todd and, incredibly, Fergie soon was staring dolefully at his jotters. This move to Pittodrie really needed to work. It would be good to have an ally.

Ironically, there was one already stationed in the Pittodrie dressing room: the equally volatile and perhaps even more voluble Stuart Kennedy. Things had moved on dramatically since their unscheduled meeting in the Falkirk rain. Kennedy's chutzpah regarding his own ability had been justified. He was now a seasoned first-team regular and had just returned from Argentina, having been one of the few Scotland players to acquit himself with some World Cup distinction. But, as ever, he was a man with an opinion and a voice loud enough in despatching these opinions to forego the hiring of a loudhailer. Would there be conflict between two men who boasted strength of character as their predominant feature? Does the Beach Boulevard lead down to the North Sea? Of course, there would be conflict, but it would be of a variety that did not necessarily leave scar tissue. Kennedy recalls, 'Willie (Miller) wisnae that vocal in the dressing room. I was the leader. And it's no' the first time Fergie would say, "I'm the manager of the club – no' you!" I'd bite back, "I don't think I'm the manager – okay, sometimes (I do). But it's no' about me and how great I am, it's about the attitude of the team." The common denominator between the men was respect. Kennedy, with two years' Pittodrie service under his belt, was the more assured to begin with. He did not require a crash course in confidence. 'Me? I've got assets: I've got a memory like Maggie Thatcher at the Question Time. I was very vocal in the dressing room and Fergie (most times) widnae have a problem with that. I was a forceful player on the training ground, on the park, in the dressing room – and on the team bus, But I had a lot to contend wi' when I was up there.' We shall inspect that latter statement shortly.

For all the bombast, Kennedy recognised the travails of his new manager and that insecurity might lurk behind that razor-wire exterior. Indeed, Ferguson's mind was besieged by the recent death of his beloved father. Also, he was still trying to divine the mysterious circumstances of his sacking by St Mirren.

But, on the plus side, it's important to remember that the tools were in place at his new workplace. Ultimately, another physiognomy would be carved on Mount Rushmore. It just was never destined to be a rush job.

So, what about those tools that were placed at Fergie's disposal? At this point, a conducted tour of the dressing room is essential, with Kennedy acting as guide. He pays tribute to the goalkeepers, first Bobby Clark, then Jim Leighton, but it's as if their greatness is such an established fact that it doesn't warrant further explanation; you suspect he'd rather concentrate on the outfield players. The analysis begins with his captain. 'Willie Miller was a loner, a very insular guy who didnae socialise with anybody. He didnae share a room with anybody until later on, when that team was broken up, he condescended to room with Big Alex. Willie was a boy who knew what he wanted. But, as far as playin' goes, I'd pick him in my team every time. He will go down in history as the greatest ever Dons player. Of course, he had a great centre half with him in Alex McLeish. For me, Big Alex was top man. How often does a combination like that come along? Miller and McLeish – Lennon and McCartney. There'll always be the two of them. And they both could play with different partners. Alex proved that with Brian Irvine. He got him nine Scotland caps. Brian got them because Big Alex was centre half. But, before that, Willie enjoyed that partnership with Big Alex, me at right back and Leighton as goalkeeper. Then he got Neil Simpson and Neale Cooper in front of him after this. Basically, Willie was a great tackler and read the game well. The two of them were no' the quickest, but positionally, they were right there. Willie, for his size, was great in the air defensively. Richard Gough always looked as if he'd get a goal from a set piece. Willie and Alex didnae have that goal tally, but they were better defensively.'

A Kennedy smile indicates a lull in the Miller-McLeish eulogy: he's thinking of his fellow full back, the steadfastly robust Dougie Rougvie. 'Hey, I gave that big man a lot of stick and he deserved it. After about 200 games, he said to me, "We're two different types of players!" I said. "Oh, f***in' hell! Really? I'm like a Stealth Bomber, You're the Chainsaw Massacre!"'

He returns to more serious business. 'Willie, Alex and Big Dougie took all that aerial stuff. And Miller's a left-sided centre half, although he's right footed. His concern was to keep his eye on Dougie. Then we had protection in front of Dougie: Peter Weir and John McMaster. So, my side of the park was open to the world. I hadn't got an outside right as protection: I had a right sided midfield player who just did what he f***in' wanted. Like Wee Gordon (Strachan). But oor team could cope with that. It worked great for us. Folk werenae sayin', "Let's go doon that wing." Naebody gets past me. I shouldnae be sayin' that. I should let other people do it, but it's a fact. I never had any bother with wingers.

So that was the dressing room. Eventually, you had two Scotland managers (Strachan and McLeish) in it and, at a later date, there was the manager himself. No bad, eh?'

The analysis leads inevitably to Alex Ferguson and a man who would howl at the moon, even if that moon was obscured by cloud. 'The Hairdryer? Hey, that's when Fergie was 60 and 70 years of age. Imagine when he was 36 or 37. He was the Blast Furnace back then! Oh, the energy of him. Here was a young manager, one who had a lot of ability, but a manager who was going to make mistakes. He's learnin' man management skills. He's got a lot of experienced players, no' just a bunch of young boys. Now you know there are ones who'll backstab you; they're all out there. They're the nine to five players: I call them that. They come in, train and go home and then dae a nice job on the park. They look after themselves and there are many of them out there. I wisna a nine tae five man. Big Alex (McLeish) was learnin' his headers at the time. I says to him, "Come back this afternoon and I'll tee them up for you." And I told him to shorten his stride a bit. Then he would get to the ball quicker. I'm thinkin', "This guy will get into the team and be your team mate. He'll be beside you." He was the top man, for me. No, you've got to think about the team, not just yourself. Other players did things like that, but not the nine to fivers. No. They just went hame.'

You imagine the nine to fivers to whom Kennedy refers would not take on their manager in an argument. Not so your man from Grangemouth. Now, the stories about Ferguson praising his former players have been often put up as evidence of an uncertain beginning. The versions I heard had Willie Miller, as captain, criticising his manager for living in the past. But was it really Miller who calmed the Fergie rhetoric? Not if you believe Kennedy's version of events. This takes you into fresh territory. 'Obviously, Fergie had affection for St Mirren players like Jackie Copland and Frank McGarvey, but he was upsetting a lot of people, big style. I mean, we'd beaten them four times the previous season. Anyway, I go to his door and knock. He always barks, "Who is it?" He's mibbe thinkin' someone is wantin' a tenner of a rise and that normally frightens them off. Of course, it can also be the chairman. When it is, everything changes. "Oh, come in, Dick." But there's no doubt he's frightened a lot of people anxious for a tenner.

'Anyway, I says, "Boss, can I say somethin' to you? You've been great to me as a player. You got me into the Falkirk first team. But there's one wee thing: you're making a lot of enemies here. You keep referring to Tony Fitzpatrick, Frank McGarvey and Jackie Copland. You're a young manager, not a lot older than many of the players. Just think about it." Ferguson, perhaps not immediately, accepted that he was wrong and made immediate plans to rectify the wrong. A night's sleep concentrated his mind. 'The next day, he says to us,

"By the way, maybe I've got off a wee bit on the wrong foot here. I was at St Mirren for a wee while and have a lot of affection for the players 'cos they did well, but maybe I've been mentioning some of their names a bit too openly. I don't want to upset anybody. If I've done that, I'm apologising. We'll start again today." And that solved it. All the sweetie-wife nonsense was finished. It was rarely mentioned again. But Fergie needed that talk and he knows he needed that. And he knows that I went in and said it.'

If the Kennedy revelation has dismantled one claim, it's only right that another is considered for demolition. One of the most intriguing aspects of Fergie's career at Aberdeen, aside from an innate genius for football management, was an alleged ability to polarise opinion among his players. Yes, Ferguson supplied the continuity that was so vital to any club wishing to harmonise with history, yet it is always claimed that lurking just behind the stability was a curious form of instability. Where was the unconditional admiration from within that was accorded the great managers like Shankly, Paisley, Busby and Stein? Those Aberdeen players won countless trophies, made impressive piles of crispies to raise their living standards, and rapidly became the recipients of Doric-style hero worship. This allegedly was not enough for some of them, however. A love affair with the indefatigable man who made it possible was said to be beyond them. But this claim was fanciful rather than factual, according to Kennedy.

'Our great team of 1980, well, I would say that naebody had a bad word to say about Fergie. I'm talkin' about the main, front-line players. The only guy who was really anti was Joe and he was venomous. The other conflicts (Gordon Strachan, Mark McGhee, Doug Rougvie and Jim Leighton) came later. Fergie wrote in his book that he wouldnae turn his back on the wee man (Strachan). Now if someone's gonny write about me in a book, I'm no' gonny like that. I'm gonny hunt him down. Maybe I'll no' come and chap on yer door, but eventually we'll come across one another. As it was, he said that I was someone he'd trust with his life. He talks big style about me. So I'm a Fergie guy. I'm also a Strachan guy. Some of your team mates you get on with better than others, but I've no' got any range wars. I just don't think Joe's attitude was justified. He was at the end of his career; he had a bad injury and was oot for a while.'

Whatever, Aberdeen tiptoed towards respectability, if not invincibility, in Ferguson's first full season: fourth in the Premier Division, semi-finalists in the Scottish Cup and runners-up to Rangers in the League Cup. Invincibility in the Premier Division, however, was parked just around the corner, ready to rumble. The next season they won that coveted title, securing matters with a 5-0 victory over Hibs at Easter Road. The scaffolding was being erected around another version of Mount Rushmore.

Controversially and without a moment's hesitation, Kennedy includes Mark McGhee and Steve Archibald in the team of his dreams, to the exclusion of Harper. 'If you're picking an Aberdeen team, without doubt they're the two strikers. I played with them. Joe's no' getting' a game. Yeah, he could score goals at Pittodrie, but against European teams, away from home, no' really. He's never gonny shut people down. Their centre backs are like midfield players, the Beckenbauers of this world. They're comin' forward and pingin' passes against you. But they've got to clear their lines, like everybody else, especially if you work them. Joe didnae work them.'

And so we arrive at the provocative statement that Kennedy had a lot to contend with in that dressing room. The friction in the dressing room came from strong-willed players like Joe Harper and Steve Archibald. 'You will be aware of the story about Archie scoring a hat-trick and Ferguson stopping him taking the ball home with him. Ferguson then finds that same ball aimed at him as he sits in his office. Well, it's true: Archie had his ups and doons with Fergie. I remember Archibald wearin' his own training kit. He said that the club kit was getting' manky and that he was gettin' too many groin rashes. Now Teddy Scott, the indestructible Teddy Scott, had two industrial washing machines and a couple of tumble dryers, but you keep washin' clothes and they do go aff. Me and Strachan would hold our noses when the kits came oot. Well, one day, Stevie arrives in like a Kilmarnock strip: blue socks, blue shorts and a blue and white top. Plus a blue rain jacket. And he wore them. Fergie told him not to, but he wore them anyway. I admired him for that. But that was Stevie; he always tried to take on the establishment. I wisnae the establishment, but he was looking for me and it went badly for him. He was a fit, tenacious guy who ended up playin' for Barcelona. I think he's the only fella who has been top scorer in Scotland, England and Spain. But it didnae wash with me. He tried to take me on and failed.'

Kennedy sets the 1978 pre-season scene. The players are locked into their Spartan week at Gordonstoun. Distractions are welcome. Archibald, who arrived at the Dons midway through the previous season, is anxious to challenge Kennedy's hegemony at sprinting. There is an eager audience – Ferguson, Strachan and Harper are in attendance. Kennedy decides that he doesn't need to be a Stealth Bomber on this occasion. He responds to the challenge with cocky aggression. 'I'll gie you 10 yards over 100 and beat ye f***in' runnin' backwards!' Kennedy justifies the proclamation, but there is still Joe Harper to convince. The show moves back to Pittodrie. According to Kennedy, Harper is going around in the background, promoting sprints in the manner of Mickey Duff. Now, new players arrive at Aberdeen every close season. Harper announces that he's laid hands on a new contender for the sprint title. The name is Derek Gibson, purportedly a Lanarkshire sprint champion. He'd dismissed the challenges of Duncan Davidson and Dom Sullivan. Now he is seeking the major scalp of Harper's old adversary.

Nothing seems to disturb Kennedy's equanimity, not even the Harper claim that he is no longer the fastest player at the club. Kennedy considers his opponent and doesn't come to a favourable conclusion. 'Now Derek's a cheeky wee guy; he's no' a wee, humble guy. Wee Joe's his Rasputin; his Svengali. Remember the snake out of the Jungle Book? "Trust in me," he says. So we're daen all that stuff. It comes down to me and this guy. I say I notice that he's been runnin' from the 18-yard line at the Beach End to the by-line at the Paddock end. I say, "That's like a ladies egg and spoon race for me. Why don't we just go by-line to by-line? It's 121 yards – I've asked the groundsman." Wee Joe's there, mixin' it. The wee boy's thinkin' he's gonny win. I do somethin' that I'm no' actually proud of. When I got to the 18-yard line at the Paddock End, I turn backwards and wave tae the boy. If he hidnae said somethin' at the start, I widnae have done that. Then I say, "Are ye happy, Joe? Keep bringin' them on and I'll keep beatin' them!"'

Joe Harper left Aberdeen in 1981, his first-class career decimated by injury. For his goal-scoring exploits alone, he should have gone in some style. Sadly, he left with scarcely a murmur – a departure he describes graphically in his autobiography, *King Joey*. An equally graphic *Sunday Herald* interview with him comes later in this book. But, if Harper was considered to have suffered a cruel fate, something far worse awaited Stuart Kennedy, at the tender age of 30.

CHAPTER 7

Gothenburg's Other Face

ON A RAIN-BEDEVILLED night in Gothenburg in 1983, Real Madrid were obliged to fume in the wings of the world football stage while occupying a role of irrelevance that was comprehensively anathema to them. That night belonged to an inspirational team which, in the haughty eyes of Madrid, had emanated from the boondocks. That night belonged to gifted representatives of youth like Eric Black and John Hewitt, et al. It also belonged to Alex Ferguson, a man who for a great part of five decades would make management seem like a walk in Seaton Park. And, of course, it belonged to a wonderful set of fans whose belief in the existence of luck returned a dividend of unimaginable proportions. If life had enjoyed any association with fairness, that night also should have belonged to Stuart Kennedy, a player who had promoted Aberdeen's cause for seven years, presenting pugnacity, loyalty, brilliance and self-aggrandisement in one irresistible package. The fact is that it didn't belong to Stuart Kennedy and, in many ways, he became just about as irrelevant as the vanquished matadors of Real Madrid. His European Cup Winners' Cup story, over the years, seems to have lost its way in terms of significance, and yet essentially it is no less significant than any other landmark in the history of Aberdeen FC.

It began in the summer and autumn of 1982. Sion of Switzerland brought their naïve brand of football to Pittodrie in the preliminary round and were skelped, 7-0, for their imprudence. There was an unfamiliar yet welcome name of Kennedy on the list of goal scorers. Sion were eventually dispatched on an 11-1 aggregate. In the first round proper, there was nothing naïve about Dinamo Tirana, of Albania. You imagine that handkerchiefs were distributed among players and spectators to absorb the cascades of homespun sweat: a goal from John Hewitt gave the Pittodrie side a 1-0 aggregate. The Poles of Lech Poznen were dismissed, 3-0, in the next round, before the Dons, awarded the role of David, were matched with the Goliath that was Bayern Munich, in the quarter-finals. Fergie waved aside predictions of a mismatch, The Goliaths were there to be knocked on their corporate arses. After a 0-0 draw in Bavaria, the Dons entertained 24,000 Pittodrie customers in a pulsating 3-2 victory. Now, it was the turn of Waterschei to be tortured and, in fact, that how it turned out, their 5-1 defeat at Pittodrie being an early form of water-boarding. But it was in the return fixture that the wheels were separated from the Kennedy wagon. The score was 1-0 to the Belgians, the damage to Kennedy irreparable. He takes up the story of a match that finished his career.

'I caught my studs and this guy fell on me. I got up and knew it was a bad one and that I couldnae run it off. I would say there was 10 or so minutes to go. We'd used both our subs. I got up and employed the Spartacus war cry. I'm the man: I play on. And, yet, after the game I got The Hairdryer, or mibbe the Blast Furnace, for no' closin' the winger doon. I says: "Gien me The Hairdryer? Me? Away and f*** yerself! There's more to it than that."

There was, indeed, far more to it than that. Kennedy had roughly three weeks to get himself up and running before their Swedish appointment with Real. He became a habitué of the treatment room, lying there staring at a knee that had the dimensions of a medicine ball. His manager came in one day and inquired about the progress of the injury. Kennedy was locked into insouciance. 'I'm actin' as if there's nothing wrong with it, but I'm thinking that I'll never be fit in time. He comes in the next day. By this time, it's getting doon to the size of a grapefruit. I says, "Fine, I'll be breakin' all sort of records on the stopwatch next week."

'Fergie wants me oot on the track and jogging up to the halfway line. It's Tuesday afternoon and there's naebody there. So we do it. Fergie is looking for symmetry – perfect symmetry – in ma runnin' style. I got to the 18-yard box and he says, "Hold it! In ye come." He asks me how it went. I says I thought it went great. He tells me to come in close to him, so that he can speak in ma ear. I went in close. "Son," he says, "Relax about yer knee – I'm stickin' ye on the bench. I'm guaranteein' you a place in the final – on the bench. So stop the charades about yer knee. How is it, anyway?" I says, "Where do ye want to amputate ma leg?" He shook ma hand and reiterated his promised to stick me on the bench. "You deserve it," he says. Now that's a fact and that was his man management. You know, Willie Garner was here in the hoose a couple of months ago, and we had this great conversation. He knew Alex was this ruthless guy who widnae carry a passenger on the bench. Willie says, "He would never have done that to anybody bar you." Fergie says it was one of the best managerial decisions he'd ever made. I'm just delighted that he thought that much of me.

'I was also delighted that I got ma winner's medal. Sure, I was disappointed I hadnae played, but I also know that if the score had gone tae three or four – a pipe dream against a team like Real Madrid – he'd have stuck me on for three or four minutes. But that didnae happen. We won after a tight game and extra time. But, hey, Aberdeen were easily the better team.'

I ask Kennedy if he felt a sense of isolation when he sat on that substitutes' bench. He agrees he did, but adds quickly that there was another massive stroke of man management from the manager. 'In the second half, it poured with rain and he said to me, "Kennedy, get yerself warmed up." Now, I have about five gallons of cortisone in my knee, but I can run straight quickly. Nae tacklin' or turnin', mind. But it had me imaginin' that they'd stick me up front. I'd get a through ball and, with ma pace, I'd score the winner. I'm thinkin' fairytale stuff when I'm doin' my warm-up. Now, I done that for a good quarter of an hour. I'm chattin' to the Aberdeen fans and sayin' how I'll come on and put this game tae bed. I was enjoyin' the craik. Then Fergie summoned me back and sat me doon in the dug-oot – and told John Hewitt tae get stripped. Obviously, being me, I complained. "I've just warmed up for 15 minutes in the rain." He says, "I just gave you a run in front of the fans." He'd noticed I had been sittin' there feeling out of it. So he got me involved. At the end of the game, when John Hewitt scored the winner, I said, "Boss, that was quite a good substitution." The fact is he gave me a run, but I did actually think I was goin' to play. But, at one each, I was never goin' on the park as an injured player. That was a piece of management that he had up his sleeve. No' many people would have been aware of it.'

When the final whistle sounded in the Ullevi Stadium, a phalanx of bodies left the subs' bench in what represented a choreographed stampede; arms outstretched, they headed to acknowledge the might of history. But something went wrong with the choreography. Kennedy recalls he tripped and that somebody fell on top of him. 'That didnae help ma knee either.'

Pictures suggest that the culprit might have been assistant manager Archie Knox. For the first time, Kennedy hesitates. 'Well, I'm no' sure. I wouldnae… I mean, Archie's fell on my wife at a Cup final dance before and that wisnae a good experience. He's quite a solid guy. But someone fell on me, that's for sure, and thae thermal jackets are all the same to look at. But you've just beaten Real Madrid, you're up very quickly and I couldnae really identify Archie as the one. But it probably finished my career.'

I have visited players when they've suffered serious injury, and sometimes it seems as if they're surrounded by a wall of impenetrable bitterness. It's the syndrome that smacks of 'why me?' But, in saying this, no disrespect is intended towards those men. You cannot blame someone for being sour when a twist of fate deprives him of his livelihood. There are no evidential signs of this surrounding Kennedy, however. He seems to be a man who has discovered a panacea for life's vicissitudes. So, his professional life was over at the age of 30: how did he handle a situation that was totally unfamiliar? 'When I was having the operations, I was in the orthopaedic ward. I went out of hospital on crutches.

I was getting congratulated on one hand and, on the other, people were feelin' sorry for me for havin' lost my career. But I've been lookin' at guys in wheelchairs with their legs missin'. And they've been talkin' to me about my career bein' finished. That puts it in perspective for me.'

I ask him to take me back to the moment he knew that the carnival was over. He reveals that he was in Foresterhill hospital and round his bed were his four loyal visitors, his wife, John McMaster, Gordon Strachan and Alex McLeish. The surgeon recommended a private audience, but Kennedy preferred that all four remained. 'He said I was no' goin' to be playin' again. That was the prognosis. Those three guys were devastated for me, but what can they say? And what can you say? That was it. I don't think I was emotional – maybe I'm emotional now talking about it. But not at that time.'

The verdict from the surgeon confused an already complicated situation. The Kennedys had just had a baby at the time and were in the process of having an old steading at Clinterty, near Blackburn, rebuilt stone by stone. This was to be their new home where they would build for the future, but now that future was as grey as the steading granite. Kennedy had just over a year of his contract to run. He would be at Pittodrie for a further 18 months, but where would he go after that? His boss had an alternative solution: he wanted the player to join the Pittodrie firm. 'I could have been an employee with Fergie for the rest of my life. He was always at me to get my coachin' badges. I mean, I was takin' the reserves and the third team after that with Archie Knox. But I felt it wisnae for me. I couldnae show the same enthusiasm for that as I did as a player, and if I wisnae able to do that, my mindset said no' tae bother. I know there are people in the game who are probably less enthusiastic than me. They're still in it and making money, maybe by pretence. But I'm a guy who judges himself on what I'm prepared to put in, and when Archie came in with his East Coast league on a Thursday night, I wisnae exactly rubbin' ma hands and thinkin', "That's great!"

'Archie thought it was great. He and Fergie were a great mix. Paddy Stanton and Fergie were also a great mix. But Archie's the best guy to take a trainin' session I've ever known. Fantastic man. Hard as nails, by the way. I wouldnae want to go up against him. He likes ma stuff, though: the bit about us being a team and no' tae jeopardise the bonus. We're on the same page. I knew if I couldnae show the same enthusiasm that he showed, forget it. Archie would come up tae me, saying "Kiddy, we're gaun doon to East Fife." Well, I've always got a razor blade wi' me – f***, wait till the wife hears that – and I'm telling' you, I'm gaun doon there with the razor blade inserted. That's how I felt. When I was injured he came roon to ma hoose. "Kiddy, I've got pages of trainin' notes. You're the man for this."

'I telt him he'd actually stopped me being a coach, He wanted to know why. I tell him we'd come back from a game at Cowdenbeath. Now we had this mini bus that we called the "Tumble Dryer". When you sat in it, it bounced all over the shop. Archie liked tae drive and didnae like anyone else drivin'. Anyway, we're back at Pittodrie and it's maybe half past one in the mornin'. It was drizzlin'. I sneaked a look at ma watch, no' tae annoy him. He said he wisnae happy with the movement of our strikers. This was just as we were gettin' the hampers oot of the back of the "Tumble Dryer". Archie was using those hampers as examples of where the strikers should have run tae. Those hampers were heavy, yet he was movin' them about in Pittodrie Street like they were feather dusters. It was now twenty to two. And the rain was pissin' doon by this time. I said to him later, "See when you did that, I knew I'd never be a coach; that I'd never have that enthusiasm." It wisnae any bother to him. It was natural. No' tae me.'

Kennedy left Aberdeen in 1985, his contract paid up, and returned to Grangemouth, where he prepared to take over the licence of a public house in nearby Falkirk. It seems Ferguson was reluctant to see a good man walk into football's departure lounge. Previously, he had called Kennedy one night and asked his former player to scout for him and also help him with the preparation for a European tie, against Dinamo Berlin. Kennedy was flattered and therefore only too pleased to help. 'Alex liked me aboot the place. He liked the confident way I had aboot me, my way of assessing things. I was good for the dressing room, even though I wisnae playin'. He felt the place was quite flat and asked me if I'd go along to the pre-match meal just to see the boys and give them a wee lift. I went along and they're all lookin' at me. I shouted, "I'm back! I'm playin'!" Obviously, Stewart McKimmie was there at that time and maybe he didn't think that was great. But the rest seemed delighted to see me. I just went aboot the dressing room, handing out criticism about people's gear, especially their boxer shorts. I kept the place laughin'. I think the game went to penalties and they lost.'

But Kennedy's connection with Aberdeen didn't experience the same fate. Kennedy told the club office not to put any more money in his bank because he was packing in scouting. Ferguson overruled this, believing that Kennedy would change his mind, and told the club to keep him on the payroll. And in some ways he did change his mind. Aberdeen won both the Scottish Cup and League Cup in 1986 and it was Kennedy who compiled all the match reports. 'Now, he's no' an easy guy to do that for. I think if it had been Jock Wallace, you could have written it on the back of a beer mat, sayin', "they're big and strong." But, with Fergie, it was pages and pages of detail. I was up for it. My wife knows. I was up to aw' the hours of the mornin' with a dictionary, makin' sure I got the spellin' right. Oh, he'd get the report, photo stat it and make a big pile, which he'd leave at the dressin' room door. He'd say to the guys, "Stuart was at the game last week, boys. Pick up a copy of his match report and have a read of it." Some would throw it away, others would read it – and criticise the grammar. There was only one thing for it. I says, "Boss, you had a public house. You always give 100 per cent when you do somethin', you're givin' Aberdeen 100 per cent as well – and I'm givin' my pub the same." That was that. He respected what I said.'

You would expect a twist in the tale of Stuart Kennedy and you are not disappointed. Modesty may not be his strong suit, but he has enough of it to leave out a hugely important piece of this story. It tells you everything about this garrulous man and it should serve as a lesson to footballers everywhere, particularly those who have done well in the game. I mention to him that he might have had a testimonial match and made his retirement from football that bit cosier. He admits that this is the case but adds, 'I've no' gone speaking about it. Yes, it was offered. I turned it down and Dick Donald looked as me as if I'd stepped out of a rocket from outer space! He asked me for my reason. I said, "I'm no' wantin' the fans to read in the paper that I made X amount from my testimonial. When are they getting their testimonial?" So I says, no, I'm no' takin' one. Now that seemingly went down as a strange decision. There are those who've had testimonials and still gone on to play. I was the poster testimonial in that I would never play again. I just wasn't comfy with that situation.'

It was a highly principled stance, I point out. And principles scarcely proliferate in the sport of professional football. He laughs without humour. 'Stick my name into the computer and it'll decide what I've done for this club. That guy who does his work and overtime and gets his wages on a Saturday, am I goin' back to the well for more money? No, I'm no' doin' it. The club paid my contract for a year and a bit. And that was it.'

Going back in time, I've always been faithful to the great love of my sporting life. And although I'm back working in London, there has been no deviation from the cause of Aberdeen FC, no question of infidelity and finding another team to support. A lifetime's habit is impossible to change, even if it's occasionally dismissed as a bad habit. But, for the immediate future, my dedication is directed at my wife and family and their needs rather than that of a football team. Given my history of bacchanalia, I vow to be a social saint: there will be nothing reprehensible about my behaviour from now on. I'm leaving the subs' desk of the Daily Express *to join its sister paper, the* Daily Star, *as a football reporter. Contractually speaking, I'm still with the* Express *when I complete my first assignment for the red top. It takes me to the house of Peter Marinello. He tells me that his poor form for Fulham can be attributed to his wife's recent illness, and the consternation that arose when she was deposited, by mistake,* *in a cancer ward. I write the story and embark on a small celebration, which evolves seamlessly into a major celebration. By the time the newspapers come off the Fleet Street presses, I'm riding on a star, never mind working for one. But, f*** me, what's this? The story has made the front-page splash. It has few affiliations with the one I originally wrote. It's now suggesting that the lady has cancer, which is not the case.*

The Star, *meanwhile, is marking its first anniversary over in the City Golf Club. All the executives are there, some of them dancing. Not for much longer, though. They scatter as I vent my spleen on them. I waken the next day asking myself if I'm certifiable. Didn't I have the newspaper world at my feet yesterday? Yes, I did. But, remember, I'm the master of self -immolation. It looks as if I'm going to be f***ing out before I'm actually in. But, wait for it, there is a God and he is prepared to lend a priceless hand: evidently, those editors are prepared to swallow a bit of drunken buffoonery and forget it even occurred. Maybe they're even more embarrassed how a bloody good sports tale morphed into an erroneous splash.*

Soon, I'm on the road and this takes me to Aberdeen. There are whispers that Tottenham are interested in Steve Archibald. I waylay the said Archie after one match in Aberdeen's title-winning season and he confirms the whispers. I write a back-page exclusive. For some reason, Archie and I seem to rub along quite well together. Now at White Hart Lane, he tells me Alex McLeish may soon be heading to join him. I take his word for it and the Star's *back page celebrates another exclusive. A push on the Scottish edition takes me up to Scotland. I'm forced to telephone Alex Ferguson to check on some story. I wish I hadn't. He fills my right ear with colourful invective. I've never heard such a diatribe before, even in the heydey of past masters like Stein and Turnbull. He totally dismisses the story as 'fantasy' and finishes an outrageous rant with the ominous words. 'Don't you f***in' darken the doors of Pittodrie again!'*

I knew he was a bolshie bugger – but a talented one, too, it seems.

Football tradition more or less stipulates that, in a managerial partnership, one half should major in the darker arts of intimidation and vituperation, providing the other holds a proficiency certificate in restoring shattered egos, and applying balm to fevered brows. It's the bad cop-good cop syndrome and it has an uncanny knack of working. But what happens if two unconditionally 'bad' hombres team up and start demanding answers in the dressing room? It was a situation that the players of Aberdeen FC were presented with in 1980, when Alex Ferguson secured a new right hand in Archibald Knox.

Pat Stanton, only a year into his role as Fergie's first lieutenant, had decided he wanted to become a manager in his own right. He left to care for Cowdenbeath, Dunfermline and, ultimately, his *alma mater*, Hibs. He had been well quoted by the formidable characters in the Pittodrie dressing room. A nice guy with dry humour, he had more than enough gifts to bring to the table. Once the iconic captain of Hibs, he never disappointed in his ideas for training, and so many players placed so much emphasis on this. Stanton was also proficient at dispensing encouragement. Indeed, it was he more than anyone else who was credited with bringing Gordon Strachan out of the shadows and into the strobe lighting of fame, something that even Billy McNeill had failed to do. But now, apparently, the time for this form of wet nursing was over. Knox teamed up with the man whose catchphrase was 'you cannae make honey out of shite.' Maybe so, but you could try. The fun was about to begin.

I need to talk to one of the most legendary figures in football. I feel I know most things about Alex Ferguson – who doesn't? – but very little about his one-time assistant. As it happens, Knox lives just around the corner from me and, with the minimum amount of fuss, he agrees to contribute to this book. Right at the appointed hour, a Porsche Cayenne sweeps into the driveway and, within minutes, he is sitting beside me in my home, about to be fortified by a cup of tea. I'm able to inspect the legend at close quarters. It takes some inspection. Kennedy was right: here is a man with whom you would not wish to take liberties. No-one, you suspect, has ever been incarcerated by Archie Knox. Now, I wish to discuss the fun and games of a regime that brought consignments of silverware to Pittodrie but had the ability to terrorise. But, before we discuss it in more detail, we should inspect Knox's background in order to know what we're dealing with.

The youngest of a family of six, he was born in the soporific surroundings of Tealing, a village slightly nearer to Dundee than Forfar. His mother and father both worked on farms, and Knox found himself in a similar career path early in life when he and one of his brothers began working in the dairy business. This meant he was milking the cows at 3.30 in the morning till about nine. He'd go home for a while, return at midday, and would remain there through to six. But Knox simply could not envisage himself as a farmer's boy. He went to live with his sister in Dundee, and trailed around the streets of that city for six months trying to secure an apprenticeship. Eventually, he was adjudged to be reliable enough to start as an apprentice joiner – an appropriate niche for someone described earlier in this chapter as being 'as hard as nails.'

The get-out clause from the mundanity of his working life was football. Knox was a doughty performer in midfield – I imagine his speciality was rattling opponents' tooth formations – but his career with clubs like St Mirren, Dundee United and Forfar was never going to give him a permanency in any hall of fame. His managerial career, which he dovetailed initially with his playing one, began at Forfar. Here, he acted as general factotum, ensuring the pitch was lined properly, putting on the floodlights, laying the strips out. During daytime, he worked in the building business of vice chairman Gordon Webster. But it was the chairman, Sam Smith, whom he thanks for keeping him in his part-time job. Forfar lost 4-1 at Brechin on one occasion and Knox acknowledged his putative short-comings as manager by offering to quit. But, under Smith's encouragement, he stayed on and slowly began to convince his players that they should not be content with squatters' rights at the bottom of the league. Knox, you discover, is someone who never forgets his roots. 'Sam was a great man. If it hadn't been for him, I would never have survived in football.' And so the word went out that this man Knox had possibilities. It reached the fertile ears of Ferguson; he was forever keen on assessing possibilities.

On Knox's initiative, the Tayside Reserve league had been started up, in order to incentivise players who could not penetrate either the first team or reserves. One Tuesday night, the mighty Aberdeen visited and Ferguson asked Knox for a word. It was to be the most fruitful conversation of the latter's life. 'How do you fancy becoming my assistant at Aberdeen?' Fergie was almost bowled over with the enthusiasm of the response. Transactions were simpler in those days of 1980. There were no lawyers, no agents and, I imagine, no contracts with release clauses. 'He asked me when I could start. I said I could start the next day! "I'll just tell them that I'm going."' And that is more or less what happened. 'There was no mention of compensation or any of that stuff in those days. You were just going to another job.' But what a job! The next day, Knox arrived in Aberdeen to find that they were playing the Dutchmen of Twente Enschede in a pre-season friendly. He met Ferguson and Chairman Dick Donald and the deal was done. 'They said they'd pay me a wee bit more than I was getting part-time at Forfar and my job with Gordon Webster. No much more, mind. And I didnae have a car. Nothing like that. So that was me and I started within a week.'

At the beginning of this relationship, as far as training was concerned, there was only one show in town. Its impresario was called Ferguson. Knox spent most of his time with the reserves but, as time went on, he felt he should be given far more responsibility. 'I was just picking the fluff out of my belly button and taking the young boys in the afternoon. It was bugging me and I just sidled up to him and says, "You'll need to tell me what the f*** I'm doing here – because I feel as if I'm no' doing anything." He says he wanted time to think about it. Then he comes to me and says, "Right, you're taking training frae now on." And that was it. Never a problem. I mean, you either take the bull by the horns, or you get nowhere. You'd just be festering. But Alex was great with that.'

Soon, Knox was doing far more than extracting fluff from his navel. He was encouraging the influx of kids at Pittodrie to adopt a disciplined attitude to their profession. And if these kids did not comply with what were classed as reasonable suggestions, there were repercussions. I suggest to Knox that the sea change in today's football must have been rather dramatic from his early days.

He doesn't waste time on equivocation. 'I wouldnae survive now. There are some things Alex and I did at Aberdeen, well, you'd go to jail for them.'

Somewhere, in Pittodrie mythology, there are suggestions that Knox occasionally carried a baseball bat in order to show players the error of their ways. It's too early in our conversation to suggest such a thing. Instead, however, he relates a story about a balaclava. 'I remember there was a young boy called Alan Lyons. He'd come in one close season and had dyed and permed his hair. Alex says, "What the hell have you done to your head?" The boy says he just did it for the summer. "Well," says Alex, "until such time you get it back to normal, you're to wear that." And he produces a balaclava – with just holes for the eyes. So, this boy during close-season training had to run around with the balaclava on. And when he left Pittodrie to get his bus, he had to wear the balaclava until he was out of sight. And it was the same when he arrived in the morning. You'd see him at the top of Pittodrie Street with his balaclava on – just in case we were passing at the time.'

(Knox, in fact, met Stuart Kennedy at a function in the last year – and the former player was quick to wind him up. '"See that new guy at Fifa, Infantino; he wants you to do a lecture on sports science, Archie. You know about it. And he wants to bring your equipment with you. We're no' talkin' Bunsen burners and that kind of scientific equipment. You remember telling me about a couple of boys with tight hamstrings. Aye. Did ye no' go oot with a balaclava on? That's equipment. And the baseball bat: that's equipment. And, being a pioneer in sports science, you gave them carefully placed whacks on the bum: the gluteal muscle. And did they no' scatter very quickly? And did ye no' say to boys who had ankle injuries, just stick them in the North Sea? Aye, freezin' cold baths in the North Sea." Hey, just aboot everyone was laughin', including Archie. In fact, he couldnae stop laughin', but some of the people at the table thought it was serious.')

Those were indeed the days. Knox continues his theme that most things were accepted in the name of professionalism. 'That was your job and it was always the case if you wanted to be a football player, you needed to make the sacrifice. You canne be like your mates, out on a Friday night and stuff like that. I can remember one of the laddies who'd been caught smoking or drinking – I can't remember which. He was sacked on the spot. That would be challenged now because it wasn't the most ridiculous offence to commit, but it made all the rest sit up. I had two wee girls at the time and Alex had three boys, so the young players had to babysit for us and you never thought anything about it. I had Eric Black, Bryan Gunn and John Hewitt and people like that. I'd say, on a Saturday, after the game, "What are you doing tonight?" One of them would come back, "Erm, I'm meeting my girlfriend." And I'd say, "Naw, you're babysitting for me!" My two girls loved Bryan Gunn because he used to take them down to the garage for sweeties.'

Knox, having occupied 15 posts as assistant manager, finds himself astounded by the way things have moved on in the game he loves. When the Dons were knocking down all-comers in the 1980s, there were four permanent members of staff: Knox, Ferguson, Teddy Scott and the physio. The doctor came in at lunchtimes. There was an office staff of just three. 'See the staff they've got at football clubs now. I'd been down seeing Eric Black recently. Southampton have a staff of 165, excluding players. When Eric was at Aston Villa, a club that was a complete shambles at the time, when he had taken over from Tim Sherwood, I went to see him at the training ground. I said there were a helluva lot of people wandering around. Excluding players, there was 168 full-time staff. And we operated with four. I drove the mini bus to the midweek reserve games and also on Sundays when Teddy always had a game. But, again, it was just accepted.'

How had Knox adapted to life in Aberdeen? 'I loved staying there. I used to get all the lads together for an afternoon session. I told them I was looking for a house and they'd better find me one.' So Neale Cooper, Bryan Gunn, Eric Black and John Hewitt used to come house hunting with me after training. Eventually, they said to me, "Why don't we go and look at this house in Burnieboozle Crescent?" I asked them if they were taking the piss. I mean, I'm gonna stay in a place called Burnieboozle. But that's where me and Janice ended up staying. It was a lovely semi-detached that backed onto the fields.'

I point out that this home search was an admirable alternative to an afternoon in the turf accountants. 'Well, exactly. They never batted an eyelid. And there would be times when we'd be coming back in the bus from training and I'd say, "Whose birthday is it today?" And we'd pick on somebody, even if it wasn't their birthday for another six months. We used to take that person down to the beach, take their gear off and throw them in the water. It'd be a different person every time. Then they'd have to walk back from the beach to Pittodrie. There were all these sorts of things which you'd get jailed for now.'

I take it these youngsters quite enjoyed the regime? 'Alex and I used to have a gym game called "Tips". We'd maybe be there for two hours playing, and we'd have all the young boys in. They had to pick whose team they were in and those teams they were supporting. I used to get them all wound up and tell them they'd be babysitting on Saturday night, whatever. Alex would fall out with some of them and say, "Get outside and start lapping round that pitch." I remember one day we were going home and suddenly we remembered, "Christ! Those two boys are still out there on the laps." And there they were, still jogging after two hours. But there was lots of fun.'

Returning to the bad cops theme, I ask Knox how they made such an enterprise work. He admits that he doesn't really know. But he stresses that even when he went up to Aberdeen after their first Premier Division title victory, there was no chance of a revolt. He never experienced any problems with Willie Miller, Alex McLeish or indeed Gordon Strachan. 'Never. It was a case of this is what we're doing for training and this is when we're leaving. If you're no' there, you're no' coming. If you see Alex's record with the top players at Man United, if he thought they were getting a wee bit above their station, then it was POOFT! But he never had that at Aberdeen. Never allowed it. It was his way or no way and everyone just bought into that.'

They also bought into his phobia about the Old Firm. These were the guys who were against them, he'd tell them. These were the guys to beat. Knox remembers a game at Parkhead where a bit of additional psychology was required. There was an infuriating habit of the kick-off being delayed in order to let the crowds in. This meant that the players, now stripped for action, would be kept waiting and maybe their concentration would begin to waver. On this occasion, however, Ferguson changed tactics and ordered his men to stay in their suits until further notice. 'He (Ferguson) had that bit when everybody in the world was against you, so you had to show you were capable of overcoming that.'

The Glasgow boys in the squad – ie: Miller, McLeish, McMaster, Peter Weir and Mark McGhee – had a toughness about them and passed on this durability to the local boys like Cooper and Neil Simpson. 'They were definitely influenced by the West of Scotland lads and Alex, of course, so they grasped that right away. We might be up in Aberdeen and be sheep shaggers and all the rest of it, but we can stand up for ourselves. You'll remember Neale Cooper's tackle on Charlie Nicholas? It was about two seconds, after they'd centred the ball. Well, Alex had been on to Neale the whole week, so you'd be walking about the place and Alex would shout "Cooper!" And Tattie would answer, "Nicholas!" So Tattie was going to be about Nicholas the whole game because he was the big hitter for Celtic.'

I put it to Knox that the perception – from afar, admittedly – was that this hard, unrelenting, unremitting regime brought success after success, but not perhaps so much in the way of laughter. He disagrees. 'There was great camaraderie to balance it. But, yes, there was a toughness. They would point the finger at each other. There was never a time when there would be an arm around the shoulder. If you weren't doing your job, you were told. There were tough boys in that team: mentally tough.'

So, who was the harder cop – himself or Alex? 'It would be Alex. As far as the younger ones were concerned, it would be me 'cos I was with them all the time. But my bark was bigger than my bite.'

Nevertheless, I suggest, he gathered a fairly fearsome reputation as an enforcer. 'Well, if getting lads in on time and getting them to do their jobs is tough, that's what I did. But it was just part of the bloody job. The same in any business. If you don't do your job, then you get the bloody sack. Was there a lot of compassion in me? Oh, God, aye. If you knew there was something wrong with some of the young lads, someone would drop you the word and you would act accordingly. Maybe someone falling out with their girlfriend.'

So, let's talk more about that compassion. Did he ever feel sorry for those finding themselves reduced as men? 'There was never an intention to do any of that. It was always a fun thing. You'd never do it to belittle them. You'd give them stick in front of their team mates about performance. But you'd never pick on them to belittle them in front of anyone. That never happened.'

It was a different matter if the performance didn't match up to Knox's requirements. Was this the time he sought the jugular vein? 'Oh, God, aye. I don't think this story's ever been told. We went down to Tynecastle on a Friday night and I'm driving the mini bus. We're 2-0 up with ten minutes to go and yet we drew 2-2. So, all those young guys are going home for the weekend, and they're down with all their gear. So, of course, I'm f***ing ragin'. So I says, "Right, the lot of you are going back up the road: we're training tomorrow morning." One of them, this boy Billy Muir, says his dad's here to pick him up. I'm no' caring. He's going back to Aberdeen.

'We get into the mini bus. Someone knocks on the driver's window. I wound it down. He says, "I'm Billy Muir's Da. You taking my boy back up the road?" I says, "Aye, we're training tomorrow morning. That's the way it is, I'm afraid." He fires back, "So he cannae come home with me?" I says there couldn't be any concessions. He could go home after he'd done his training. "Well," he says, "that's what I've always f***ing thought about you. You're a f***ing eejit!" I says, "Well, I might be so, but he's still going back up the road." I was pissing myself laughing. Ye cannae get better than that.'

So, the youngster was returned to Aberdeen? 'Aye, he was. But, hey, I used to do that with the first team. I mean, we never really lost at Parkhead or Ibrox, but if we did, it was back up the road. And some, like Peter Weir and Billy Stark and others who stayed in Glasgow, were waving to their kids out of the bus. There was training in the morning.'

Was there any defiance? 'Not a chance. Never came across that, no.'

Such tactics were effective, then? Knox insists that they were. He adds that fights between the players in training were rebooted in the dressing room. There was only a single pair of boxing gloves, so one player would take the right glove, while a second player would take the left. They would be obliged to put their other hand behind their back. 'They'd be jabbing away and then you'd stop it when it started to get really serious. I used to go into the boot room and say, "Oh, ye wanna fight, do ye?" I'd take a baseball bat in with me, stuff like that. I'd put the lights out and swing the bat. "Oooh Ya!" you'd hear. But it was never a full-blooded thing 'cos you'd have killed them.'

Ah, so the story about the baseball bat does not belong to mythology. Archie Knox, like Pat Stanton before him, imagined that being his own man was an option he should explore. So, in 1983, he directed his car the 68 miles down the A92 towards Dundee, where he spent two and a bit years trying to stem the massive tidal wave that was Jim McLean and Dundee United. He met Ferguson at the World Cup in Mexico, and Fergie presented him with an offer that was difficult to refuse: return to Pittodrie and they would be joint managers. Joint managers? If you say so, Alex. But, aside from the spurious title, Knox wanted to place his hands on silver again. He'd scarcely had time to position his feet under the table when Fergie was lured by Manchester United. It was on the afternoon of 6 November 1986 that Knox remembers being up at Seaton Park and seeing Fergie's silver Mercedes racing along the small track.

'My mother hadn't been well at that time, and I thought, "Oh, Christ, he's got bad news for me." So I run up and ask him what's happened. "We're going to Man United!" he says.

"When?" I asks.

"Today," he replies. "I know they're going to offer you the job here, but what do you want to do?"

'I says, "I'm coming." And that was it. There was no discussion with my wife, or anything like that. I just carried on with training. Then I met Martin Edwards and Maurice Watkins at night. I don't even think I knew what I was getting paid, or the length of contract. We just said that was it: we're going.'

Aberdeen's world was in danger of implosion. Knox's departure was delayed as the club scoured the country for a new manager. He remembers walking out for the visit of Clydebank on 17 November. The crowd's mood was ugly and unforgiving. Amid the booing, there were shouts of "traitor" and "Judas."

All these years later, I ask Knox for his verdict on the fans' outrage. I'm not surprised when he suggests it was of little consequence. Knox had a booking at the Theatre of Dreams and he was already dreaming of first nights and fantasies.

There again, he had so many pleasant memories upon which to look back. 'I remember one Christmas when I knew there was something on the go. I could sense it. About five of the players grabbed me after training this day. They set about me and stripped me naked in the dressing room. There was six inches of snow at the park. They (Black, Gunn, Simpson, Cooper and Hewitt) carried me onto the centre circle and dumped me there and started chucking snowballs at me. They were all going home for Christmas.'

I have only met Knox once before and it was the briefest of affairs. I've now known him for an hour and it's difficult not to warm to him. You get the sense with him that even the bad times were good. Right now, he's remembering one more story that he tells against himself. It involves a chairman in Dick Donald who was just as cute as the men he employed:

'Dick fully understood it when I told him that while I appreciated the opportunity of maybe managing a club like Aberdeen, I couldn't really turn down a club like United. He was a great man. He never used to have board meetings, or anything like that. He used to sit at lunchtimes and Alex would be going on at him. Alex would say we needed a left winger.

'Dick would say, "How many players have we got, Archie?"

'And, of course, I would go through them all, the young ones and that. Dick would turn to Alex and say, "There you go. Do you not think you've got enough players?"

'And, of course, after the meeting was finished, Alex would turn to me and say, "F***ing shut the f*** up! Don't f***ing tell him how many players we've got!"'

An authentic hard man? Certainly. Argumentative? Sure. Pejorative? Absolutely! Driven? You'd better believe it. The fact is they just don't make them like Archie Knox any more.

CHAPTER 8

Super Trooper Cooper

FIVE MONTHS BEFORE FERGUSON and Knox travelled to what they believed would be a Mancunian El Dorado, another young man had left Pittodrie for England. This was a young and accomplished man in every sense. Neale Cooper was only 23 and had achieved everything: two Premier League titles, four Scottish Cups, one League Cup, one European Cup Winners' Cup and a Super Cup. He had never lost in the final of anything. But it wasn't as if he was slumming it: he was going to a club that had won the European Cup in 1982; would he be going on to even better things? Sadly not. Aston Villa were in a state of transition as far as managers were concerned – Graham Turner was replaced by Billy McNeill, who was succeeded by Graham Taylor. But, far more important, was the fact that injury and burn-out had established themselves in Cooper's world.

But before we address those issues, it's important to explain the Cooper background. You might say he had been born with a silver teaspoon in his mouth. The son of a tea planter, he was raised in Darjeeling, India, and was brought back to Aberdeen five years later. But silver teaspoons are of no consequence when tragedy calls. His father, Douglas, opened a post office-cum-delicatessen in the leafy suburb of Bieldside. A week later he died of a massive heart attack. He was 42. His mother, Anne, went back to her job as a teacher and the family moved to Airyhall. The hard shift of life had begun.

Cooper was kicking a ball about at school one day when he was spotted by the janitor, one Ernie Youngson. The latter approached Mrs Cooper and asked if her son could attend football training. Youngson became his mentor and sort of surrogate father. But there would soon be another man in his life: Teddy Scott. With Cooper establishing himself as a Pittodrie ball boy, he signed schoolboy forms at 14 and, two years later, broke through into the first team. Scott was there every step of the way.

'You'll never meet another Teddy Scott: they just don't come along like buses. He lived and breathed the club and I just loved the encouragement he gave me. He was such an important part of Aberdeen's success. I mean, if someone asked him to play a game, say at Auchtermuchty, he would put a team together. Sometimes, he would return late at night and not bother going away out to Ellon, where he lived. He would just make a bed up for himself in the physio's room. That was him. You had to keep in with him, mind, or else you got the rubbish boots.'

This interview is being conducted on the telephone. When I first approached Cooper, he was lying in a hospital bed, being treated for a leg infection. He was originally booked in for a couple of days, but his condition worsened and he was hospitalised for over a week. He is still in the throes of recovery, but insists he is happy to talk. He tells me about playing reserve-team football – which many people would like to see reinstated – while still at school. He was only 14. 'It was strenuous stuff, incorporating all the players who couldn't get into the first team, and those who were coming back from injury. Often, it would be the case that you were playing with half the first-team squad. There were no concessions made for my age. I grew up quickly.'

Neither were there any allowances made in-house. 'If you were young but mentally strong, you got a chance. If you weren't you were out the door. I remember making my first-team debut: I was cleaning the toilets on the Friday afternoon. He (Fergie) just walked in – I hadn't even trained with the first team – and told me to get myself home. I pointed out it wasn't even five o'clock yet, but he said this was different: I was playing against Kilmarnock the next day. I was 16 and I thought, "Wow!"

'I played centre half that day. Okay, if you were in midfield or a striker, you can get by, but playing against big, strong players was hard, you know. And Kilmarnock had a really big striker called John Bourne playing for them. I turned up for the lunch on the Saturday, and the boys were asking what I was doing there. I told them the manager had told me to report because I was play-ing. They went, "Aye, good one." Anyway, I deputised for big Alex McLeish. It wasn't my sort of game. I was more like Willie (Miller), trying to reads things. But Willie helped me a lot. I knew I would be in and out, though. I was still 16 when I played against Celtic at Parkhead. We won 2-0. That was another late call into the team – on the Saturday morning. Willie pulled out after training. I was only down there to help Teddy with the kit. I was standing with him when Fergie named the team. I wasn't even listening. Teddy says, "I think he men-tioned your name then." I didn't think so. Teddy went up to the manager and said, "Did you say Big Tattie was playing?" The answer was yes: I'd be playing centre half alongside Alex McLeish. Oh, my God, it was panic stations. But that was Fergie. If he thought you could handle it, away you went.'

Tattie was the nickname bestowed on him by McLeish, Neale being Potato Peel in rhyming slang. I tell Cooper it is a story worthy of the front page of

Roy of the Rovers. He agrees. He also accepts the fact that he was too young to have secured his place in the team: Miller and McLeish were the centre halves and could not be replaced. But Fergie was keen to get the boy involved. Could they try him in midfield? You bet they could. The Scottish Youth captain was strong, physical and one day he'd be likened to Franz Beckenbauer. He played alongside Neil Simpson in the role of attack dog.

As we mentioned in the previous chapter, Fergie psyched him up for the stringent tests, such as Charlie Nicholas. The manager would bellow his name: Cooper would respond in kind by shouting Nicholas's name. 'He told me that Charlie was a dangerous player, a real threat who liked to drop off in midfield. When he did that, I had to make sure I got in about him. So this carried on all week. I was, like, brain-washed. On the Friday, I was waiting at his office: he didn't have to shout at me. He just told me to go home and relax. The next day, there was a full house at Pittodrie, and Archie McPherson was commentating. Frank McGarvey pushed the ball to Charlie and I whacked him right on the knee. A beauty, you know. That was after three seconds: the referee couldn't see because he'd turned away after blowing the whistle. I never got booked. I'm thinking, "What have I done?" My team mates were asking the same question. I looked over at Fergie, and he's going, "Good lad!" It was a mental thing. He definitely tried to brainwash you.'

Simpson and Cooper provided the midfield engine, as Fergie described it. 'Physically, we'd protect matters. I'd be more defensive than Simmy, sit in front of Alex and Willie. And when you did win the ball, you had Strachan and Peter Weir either side of you. The theme was you'd supply them and sort of protect them.'

But there was no protection against Ferguson and Knox. 'The thing is if Fergie came in and slaughtered you, you were hoping that Archie would back you a little bit. But then he'd slaughter you, too. But they were both superb as coaches. They were great together, massive together. Total quality. At times they were supportive and would back you accordingly, but I was scared of them at other times. If you weren't doing well, you didn't want to lift your head up when he came into the dressing room. But he'd be straight into your face, giving you "The Hairdryer" and shouting, "You're a disgrace. With your big, blond hair, you're a Jessie. You couldnae tackle anybody." But then, I could react to that: I'd go and perform and play better. It was a test of character. The point was: did you react positively, or did you slink away and hide? If you did that, you were out the door. Some couldn't handle the stick.'

But Cooper could handle the abuse, even when it came raining down on him, monsoon-style. He was 17 when he counted his savings and bought a flat in Great Western Place. He moved out of his mother's home in Airyhall, although he would return there at meal times. He had been there about six weeks when the manager pulled him aside at training. Ferguson told him he'd been seen coming out of the flat. Cooper, flustered, asked him if there was anything the matter with that. 'It's mine. I bought it.'

Ferguson was not convinced. He ordered him to return to his mother's house. And this state of affairs lasted until he was 21. 'I thought I was Jack the Lad with my flat, and I was obviously annoyed when he ordered me back to my mum's. But he didn't like any distractions. Even at 21, I had to ask again if I could go and live in it.'

Cooper emphasises that Ferguson's demands were rarely met with defiance, such was the respect in which he was held. I mean, as much as he would have liked to, he couldn't replicate a Gordon Strachan outburst when he had told Ferguson to 'shut his f***ing face.' Cooper shudders. 'Fear stopped me doing that. As a young boy, you just had to take it in.'

And yet the Fergie's laws of prohibition were more stringent than 1930s America. Players were allowed only one night out a week and that was only a Saturday. And if someone had not played well that day, he was made to feel guilty about contemplating that leisure time. Of course, there were ways that Cooper could find a voice of resistance, even if it couldn't be described as outright defiance. 'Fergie would get players' names wrong. I would start laughing and he'd pull me up. I'd tell him that this wasn't what the player was called and that I was just laughing at him saying that name. "Oh, you think that's funny?" he'd say. "Well, go and stand outside the changing room." So you would, like a little boy. Aye, sometimes I had to go and stand out in a corner in the hallway.'

Perhaps it was when he stood in that hallway that Cooper perfected the Ferguson imitation: the speech impediment; the habit he had of rolling his r's. Cooper was the one with the voice and the mannerisms to impersonate his boss. 'The boys used to ask me to take him off. I used to do him quite well. And he knows it. When I bump into him, he still laughs about it.'

In the summer of 1986 – some people claim this was the time Fergie's eyes began to contemplate the main course of Manchester United – Cooper decided that a change of scenery would benefit his aching limbs. His contract was up and it was time to go. Three hundred and fifty thousand pounds would exchange hands in his transfer to Aston Villa. He would continue playing for many years but the football was ostensibly burst. He appeared 20 times for Villa, 17 times for Rangers, missed out altogether on a brief return to Aberdeen, seven for Reading and 101 for Dunfermline over five years. The conclusion was five games as player-boss of Ross County, whom he managed for six years.

Today – a major operation on his foot, two on his back and four on his knee later – he admits to burn-out. 'It was hard. I was saddled with a lot of injuries after that. I was just overplayed by Fergie, which he realises now. Simmy struggled with injury, John Hewitt and Eric Black the same. So did I. There were four boys who played all the time. We played when we shouldn't have played. You just don't realise it at the time. I still struggle with injury. For example, I couldn't go for a run, or anything like that. No chance.'

I suggest to him that the original Life of Riley became a life of pain. He concurs. 'Yeah, to be honest, yeah. Fergie learned that when he went to Man United. He admitted that he over-played us. We played with injuries because we were forced to and, at times, he'd push you, calling you a big softie. I'd gone somewhere else and I remember someone asking if I knew I'd cracked my ankle. I said "no". But I'd been playing with it. The medical side of it has improved since.'

We're almost done here, but there's one vital question. I ask him, given the knowledge that he possesses now, if he would do it all again. 'Listen,' he says, 'I was so fortunate coming in at 16, debut 17, by 20-odd I'd won everything. Some players never win a thing. People talk about the money now. Well, that's life. That's the way it was back then. You were making about 300 quid a week: people before us were earning a lot less than that. I'm just so grateful that I had the opportunity. But, do you know, my Dad was a good guy. We were never a football family – it was always rugby. He played for Gordonians. See those medals and honours – they're in a safe in Aberdeen – well, I'd give them all up if I had my Dad back.'

*Neil Cooper was hospitalised after suffering a heart attack in June of 2017. I wish this splendid man a speedy recovery.

* *

IT DIDN'T SEEM TO MATTER who was deployed in the role of assistant manager, whether it was Pat Stanton, Archie Knox (twice) or Willie Garner, no one seemed capable of impeding Aberdeen's progress in the seventies and eighties. The common denominator was Alex Ferguson, incisive and imperious, but also endlessly autocratic. In the early chapters of his reign, a resistance movement had been led by Joe Harper. Unsurprisingly, the striker did not have a surfeit of allies. Initially, as previously mentioned, there had been occasional flurries of defiance from Willie Miller and Gordon Strachan, but as time moved on, Ferguson's autonomy had become more or less absolute. However, in 1980, with Harper preparing to exit stage left, that resistance movement was re-invigorated by someone who did not even play for the Dons. Frank Gilfeather, a young man with with exceptional skills in journalism and communications, joined Grampian Television as a sports presenter. A Scottish amateur lightweight boxing champion who represented his country 16 times, Gilfeather had been teammates with Dick McTaggart and Ken Buchanan. He also trained and sparred with Walter McGowan, before being indentured as a journalist and working for *Aberdeen Journals* as first a news reporter and then a sports correspondent. He'd resigned in 1977 in favour of the freelance option, but now he was back in pensionable employment and had reverted to sports reporting. It was a move he'd come to regret. Gilfeather was very much his own man and therefore not easily intimidated, his boxing education bolstering that sense of independence. But even he admits now, 'It was like being involved in guerilla warfare. You never knew when the fire was going to start, or when you were going to be ambushed.'

The emergency services were dispatched early on in their relationship. Gilfeather, ever the ideas man, believed that a five-a-side football competition, staged at the Dewars Sports Centre in Perth, could be productive for his new employers. He sent a letter round to all the SPL clubs and received enthusiastic replies from nine of them. The only one failing to respond was Aberdeen. Gilfeather spotted Ferguson in the corridor after one home game and asked him why the club hadn't replied. 'Oh, Ferguson just let rip. He said he'd no intention of putting a team in. I said that was fine, but pointed out that they had ignored the letter. He went into one of his rants about how dare I question him. Actually, the match commander was standing nearby and his jaw dropped. The conversation ended when Fergie said, "Well, you're not getting a f***ing reply. That's my reply."'

I meet Gilfeather in the Ferryhill House hotel. Currently standing as a Labour candidate in the local by-elections, he is out in the campaign trail every day, and so I'm grateful to him for affording me his time. He emphasises that his collisions with Ferguson didn't happen on a daily or even weekly basis and, indeed, there were times when their meetings were serene and pleasant. But he claims most of the disagreements were fuelled by Ferguson's financial expectations and were fairly spectacular as a result. Gilfeather blames himself to some degree. He remembers meeting the manager on the day Grampian's fiscal figures had been announced: they'd made a £5million profit. As the two men went into make-up, the journalist told his companion that these were fantastic numbers. He realised, simultaneously, that he was fashioning a rod for his own back and that this might only encourage Ferguson to ask for more. Eventually, he raised the matter with director Chris Anderson.

'Chris indicated that Fergie was a megalomaniac. He told me Alex was on £50,000 a year and that, it was expected, would take in him promoting the club in TV interviews and so on. He claims Anderson added that Ferguson wanted to control everything at the club; the media, what went into the papers, what stayed out. Gilfeather asked him why the club didn't do something about it. Anderson replied, 'He's a winner. We don't want to upset him.'

Gilfeather apologises if the emphasis is on the fractious parts of their relationship, but insists it's these he remembers most. 'Sometimes, you'd come back from work after a row and say to yourself, "I don't need this." On the other hand, he could be very friendly and personable, liked a laugh, all that kind of stuff. But my problem as that I don't have an empathy with these guys. If I'm in a footballer's presence for more than a minute, I begin to wonder what we're going to speak about. You'd go to dinners with him and, out of the workplace, he was a different guy. But, in the press room, he had his friends, the ones he could rely on. They would be pliable and he could get away with murder with them.'

The antipathy was not always derived from finance. One Saturday, the party line suggested that Jim Leighton, the Aberdeen and Scotland goalkeeper, was injured. This was an expedience and saved the player from embarrassment. It was also untrue. Gilfeather was informed by a director that the player had been dropped and this information was promptly downloaded to listeners of Radio Clyde. 'I never thought of the next stage, which was Armageddon on the Monday morning. The phone was red hot in my office: everyone was looking and thinking, "Bloody hell!" I stayed calm and just let him rant. "Is that you, Alex?" I said, knowing full well it was. Ferguson told him he was banned. The journalist queried the terms of the ban and was told that this meant he couldn't talk to the manager after games. To which I replied, "Oh, I thought it was something serious." He went absolutely nuts. The guys could have come in with the white coats and taken him away. And then I said to him, "Alex, don't ever presume to phone me and speak to me that way. My father wouldn't speak to me like that and you will certainly not get away with it."'

There were other disagreements. When Aberdeen played Liverpool in the European Cup, Gilfeather, a Dundonian, found himself being accused of lack of sympathy towards the club. 'You're not an Aberdeen man.'

In another instance, after a TV interview with Dom Sullivan, Ferguson warned him against approaching his players without permission. Gilfeather responded that it wasn't his responsibility to ask for an interview and that it should be the player who contacted the manager. Eventually, he had to concede territory in this dispute.

We return to the other side of Alex Ferguson. Gilfeather recalls, 'I remember sitting at traffic lights; I was in the car with my children. Fergie drew up alongside me. He was beep beeping and waving – and so were my kids. And the kids were excited and saying, "There's Alex Ferguson!" He was like that. I saw him in action with lots of people and he was fantastic with them and made sure they had their place: ordinary people, poor people, it didn't matter. He was great like that and I admired him for it. But the other side was that if you dared question what he was doing, or raised an eyebrow, then... the more accurate picture would be this: "If you don't accept what I've just told you, then you're not on my side." In my opinion, it's all about megalomania and insecurity. You've got to recognise that people are there to do a job and you can't fall out with them because they're doing that job. The trouble is that clubs would like nothing better to get all the coverage in the world without having to actually meet the media. I honestly think there should have been a backlash about this long ago, but people are weak and allow it to happen. As for Fergie, just look at him with Rock of Gibraltar. I think that tells you everything you need to know about him.'

The men were never destined to become buddies of the bosom. Ironically, matters improved after Gilfeather snubbed the manager's attempt at a reconciliation. Aberdeen, in their successful Cup Winners' Cup campaign, had recorded a 0-0 draw at Bayern Munich. Everything worked in terms or tactics and Ferguson's mood was benevolent. He put a fairly impressive sum of money – in Deutschmarks – on the hotel bar and instructed the barman to use that as a kitty for the press guys. 'He came over and asked if I would have a beer. He put his arm around me. I told him I was really pleased the way it had gone for him – it was a pretty special night. But I added, "Please take your hand off my shoulder." He said, "What's got into you?" I told him he had a short memory and didn't he remember he'd been screaming down the phone at me the last week? "Now you want to be my pal, but we're never going to be pals." The hand was off my shoulder then. After that he gave me anything I wanted. He was practically suggesting players for the programme.'

You imagine Gilfeather was relieved when Ferguson left in 1986. He suggests he was 'scunnered' by then not only with the manager but with sport itself. He suggested to Alistair Gracie, the Grampian head of news, that the format be changed on the Friday programme to encompass leisure, entertainment and the arts. 'I had a greater interest in that than in football. Subsequently, I had some fabulous interviews with authors, actors and comedians. It was good fun. I repeat: the aggro hadn't been on a daily basis, but I couldn't pretend that I enjoyed what I was doing. It affected the love of my job – and I loved my job. I look back and remember that often it was a difficult and horrible time.'

On 6 November 1986, I'm flying to Aberdeen, contemplating a rather incomplete brief regarding the futures of Messers Ferguson and Knox. The Daily Star *suspect something is going on and have sent me to sniff around, like some bloodhound. There is a squad of Fleet Street journalists on the plane, intent on writing about tragedy – and the Chinook helicopter crash in the Shetlands that has claimed 45 lives. They're drinking up a storm and, as it's my 42nd birthday,*

I join them. The fragility of life, as demonstrated by the crash, encourages me to do so. By the time I reach my home city, I'm attached to Cloud Nine. There's a message for me to phone the office. This sounds like bad news. It is. Ferguson and Man Utd representatives are closeted somewhere in the city – but no one knows where.

The inclination, if I were sober, would be to panic, but three or four miniature bottles of white wine have eradicated this temptation. I grab a taxi and recommend that we visit Pittodrie. It's quieter than Oliver Goldsmith's Deserted Village. *Not a light is showing, not one Mercedes parked outside. I tell the taxi driver to take me to my favourite hotel, the Atholl. As I fill in the registration form, I ask the receptionist if she could find out where a Mr Alex Ferguson and party are booked in for dinner. A bottle of champagne shall be hers if she is successful. I repair to the bar, fling down a couple of pints of lager and contemplate my good fortune. I'm back in the game: I'm now Chief Sports Writer of the Daily Star and life is a whole lot better than when I was scuffling around Stirling's Raploch trying to sell penny insurances.*

There is one cloud disturbing the horizon, however: I collapsed after attending the 1986 Commonwealth Games in Edinburgh, spent a few days in intensive care at Kirkcaldy Royal hospital and was later referred to the world-famous Harefield. They told me I must never drink again because of an enlarged heart muscle: if I do, they will not put me on the transplant list. Right now, however, I'm occupying a blissful little oasis of insouciance. In other words, I couldn't give a f***. I'm on my third pint when the young lady appears, looking, quite rightly, triumphant: the party to which I have referred is booked in for 8pm at the Holiday Inn at Dyce. She is worth the champagne reward. I phone the office and tell them that I may, repeat may, have found Fergie's destination.

I imbibe more modestly and recall my history with this manager. I go back to Glasgow's Albany hotel. It's 1979 and I'm interviewing Ally McLeod, raking over the debris of Argentina. Suddenly, I espy Ferguson walking down the corridor and disappearing into the gent's toilet. The wounds left by the Archibald affair are still tender. I excuse myself from McLeod and give pursuit. I stand next to Fergie and slowly turn my head towards him. I ask him if he knows who I am. He nods his head. There is, thank f***, no hostility showing. I ask if I can call on him one day. The door to the Blast Furnace stays closed. And thus a tentative relationship is formed. I fly up for a home match and, as he is dispensing drinks in his office, ask if he can give me some of his time. He's busy and looks perplexed, but suggests I return the next day – a Sunday. I do as I'm bid and am given a really nice interview. We are the only occupants of the stadium. He is fascinated that I have arrived in a light blue-coloured taxi and insists on having his photograph taken standing in front of it, perhaps emphasising old leanings towards Rangers.

After Jim Leighton drops his contact lenses during the World Cup qualifier in Cardiff, I return to Aberdeen sensing a scoop. I knock on Pittodrie's front door – Fergie opens up. Christ, it's just before 8 o'clock. He invites the photographer and me inside and, before we know it, tea and toast is being supplied. There's another supplement: a good insight into Leighton and permission to talk to the man when he arrives. Leighton duly panics when I mention contact lenses and virtually runs away from me. There is no recrimination from Fergie. Now, we have not exchanged droplets of blood and it would be wrong to call him a friend. But there is some semblance of a relationship. I'm hoping it will pay dividends tonight. When I walk into the Holiday Inn, Dennis Sheriffs is there to greet me, an old associate from my days on Aberdeen Journals. How the f*** does he know about this? He tells me he rang John Mann, one of our reporters, and siphoned the information from him. We are still debating the whys and wherefores when the automatic doors open and a smiling Alex Ferguson enters the foyer. He doesn't seem in the least discombobulated by our presence.

'Am I talking to the new manager of Manchester United?' His smile almost knocks me over. 'Yes, you are,' he retorts, before giving us a few minutes of quotes. Before he leaves, I ask him if he will give me an interview later on. His reply is equivocal but that smile suggests that this will not be out of the question. Then he and the United entourage, including Martin Edwards, go off to dinner. Extraordinarily, Dennis and I are the only two reporters on the scene and we quickly file our stories and then repair to the bar. News must travel slowly in Aberdeen. We are joined by reporters from the other newspapers, but this is over a period of a couple of hours. Later, Ferguson surfaces from the dining room and gives a general press conference. Even later, he gives me what is termed a one to one. He is three-parts pissed, but then so I am. It has been one eventful day.

CHAPTER 9

Crying Like a Baby

THE MORNING AFTER THE surreal night before was positively anti-climactic. Around 9.30am on 7 November, 1986, two sports journalists – Jim McLean, of the *Scottish Daily Express*, and me – stood chatting in a more or less deserted Pittodrie Street. A handful of hours earlier, Alex Ferguson had transferred from one natural habitat to the ultimate natural habitat of Manchester United, but it seemed that the city of Aberdeen had still to engage with this disturbing development. You imagined that such a high-level exit would have guaranteed a commotion in other football cities, with crowds not only mourning the departure of an icon but also demanding to know the terms of succession. Aberdonians, however, are not easily associated with hysteria and no such frenzy of declamation or anticipation materialised on that cold, flinty morning, as we watched the players filter in for training.

Some, like Willie Miller, were reluctant to pass comment on what had occurred the previous evening. Miller delivered some sarcastic remark about the presence of the national press, before moving on quickly. Davie Dodds was noticeably and predictably friendlier. He called over to us from the car park to ask if any decision had been made as to Fergie's replacement. My colleague McLean tossed back a verbal grenade.

'You'll never guess – Jim McLean!'

Dodds, who had arrived at Pittodrie only earlier that year, feigned a seizure and pretended to get back in his car, no doubt reliving his history with Dundee United's controversial manager.

So, who indeed would replace Ferguson? If the information had been correct regarding his career move, my mind was a blank page as to any future appointment. Ferguson had won four Scottish Cups, three league titles, one League Cup, one Cup Winners' Cup and a Super Cup. It would have been no surprise if a partridge in a pear tree had also taken up residence in the trophy cabinet. The general expectation was that one leviathan would be supplanted by another. The snag was: would anyone of established substance wish to put their reputation at risk? As it turned out, Jim McLean's flippant remark about his notorious namesake had not strayed too far from reality. The job was offered to Motherwell's Tommy McLean, brother of Jim, but he allegedly stepped away from the temptation for reasons that were never made public. Within a short time, however, a reality check was deposited into our hands: Ian Porterfield was the manager designate. No disrespect intended, but the earth scarcely moved for me nor, I imagined, for thousands of my fellow supporters. What I knew of the Kirkcaldy man's history would have represented one line on a page of A5 note paper. I remembered him for underwriting a great Saturday night out in London back in 1973, when he accessed his 'standing foot' and volleyed the winner against Leeds in the FA Cup final. I think the bookies' odds on Sunderland creating an upset that day were 7-2, and thus I converged on the Rheingold Club, just off Oxford Street, to sup multiple pints of German lager.

But such an instant judgment was perhaps unfair on Porterfield. Further investigation positioned him in a more favourable managerial light. He had proved, albeit at a modest level, that he had a flair for this paranoia-producing profession. Unfashionable Rotherham won promotion from England's old Third Division under his bailiwick. So he moved six and a half miles down the road to the more fashionable centre of Sheffield. Thereupon, the giants of United were partially cured of their sleeping sickness and lifted from the Fourth Division into the Second. When investment dried up, however, Porterfield experienced the predictable frustration of a flaky boardroom and was dismissed. Now, eight months later, he was being asked to replace the most accomplished manager of that particular era. Time would provide the evidence whether he was equipped for such a gargantuan task.

In fairness, Porterfield was his own man and, unlike many of his managerial brethren, resisted any temptation to pick up the phone and elicit advice from Alex Ferguson. An onerous job became even more difficult when, for the first few weeks, he worked without an acknowledged deputy. He interviewed a few candidates, including Mick Buxton, who had been manager at Huddersfield Town. Then, in the January of the next year, he alighted on a trusted amigo, the committed, energetic figure of Jimmy Mullen. The latter had put in 10 years as captain of Sheffield Wednesday before replicating those duties under Porterfield at Millmoor. When he received the phone call from Aberdeen, Mullen was player-manager of Newport County. Money was at a premium in that part of South Wales and consequently this was a job that carried no cargo of expectation. He was asked if he would be interested in joining Aberdeen. His answer indicated that he'd just had become a football pools winner.

'I'd walk up! Give me three weeks and I'll be there.'

It wasn't quite so simple. The directors of Aberdeen, having taken a chance with Porterfield, wanted to interview his potential assistant. Mullen told his employers that he needed to go up to London and watch a Football Combination match between Spurs and Chelsea. Instead, he flew up to Aberdeen and met Dick and Ian Donald and Bobby Morrison in a hotel. The meeting lasted two hours and he was asked a succession of questions. When Porterfield later ran him to the airport, Mullen asked him how he'd fared and the response was most encouraging. He'd impressed as a bubbly character who had supplied all the correct answers. When he arrived back in Wales, Porterfield rang to say the job was his. That night, Mullen looked back, perhaps wistfully, at a career that, while admirable in its own context, had fallen short in terms of honours and silverware. Now, the 35-year-old was elated. Scottish football, at the time, was beginning to regenerate and discover its former glory: this was the chance to close in on the big time.

I track Mullen down through Burnley FC, a club he eventually managed for five seasons during the nineties. We know each other, having met twice in circumstances which will be explained later. Burnley call me to say he is happy to talk on the telephone. It's appropriate that we do so, for this year of 2017 marks the 30th anniversary of his Pittodrie appointment. So, after a few preliminaries, I ask him how it was to replace Alex Ferguson and Archie Knox. He can almost visualise him nodding his head.

'I told my wife that would be one of your questions. It was always going to be a really tough situation. We both knew it. Fergie's influence at that club was absolute. I didn't realise that until I was in it and working with people on a daily basis. Obviously, Archie had the reputation as the rough and tumble type, and we knew that Fergie wouldn't hold back, either. Ian was a different kind of manager to that. He could raise the roof when he wanted to, but, from what I remember at Rotherham, he also used to be able to put his arm around players. Talk to them – manage in a different way to what you'd expect Alex Ferguson to manage.'

This raises an interesting point. The story goes that the Aberdeen players had become so accustomed to the brand of tough love dispensed by Ferguson and Knox that they found Porterfield's emollience strangely anathema to them. Alex McLeish, for one, allegedly wanted Porterfield to be more ruthless. I put this to Mullen, but he refuses to confirm it. There again, he doesn't deny it. I try another track: had Mullen discovered any difficulty from his own standpoint?

'I think the first couple of days were important to me in terms of how I handled myself. Vitally important. They knew I could hold my own in how I came over to them, but I gave them the utmost respect. Quite rightly so. For goodness sake, when you're working with players like Miller, McLeish, Leighton, Bett, the little boy, Joe Miller, the right back they signed from Dundee, Stewart McKimmie – I mean, they'd been there and done it. They were heroes, absolute heroes. The one thing I realised was that you couldn't go in there with a crash, bang, wallop attitude, saying you wanted f***ing this and that. They'd just turn against you straight away. So I had to earn their respect by the work I did with them.'

Had there been any difficulty with Willie Miller?

'He was a big fan of Alex Ferguson. He'd an absolutely massive influence in the dressing room and you knew straight away how you dealt with this fella was going to be very important. I could tell you a few stories about what happened at half time and you thought to yourself, "F***ing hell! Just let him get on with it." We'd been led to believe that Fergie would lose the head and so would Archie, and these players knew if they didn't put in a performance, they were going to get absolutely roasted. We knew that if we continued with the style of play and that style of coaching, but without the tumult, we could keep them going. Willie was always given the opportunity to say something, and he was always very short and very direct. You knew straight away that the players were listening. Yes, his performances on the field ensured that he was a huge influence. People used to say to me, "he's not a good defender." Well, there were games when he was one on one and he wasn't the quickest. But the thing was I never ever saw him get done in that kind of situation. His partnership with McLeish was absolutely phenomenal.'

Mullen does not seem inclined to elaborate about the Miller's tales at half time, but instead takes another tack. He reveals that he came to know Ferguson in his spell at Aberdeen, because the latter hadn't moved his family down to Manchester by then. In the summer of 1987, Mullen attended a lot of functions and the United manager was at quite a few of them.

'We'd sit down and he'd openly ask me if I was settling in, this, that and the other. It didn't take a genius to know that he kept in touch with the players, so he knew a lot about what was going on. And also one of the biggest things I found during my time at Aberdeen was the press: they were a huge influence, not just in Aberdeen but in Scotland, with the Rangers thing taking off under Graeme Souness and them spending fortunes. The number of times I'd sit and listen to Ian on the phone on Fridays to the big papers in Glasgow. He was so guarded about giving anything away to anybody. But I imagine it was the same at all the big clubs. When you think of it, any one of Rangers, Celtic, Hearts, Dundee United and ourselves could have won the league. The competition was unbelievable.'

It was, indeed. Under the Porterfield stewardship, the cock rooster that was Aberdeen, while some distance from achieving the status of a feather duster, lost its ability to strut arrogantly around the farmyard. Graeme Souness and an enlightened chairman called David Holmes had made the difference. In all three of the Dons' three title wins in the 80s, they as good as owned the Ibrox side. Indeed, during Ferguson's eight-year reign he only lost four League games to his former side, winning 17 and drawing 12. Now, there was a dramatic change of ownership. In Porterfield's 20-month segment, the Dons could finish only fourth in successive Premier Division years. They reached the final of the League Cup in 1987 and the semi-final of the Scottish Cup a handful of months later, but their pre-eminence was threatening to filter into history.

Mullen describes the League Cup defeat by Rangers (who won 5-3 on penalties, having drawn 3-3 after extra time) as the greatest game of football he has ever seen. He is desperate to get a video or CD of it.

'I'm sure I can get one from somewhere.' he says, hopefully.

Why remind himself of heartache? He is not listening.

'Ally McCoist broke our hearts with the penalty. McLeish and Miller had done a fantastic job on him that day. But it was like the world fell out below us. I remember being in the dressing room and it was absolutely silent. Ian didn't say anything. And if Ian wasn't going to speak, neither was I. Willie Miller, for once, was lost for words. McLeish and Leighton, too. If we'd won, them three would have been dancing around the dressing room.'

Porterfield, in his reflective moments, claimed that Ferguson's bequest had been a team teetering on the slippery slope of decline, but he was perhaps forgetting to factor in his own contribution to the deterioration. He imported players who scarcely promoted a hysterical reaction from the fan base: Keith Edwards, from Leeds; Tom Jones, from Weymouth; Gary Hackett, from Shrewsbury. In contrast, Porterfield was far more on the money with the robust-tackling Peter Nicholas, a £350,000 purchase from Luton, and somewhere near it with Charlie Nicholas, who came complete with a Bono-style hat and attitude from Arsenal. The price: £400,000. However, the capture of Nicholas from the high-end streets of London came as a complete surprise to Mullen.

'I've got to be honest; I didn't know what was happening. But I knew something was going on, because Ian was being very, very secretive. That was the first time he didn't want to tell me anything. "What's happening?" I asked him. "You're up to something." He just looked at me, winked, and said, "Wait and see."'

Mullen did not have long to wait. 'We came in on the Monday morning and found it had all gone off on the Sunday night. They'd met up in Glasgow. I think Ian Donald went with Ian to sort out the money side of things. Just before the press conference, I said to him, "You bugger! How did you do that?" He just said it was an opportunity. You know, a lot of people had said not to go near him (Nicholas). Not to touch him. Why? I don't know. Possibly it was his lifestyle.

He was always on Page 3 with a half-naked girl. It seemed his lifestyle in many ways in London was like that of a playboy.'

I'm listening to Mullen and I'm smiling. I remember meeting Charlie one Friday night in the manager's office of a West End club. He was drinking champagne. I asked him if he had been injured in training that day because I hadn't read anything about him being out of the Arsenal team. Nicholas looked surprised and told me he was fully fit. I pointed to the champagne. He said he often had a couple of glasses of bubbly on a Friday evening, whether he was playing or not.

I can tell Mullen is unimpressed by this. 'Dear, dear...' he says. 'On the night before a game?'

Then I describe another meeting, much later in life, with Nicholas, this time regarding his time at Aberdeen. Charlie explained that he was sitting watching telly in his hotel bedroom when he heard stones being thrown against the window. He claimed that it was the manager, Ian Porterfield, who was allegedly desperate for him to come for a drink. This was one offer that was refused.

I ask Mullen for his version of the Charlie Nicholas story. He delivers it without too much enthusiasm.

'I was always wary of him because of his reputation at Arsenal. I'd heard all the stories, of course, and the Millers, McLeishes and Betts would have heard them as well. But he was bought and we had to get on with it. Did he fit in? He did pretty much what he wanted to do and was allowed go get away with it. I was under the impression that he didn't fancy being there and that he'd been hoping that Celtic would come back in for him.'

The time has come to remind Mullen of another Friday night, this time in Aberdeen. But, first, we must retrace our steps to a situation earlier that same day in March of 1988.

I'm stationed outside the main doors of Pittodrie. It's the same place I stood three and a half decades ago when I was a wee laddie ferreting around looking for autographs. This time, I'm seeking a major exclusive rather than players' signatures. My old compadre, Tommy Docherty, has given me the starter for ten. He's told me he attended a recent dinner in Aberdeen – and Ian Porterfield had admitted to him that he'd attempted to resign due to a host of problems. The Doc could not envisage this situation lasting and emphasised that the Porterfield reign would be brief. As ever, he reached the point quicker than most human beings. 'Get yourself up to Aberdeen and you'll get a story.'

I land at Dyce 24 hours later, check into my lucky Atholl hotel, and meet a contact, who has further information to validate the tale. So here I am on a very cold Friday morning, waiting for it to break. I'm clad in a pin stripe suit, white-collared shirt, with obligatory tie and handkerchief. No overcoat. That would spoil the effect. People, particularly reactionary football directors, are not inclined to take you seriously if it seems you've fallen off the back of a potato lorry. But, I've been here for over an hour and no-one is taking the presentation seriously. It is time for desperate measures. I send a note into the secretary, Ian Taggart, that I need to speak to the club directors, as I would like their response to a fairly explosive story concerning Ian Porterfield. In the time it takes Kylie Minogue to sing I Should Be So Lucky, *I find myself in the office of the said Taggart. I tell him my tale. Pale-faced, he leaves the room, but returns after a few minutes. 'The directors will see you now,' he says.*

And they do. I'm led into the wood-panelled boardroom. The directors are seated: Dick Donald, in the middle, flanked by his son Ian and Bobby Morrison. I know Bobby of old because I used to place bets in his turf accountants' office in the east end of Union Street. Before that, I worked for Campbell and Sellars taxis during my school holidays and, on several occasions, picked him up. I'll bet he never envisaged us meeting like this again. Ian Porterfield stands with his back to a radiator on my left. He looks as if he's had more profitable days. The chairman encourages me to present my case. I do so and explain that I could, if so inclined, publish the story without reference to anyone. But I wish to pursue the correct protocol and hear the other side of matters in order to achieve balance. Knowing the composition of the directorship, I'm not overly optimistic but, possibly against the odds, I get the result for which I'm looking. The chairman says I have been very fair in my approach and therefore I should be given access to his manager. In a way, I'm beyond being surprised: I'm stunned. How times have changed! This same chairman once denied me access to the building after an evening match in the mid seventies. He insisted if I had been one of the more recognisable faces from Glasgow, such as Alan Herron, then it would have been a different matter. Today, figuratively speaking, he is opening the secret vaults to a really big football story. I wonder whether Bobby Morrison has vouched for me.

There were no preliminaries when Porterfield and I reached his office. The interview, if it could be described as such, began even before we were seated and I'd activated my tape recorder. He might have erected a barrier of suspicion with others previously. He destroyed that same barrier on this occasion. There was scarcely a requirement for me to speak. The manager rummaged through the right-hand drawer of his desk and blew the dust from a photograph of his then wife. He indicated that most of his problems were rooted in a fractured marriage; that his wife, Isa, had run away with a butcher. He claimed that lies had circulated in Aberdeen about his drinking and his private life. So many lies had been told, he insisted. A monologue was on the lips of a desperately unhappy man. I left him possibly 45 minutes later. Porterfield had unburdened himself and had looked almost relieved to have done so. Soon, I was back in the Atholl hotel, transcribing the tape recording of our meeting, then writing a back page splash and an inside spread for the *Daily Star*.

If I'd landed such a story, in the carefree days of the seventies and early eighties, I would have been at the mercy of Bacchus and enjoyed the chaos of celebration. But problems with my heart meant that any such indulgence was denied me. Michael, my older brother, joined me for not only dinner but also for an interlude of temperance. He and I had occupied two very different worlds: he had been a waiter on the cruise liners and then a taxi driver in the city. A heart defect, one that was even more serious than mine, had forced him into early retirement. In 1984, after the diagnosis, the consultant solemnly explained that he had five years to live, but offered him a place on the transplant list. Michael, consumed by terror, had declined the offer. Now he was only one year away from a very personal doomsday scenario, and the terror had never left him. There was an 11-year age differential between us and this ostensibly was the first evening we had ever spent together, sober and reflective. That night, we visited our respective pasts and stared, nervously, into indeterminate futures. We discussed everything from mortality, to our late parents, to our married lives – and concluded with remembrances of those riotous times when we both could drink for Scotland. Sure, our existences had been eclectic, but this was a glorious interlude of fusion. We laughed. We cried. We fraternised like brothers should. Earlier that day, I had written a story about a man whose professional and private lives were on a collision course. The man seated next to me had a year to live. It placed everything in perspective.

The sombre mood was broken when we were joined in the bar by Porterfield and Mullen, who were also staying at the Atholl. It was obvious that they had not aligned themselves to temperance that evening, but their behaviour was nevertheless impeccable. I might have expected a reaction from Porterfield, but there was not the slightest evidence of animosity from either man. Michael was also staying and, at around midnight, we excused ourselves and went to our bedroom where I had booked two single beds. The Aberdeen management team insisted they would be turning in soon afterwards. At around 3pm, I heard a commotion in the corridor. Opening the door, I espied Porterfield and Mullen making their way, noisily and unevenly, to their respective bedrooms. I realised then that this was a situation that was never going to last. It didn't. Only a few weeks later, it was announced that Porterfield had resigned. I might be wrong here, but I imagine a gun was pointed at his temple. Only a week before this, he'd held a meeting with the team and indicated that he was about to change the whole system. He clearly thought he had a future at Pittodrie.

Mullen takes up the story here.

'I was down in the north-east of England at me mam and dad's house when Ian rang me to say it was all over with Aberdeen. I cried me bloody eyes out that night. Oh, I did. Aye. That was the end of another season and I was thinking, "Let's get ourselves a good summer and get started again. Let's have another crack at it." Then comes a phone call sayin' it's all over. He told me that he'd resigned and a new management team would be put in place. And he added, "They've asked me to tell you that you'll be leaving as well." It broke my heart. I cried like a baby.'

If two careers had been punctured by an attempt to emulate the management skills of Alex Ferguson, the entry wounds were quick to heal. Porterfield was soon installed as assistant to Bobby Campbell at Chelsea, and he went on to have coaching and managing stints with Reading, Chelsea, Zambia (twice), a club side in Saudi Arabia, Bolton, Trinidad and Tobago and finally Armenia. Tragically, he died aged 61, of colon cancer, in a Surrey hospice. Mullen attended the funeral in Bagshot.

'I didn't get a chance to see Ian before he died because the illness was so quick in the end. The amount of people who were there that day was unbelievable. It told you plenty about the esteem in which he was held.'

But what of the second lieutenant who had found his dreams torn asunder by fate? Mullen also resurrected himself in some style, notably with a five-year stint as manager of Burnley. But in his last year at the Lancashire club, he made national newspaper headlines in the most unfortunate fashion: his wife Sharon had her dress set alight by fans outside a Chinese takeaway. He describes it, stoically, as a 'difficult time.' He resigned soon afterwards. Predictably, our conversation ends with a reference to a club he came to love.

'As for Aberdeen, it was my best experience in football and, in the end, my worst. Without a doubt. I'll never forget it.'

History explains that anyone replacing Alex Ferguson was about to have his heart broken. David Moyes and Louis van Gaal can provide testimony to that. Ian Porterfield and Jimmy Mullen were simply in the appropriate place at an inappropriate time.

* *

WHO WAS RESPONSIBLE FOR the importation of Charlie Nicholas to Pittodrie, and why had Porterfield been so secretive that he couldn't even tell his No. 2 what was about to occur? Those questions hopefully will be answered in due course but, first, it's necessary to give the background to this unlikely tale. I have known Nicholas for 35 years, initially visiting him in the early eighties at his parents' home in Maryhill; back then, he was making a nickname for himself with Celtic: the Cannonball Kid. He was a refreshingly engaging young man who had the football world positioned at his feet. All he needed to do was steer it in the right direction.

I met him on several occasions as he debated his career path and I even recommended an agent – Bev Walker – to him. There were several alternatives regarding that future. Bob Paisley was keen to take him to Liverpool. Ron Atkinson sensed he would look the part in a Manchester United jersey. But there were problems with both these clubs. Liverpool was the obvious choice, but the player felt that he might be eclipsed by the long shadow of Kenny Dalglish. How was he going to displace the man who had become a folk hero on Merseyside? Manchester United? Chairman Martin Edwards and Atkinson took him for lunch, an event, seemingly, bearing the hallmarks of anti-climax. 'Ron's conversation was fine and he was a big personality,' Nicholas remembers, 'but, when you asked him about football, he didn't have an idea about what his team was going to be. He talked about Bryan Robson and Norman Whiteside, but it was as if he was trying to remember the names of his players. Where was I going to play in his team? There was no real answer. I probably wanted to go to Manchester United. But he was so unconvincing.'

So, with Bev Walker's assistance, Nicholas opted for the tradition and bespoke reputation of Arsenal, whereupon he allegedly became the highest-paid footballer in Britain. Unfortunately, his social exploits were said to have overshadowed his on-field expertise and the nickname had changed to his detriment. The Cannonball Kid was now Champagne Charlie, with two drink driving charges to his name and a reputation for a love of London's night life. Originally, his manager was Terry Neill, but anaemic performances from the team meant changes in this department. Don Howe came in for three years, but was then replaced by the Millwall boss, George Graham. How would Charlie fare with a man accused of being an autocrat? Now, football is a game that invents conflicts, but this one was destined to become the progenitor of all sporting conflicts. I met Nicholas in a Glasgow restaurant some years back. He downloaded his story as the oysters were served.

'By the time George came long, I was pretty well controlled as a single lad at the time. Claire was in Scotland and we didn't see a lot of each other. I had a nice lifestyle. The only thing was I made it a wee bit more private and, at that time, I was seeing quite a few different ladies. The Press weren't getting a hold of it and I thought that was good. I was starting to enjoy life again, starting to feel better about myself. I went to the World Cup in 1986 and it was problematic because I got injured in the first game against Denmark. I came on for 20 minutes against Uruguay in the third game. But away from the football, I got on so well with Alex Ferguson, Walter Smith and Archie Knox. I thought I would have problems with Fergie, but I had to pinch myself some days at how unbelievably well I was getting on with him. It was then I started to realise that the Glaswegian moulds were virtually the same. I started to get educated on that trip. Wattie was taking me out for a glass of wine. I was getting these older figures to talk to. You know, I love talking to older people about the ways of life. I find it educational.

'I still had problems with the ankle, but I came back refreshed. We always used to meet George Graham and Frank McLintock in a local boozer on Saturdays after games. They were at Millwall at the time. George used to say to me, "You've never been an Arsenal-style player. You should have gone to Liverpool or Man U." I thought he'd made a fair point. I look back now and, football-wise, yeah, I should have definitely gone to Liverpool.'

It was destined to be a marriage without a honeymoon. Nicholas had been an automatic choice and, because of his intuitive approach to football, the darling of the North Bank fans. But Charlie was far from being the darling of George Graham. His place in the team could no longer be guaranteed. There was the odd delicious moment, of course, notably in the League Cup final of 1987 when Nicholas scored two goals – one of them an assist from Ronnie Whelan – to give Arsenal a 2-1 victory over Liverpool.

Two weeks in from Graham's arrival, Nicholas admits that he knew he was in for a hard shift in the salt mines. There was a temptation to return to the wine-bar existence as percentage football began to be the theme at Highbury, but Nicholas was more in control of himself by then. He tried to seek confrontation with Graham, but the manager was apparently uneasy with confrontation. Nicholas was sent to train with the reserves and eat what he considered to be pay dirt. He considered this demotion to be pathetic. But, looking back at the battlefield, he claims the problem between them was not just the style of play. It was far more personal than that.

'I got up his nose for three things. Firstly, I was better looking than him. Secondly, I was a far better dresser than him and, thirdly, I was pulling better birds. So, he had three things to deal with that he must have found impossible.'

Nicholas, in Graham's hypercritical eyes, had not shaped up. It was time to ship him out. The player flew to France, together with his new agent, Jerome Anderson, and secretary Ken Friar, to discuss terms with Toulon. They spent two days in a beautiful villa in Nice trying to reach an agreement. The deal was to be an installment plan: three payments up to £400,000. No deal was struck. But there were other suitors: Derby, Brian Clough's Nottingham Forest and David Pleat's Spurs.

'George killed the Toulon deal. I don't know why he did it, but it really stuck in my throat. A pay-up plan wasn't an issue for Arsenal. To make matters worse, George still wouldn't meet me. All it did was make me tougher, but I don't compliment George one minute for making me stronger. I got through it on my own on what was a very important time of my life. I was very much a single man, trying to calm things down and focus on what was important. Then Aberdeen popped up. If I'm honest, I didn't really want to go there, but getting back playing football had to be the right decision. I said a fond farewell to the Arsenal players. I was quite emotional: there were tears in my eyes at London Colney. I'd genuinely fallen in love with them. I knew Graham had ripped that love apart. It was over, but it was hard to let go.'

Cosmopolitan Aberdeen was accustomed to cigar-chomping Texans, but the new purchase was something else. He had bought himself a large, Bono-style hat and favoured a long, leather coat and the wearing of an earring. It almost embarrasses him nowadays. Concentrate on the word 'almost'.

'I blame those Spandau Ballet boys and those eighties types. I had a great time back then, but we were all a bit effeminate. Remember the big hair – you looked bloody daft. I laugh because my wife was talking about those Football Years documentaries, and I'm walking around in my underpants with a couple of blondes. My daughter asked me about playboys. "Certainly not me any-more," I told her.'

So, let's have the answers to those initial questions: who was responsible for taking Charlie Nicholas to Aberdeen? The answer is emphatic. 'It was the board that brought me in. Ian Porterfield was obviously involved and I reckon he was quite pleased, but the board were pretty strong about it. I met them just before New Year. I was really taken by Dick Donald – a wonderfully down to earth, simplistic man.'

In spite of the initial misgivings, Nicholas was beginning to appreciate his surroundings. 'I looked around me and there were predominantly good play-ers – Willie Miller, Alex McLeish, Jim Leighton and Jim Bett. I always loved my training and was never frightened of hard work, I didn't go through the motions, but I was starting to get problems with my hamstrings, and felt I was beginning to lose my edge with my sharpness. That was telling me I wasn't a main striker anymore.'

You suspect the departure of Porterfield and Mullen suited Nicholas. Now he was riding on the tandem of Alex Smith and Jocky Scott. 'You know, Jocky is one of the best coaches, if not the best, I've played under. He was not everyone's cup of tea, but he was certainly mine. I had a fabulous two years there. Willie Miller and I became great friends. People found that a strange partnership, but I just love the man. He's a fabulous individual. I settled down. Claire came up from Stirling; we married in 1989 and built a nice, big house in Peterculter.'

Life retains that ability to perplex. As Nicholas found his family feet, he felt that the fortunes of the team were beginning to sag. He was delighted with the purchase of Hans Gillhaus, but was surprised nobody in England had picked up on his talent. 'He was that good.'

But elsewhere, to Nicholas' way of thinking, things were perhaps not so good. Miller had a problem with his knee; Leighton had moved on to Manchester United, and both Bett and McLeish were approaching the veteran stage. 'And the young batch of players coming through never looked likely to attain Aberdeen standards. I could see it coming. The following season, they panicked at Ibrox when they should have won the championship.'

After two-and-a-half years in an Aberdeen shirt, Nicholas returned to his old club, Celtic, in the summer of 1990. But not before he had won winners' medals in both the League and Scottish Cups. Victory over Celtic in the Scottish Cup final gave him particular pleasure.

'Aberdeen? I enjoyed the people and probably one of my proudest moments was the penalty shoot-out. If I'd missed, Celtic would have won the Cup. By then, I more or less knew I was going to Celtic. But I stood up and probably hit the best penalty of the day. My memories take me to an open-topped bus and lovely cheers from the punters. A lot of people from Aberdeen – although sometimes I'm critical of them and sometimes justifiably – would remember me. They'd tell you that I scored a penalty for them against what was my team.'

CHAPTER 10

The War Zone

It would be nice to bottle certain years of your life, like good wine, and perhaps even label them as vintage. Unfortunately, you won't find the year of 1990 in my cellar. It's vinegar as opposed to Chablis. My tournament begins well in that I'm going to the World Cup as Chief Sports Writer of the Daily Star. *I perform fairly creditably, fly all over Italy and pull a few stories: Maradona has become the* de facto *manager of Argentina; the Cameroon goalkeeper who is terrified to return to his homeland; how Mick Robinson has turned into the outcast of Jack Charlton's Ireland. My tournament ends badly when my body demands rest: I phone the office and ask whether I can cover the Argentina-Italy semi-final on television, rather than travel to Naples. I am immediately transferred to the chief's office. His opening words are not encouraging. 'What is it now?' There is no mention of the fact that I haven't had a day off for five weeks. I am immediately summoned back to London, presumably in disgrace for feeling unwell.*

Now, this Sports Editor and I share a history of conflict and I must admit, there's culpability on my side: I think the man behaves like an absolute moron and it's a suspicion that I find unable to keep to myself. This is where the fun begins in earnest. A demotion arrives in the post. The company say it's in my interests, of course; to help me with my illness. I respond with a writ to the Editor. Oops! I've made another enemy. There's now enough bad blood flowing in our Blackfriars Bridge office to rival the Rambo film series. But, hey, I'm now Chief Sports Columnist. Impressive, eh? Not really. It's one of these spurious titles that abound in the Street of Shame: the only thing that is invariably missing from my professional life is… a column. Oh, I write quite a few, but most of them land on the dreaded spike. So, now we're onto the lost years of my professional life. The only thing I have going for me is my beloved football team. The Dons are desperately trying to re-discover the secret recipe for football domination once devised by Alex Ferguson. Porterfield didn't find it. Now, it's the turn of co-managers Alex Smith and Jocky Scott. I'd love to be up there, supporting them, but it's not feasible: I'm too busy hanging onto a job that means bugger all but pays the mortgage.

WITNESSING ENGLAND'S FOOTBALLERS experience any form of hardship can only enhance the life of any self-respecting Tartan Army fan. But what transcends euphoria is witnessing them being humiliated by a team of a modest international pedigree. You may remember, then, that the 2016 European Championship became the year of the Icelandic Clap. England suffered two reverses that day – on the pitch and, even more emphatically, in the grandstands. The measured, inexorable sound was apparently invented by fans of Motherwell FC some years ago – and duly customised with a war cry by the followers of Iceland. They were desperate to celebrate their 2-1 victory and announce to everyone that they had arrived on the centre stage of world sport.

By contrast, let's shift the focus from a frenzy to the domesticity of a house in Reykjavik in this year of 2017. Former footballer Jim Bett and his family are sitting down to dinner and, as usual, it is a fine dinner. It only requires something other than a sweet course to round it off. Bett's four-year-old grandson alights on the perfect recipe. He suggests it would be good if he and his five dinner companions executed the Icelandic Clap. Which is what they do. Inhibitions discarded, six smiling people of various ages sit clapping their hands rhythmically. Bett still savours the moment.

Apologies for disrupting the mood, but we must return to another frenzy. Bett is about to be transported back to a time, a place and an atmosphere that relegates the Iceland Clap to the material of children's books. The date – 11 May 1991 – is seared into his memory. This is when he and his Aberdeen FC colleagues went to Ibrox requiring only a draw to lift their first Premier Division title in six years. Rangers had won the title in successive years and were determined to complete the hat-trick. Their fans shared that determination. Aberdeen's belief was that they were going to a football stadium; the reality was that they were entering a putative war zone.

'You could cut the atmosphere with a knife that day,' Bett remembers. 'Rangers needed to win. We just needed a point. Yeah, it was incredible. I don't think I've ever experienced an atmosphere like that before or afterwards. It was ready to explode and I think if we had scored, there would have been bedlam. I don't know if the referee handled the game that well, 'cos I think he felt the heat as well.'

I have telephoned Bett in order to appreciate the career of one of Aberdeen's greatest-ever players. He will deliver a somewhat controversial account of his time at Pittodrie. We will be back with him shortly. But, to elaborate on this segment of the story, we must return to Jocky Scott, who meets me in a Broughty Ferry pub. He was co-manager with Alex Smith at the time of this momentous match. Co-manager was a rather spurious title. In effect, he was coach and Smith, the Mount Rushmore of Stewart Kennedy-speak, was the manager – a manager, it should be emphasised, who had reinvented the Dons with his astute signings from abroad. Scott remembers the atmosphere that day as being 'something else. When you talk to our fans, who were involved with thousands and thousands of Rangers fans, let's say it was not a good environment. It was very intimidating.' Some of those supporters, it must be said, were fearful of their health and safety.

But what of the team? Scott emphasises that confidence was spread liberally throughout it that day, and that matters might have been vastly different had they seized upon two wonderful chances to score early on – chances, significantly, that went to Bett and Dutchman Peter Van de Ven. 'You look back and you wonder: if we had scored with them, we would have gone on to win the game.'

But the star signs were stacked heavily against Aberdeen that day: no-one in a red shirt was destined to score goals. Concession of them was another matter. First-pick goalkeeper Theo Snelders was injured and Michael Watt was called up as his replacement. Rangers, having survived the two attacks on their goal, tested the litmus paper regarding the young keeper. Scott takes you back to the action.

'With about 15 minutes gone, Wee Mark Walters got the ball on the left wing and crossed high; Michael came for it and stretched. Meanwhile, (Mark) Hateley ran from 15 yards and just battered him. That's the word – battered. His elbow went right across Michael's face. The referee gave a free kick but nothing more. Nowadays, Hateley would have been banned for three or four games. If he'd done it in the street, he would have been lifted. Both Alex and I were going daft at the referee and linesman because it was an obvious assault. Michael was down on the deck for quite a while. Five minutes later, Walters, along the by-line, chipped the ball in. We were waiting on Michael coming for it. But he didn't come. Hateley – bang! One nothing. And that, unfortunately, set the tone. But, put it this way, it wasn't a surprise that Michael didn't come for that next cross ball.'

Hateley added another before half-time to clinch the deal. Now this game, possibly more than any other in the history of Aberdeen FC, has turned into a trade fare for older conspiracy theorists. The most persistent is that the co-managers were at odds, with Smith urging caution and Scott recommending adventure. I was not there, but listened, fearfully, to every second of it on the radio from far-off Buckinghamshire. I'm taking neither side. All I will say is that the major players have had over two and a half decades to get their stories straight.

Back to Scott. 'Alex and I went into the game positive and stressing to the players that we needed to win. We couldn't go there and just play for a point. That wouldnae have worked. Anyway, we couldnae do it with the type of players we had at that time' (nature has not given Scott a happy face, but he smiles intermittently as he is subjected to a detailed line of questioning. You will have to go figure why).

There was always speculation over the formation: was it wrong? There is a pause which is so long you might have thought a toilet break had been declared. 'Formations and systems don't win games. Players win games.'

So the speculation was wrong? 'No, regardless of formation, we could have played two or three different formations and it might have been the same result. One or two things had been said, sorry, leaked out, whatever. And people started adding bits and pieces to them.'

What was the formation? 'I'm sure it was 4-4-2. Gillhaus and Jess up front. Mason, Bett, Connor and Van de Ven in midfield.'

So, there were no arguments? 'No, no. There certainly weren't any arguments like the players saying to us... '

What about you and Alex? 'Nope.'

Why are you laughing? 'Because that's one of the things that came out afterwards – that there was an argument between Alex and myself.

Is it true, then? 'No, we never argued. We discussed.'

So, there was a discussion? 'There was one before every game. As to which players should play and how we should go about it. Drew Jarvie was involved as well. When we started off (at Aberdeen), Alex was looked upon as the manager; I worked with the players, so we would discuss the team during the week and on a Friday night. Alex would throw out what his team would be; I'd throw out what mine would be and Drew would do the same for each particular game. And 96-97 per cent of the time, we were always the same. Then you'd get one or two games where we would differ.'

Are we speaking about one particular game? His chuckle turns to laughter. 'Ach, no. I'm no' gettin' into that. It had nothing to do with losing the game.'

I return to the land of the Icelandic Clap to ask Bett for his view of the tactics that day. He thinks they were good, but he says it without any great enthusiasm. He adds, 'With us needing a point, you have to ask yourself: do we go for a win, or do we sit back? Our style was not for sitting back and letting teams have the ball. I think you must play to your strengths. It just didn't work for us on the day.'

But, did he not think that the Dons sat back? 'Yes, we did. I think it was a mental thing. When you need a point, you have to be a bit wary. To be honest, it wasn't a great game. There was too much at stake for the clubs. I don't think it was our intention to go out and defend. If you do that, you're up against good players; you give them the ball and get punished for it. I don't think we were that kind of team, but, obviously, you had to be wary.'

I suggest that Smith and Scott had differed over tactics. 'Aye. Well, I don't really know too much about that, but obviously you're going to get speculation. After the game, it's always about you should have done this or that. It's so easy in hindsight.'

Bett refuses to be drawn over the three per cent differential in disagreement to which Scott alluded. He laughs nervously. 'I'm no' getting into that. What I will say is that it was certainly a huge disappointment for those who played. I know it was the worst moment in my career.'

I won't overburden you with the Ibrox aftermath: the shattering sound of silence, the faces of the players that were as blank as the pages of a man with writer's block. It's sufficient to say that defeat did not become Aberdeen FC in those days. So, it's time to leave a story that has been classified under Pittodrie's very own Official Secrets Act, and concentrate on this man Bett. There were, in fact, very few negative moments in a career that can be characterised as stellar. This charismatic midfielder was playing for Belgium's FC Lokeren after leaving Rangers. There were several options on the table for his services, so many in fact that the woodwork was buckling under their weight. But, in the long run, the player discarded the English options and narrowed the choice to two Scottish clubs, Rangers and Aberdeen. But he'd given his word to Alex Ferguson and didn't want to renege, although the intimidating figure of Jock Wallace was proposing an impressive case for Rangers.

His faith in the Ferguson way was speedily justified when Aberdeen won both the League and Scottish Cups in 1985. Gordon Strachan had departed for Manchester United a year earlier. The midfield needed strength and vision. Bett provided both. Unlike some of his colleagues, he appreciated Ferguson's hard-line direction, at least he did until he went to Mexico with Scotland on World Cup duty and found himself surplus to requirements.

'I was a bit upset about that,' he recalls. 'I'd played in all the qualifying games and expected to play over there. People say that this is life and you've just got to get on with it, but it doesn't mean to say you need to be happy about it. When we got back, I went into Fergie's office and asked for a transfer. My reception? As far as I can remember, it was quite friendly. I thought I should have been playing, like all players do. He didn't. He just told me there and then that I wasn't going anywhere. He told me I needed a few weeks to calm down. Obviously, I did calm down a wee bit, but the annoyance was still there. Transfer request denied.'

The revolution at Rangers needed new freedom fighters. Bett was asked to sign up to the cause. He declined, chiefly because he wanted his children to be free of the sectarian divide. But Bett's defiant interlude with the manager was unusual for him. He was normally a phlegmatic kind of guy who accepted both sides of life: rough and smooth. So, what was his reaction when Ferguson, having vetoed any move, took himself off to Manchester United a few months later? 'Hey, this was football and you prepare yourself for anything. Sure, it was Fergie who got me there in the first place and here he was leaving. I suppose you could look at it that way. It was a wee bit of surprise. There again, it was Manchester United. He might never have got that chance again.'

Ian Porterfield had walked into a blizzard of expectation from the supporters. The criticism began if the team lost two games in a row. He lost his directions in that blizzard. But Alex Smith and Jocky Scott knew their way around storm conditions. Bett unequivocally recommends both men. He describes them as great and refreshing operators. 'It was a new start for the team because Alex had contacts in Holland. He managed to bring in some really good players – Hans Gillhaus and Paul Mason were two of them. Then there was Theo Snelders. I mean, Aberdeen always had great goalkeepers – Jim Leighton was one. But Snelders was every bit as good. Gillhaus came in for £650,000, quite a fair amount for Aberdeen at that time. They got Mason for £200,000 and added Theo Ten Caat – with the great left foot – and Bobby Connor, another excellent player.'

Scott, meanwhile, underscores the contribution of the chairman, Dick Donald in these signings, especially Gillhaus. 'We'd been told there was a striker worth looking at. I went out two or three times, came back and told Alex, "yeah." He went to the chairman. Now, me being an Aberdonian, I knew all the stories about him being so grippy and how he wouldn't spend his money. I had to go in with Alex to see him. He asked how much Gillhaus would cost. "Well," says Alex, "we're looking at 650 grand. It might be £750,000." The chairman asked if anybody had been over to see him. "Yeah, Jocky has."

'Over to me. "Aye, good player, chairman." He asked if he was worth it. "Aye, he is." That was it. End of story. And he did it with every player we asked him to buy. He wouldnae spend the money unless you convinced him it was worth it. He was brilliant, the best chairman I've ever worked with. And never once did he criticise, or ask why we'd played a certain player. He always said, "That's your job. You live and die with it."'

Scott is not a loquacious man, but words are spewing out of him, and it would be rude to interrupt. 'The story goes how Mr Donald became chairman. He'd been invited onto the board when Aberdeen had got into financial difficulties back in the sixties, when there wasn't the same kind of money that there is now. They went to Mr Donald and said they would like him to be chairman. He said he wasn't interested. They told him they were in difficulties and he was the man to seem them through the storm. Again he said no. Eventually, it came round to finance, and he was the richest of the lot. The club was 25 grand in debt. He said to them he would do the job on one condition: that he'd pay it off and the club would never go into debt again. And they only did when he passed away, in 1993. The one thing that I found remarkable when I went there was that every player – and 95 per cent of them were internationals – was on the same wages: same basic wages, same bonuses, and same appearance money. Where it differed was when they signed their contracts. That's when they got weighed in with money, when it became different depending on who the player was. I couldnae believe it. But that's how they were able to maintain a balance, not getting into debt and stuff like that. They managed their money appropriately. When the chairman passed and his son Ian took over, the wages started spiralling. Unbelievable. Sad, but true.'

The controversial defeat to Rangers in May had a fairly seismic after-shock, one wheel falling off the Smith-Scott tandem in September of 1991. A job offer came in for Scott from Dunfermline, giving him another chance to become a manager in his own right. He seized it with the relish of a dog that hadn't chomped on a bone for months. Very shortly afterwards, he was staring at the contents of his stomach. He admits now that he was too hasty in his decision making and admits that he shouldn't have taken it. He adds, rather mysteriously, 'Discussions had taken place and I wasn't happy with the outcome. No, money was never a problem. But, stupidly, when the first offer of employment arrived, without thinking about, I went for it. It wasn't anger. It was just stupidity. It was something – how can I put it? – I thought I deserved and didn't happen.'

Due to the unofficial secrets act, we shall probably never know why Scott allowed a hasty heart to determine his future. But I'll propose a conspiracy theory. Did his decision have any derivations in what happened at Ibrox four months earlier? Don't blame me for posing that question; rather blame the principals for being so impenetrable. Whatever, the departure had repercussions. Willie Miller was installed as coach and in a UEFA Cup-tie against BK Copenhagen, which Aberdeen lost 1-0, the crowd turned on Smith whilst simultaneously lauding the hero of Gothenburg. The boulder of discontent was now careering ominously down the hill, as far as the Stirling man was concerned. The league form, mercurial at best, dipped dramatically in November with five straight defeats. Eventually, three months later, the directors felt the time was appropriate for remedial work: Smith, a man of unlimited experience, was out, Miller, the man of no experience at all, was in. The decision may have appeased the fans, but it infuriated even the phlegmatic Bett.

'I think that was the worst decision Aberdeen had made for a long time. The guy (Smith) had built a team which was strong and great to watch. People enjoyed going to games on a Saturday because of that. Maybe we didn't start the season very well, but it was a strange decision and I felt very upset about it. Alex Smith was a really decent, nice guy who was great to work with. The place was always buzzing on a Saturday and the players were happy: they knew there were going to be huge crowds. We were always going forward and attacking and a good time was being had by all. It was an incredibly bad decision by the board of directors. I just couldn't believe it.'

Bett makes a staunch and impressive defence of Smith, and yet he has his wires in disarray regarding the crowds. The fact is attendances were sometimes pretty dismal, with six, seven and nine thousand a norm rather than an exception. But his take on the broad concept of sacking Smith is at least adjacent to the truth. 'I don't know why they did it, but I do know that they've never recovered properly from it. Okay, they've won a couple of cup trophies since, but I don't think the team has ever been as exciting to watch. (Prior to Smith's sacking), when you got up on a Saturday, you were looking forward to the game because you expected to win it. I think that kind of thinking went out the window for a while. It took them ages to get back to ways of winning and putting a decent team on the park.'

It is a swingeing endorsement of Alex Smith's capabilities and a justification of Stuart Kennedy's reference to Mount Rushmore. On the other hand, you don't need to look closely that it scarcely vindicates Willie Miller's brand of management.

I ask Bett if he can compare Smith with Ferguson. I hear no ironic laughter down the telephone line. 'Fergie was more volatile. Alex was good at man management, getting players to play, and feel better about themselves, and getting the best out of the team. Fergie had a brilliant team, the best Aberdeen there's probably been. But we had a great one as well, and that was partly because of Smith's man management style. He dovetailed well with Jocky, and that's why I was disappointed when Jocky left. They worked well together. But Jocky wanted to be his own man. Alex had a hard job as well, bringing in all these players and managing to blend them. We had a great bond at that time. The team went out together and enjoyed each other's company. All the players were happy together as a group. Obviously, we went out and had a few beers, but it never got out of hand. Importantly, the experienced players were good at bringing the young guys through. And there were a lot of them.'

The enthusiasm in Bett's voice seems to wane when we discuss the Miller regime. This was his fourth manager in six years. 'What can I say? I was thinking about leaving after Alex's departure. I was injured quite a lot and didn't really enjoy the style of football that was there. It went more long ball and didn't suit the ball players. In my opinion, we had too many good players to play that way. You need to look forward to games. My family was happy but I wasn't really enjoying my football at that time. I think I was there for a further two years, but the dream had exploded when Alex left. I got on all right with Willie, but if you're not enjoying your football, you're not looking forward to playing. I didn't enjoy playing under him because of the style of football. It just wasn't for me.'

Bett left Pittodrie in 1994, along with others like Alex McLeish, Robert Connor, Lee Richardson and Mixu Paatelainen, as Miller called for an infusion of new blood. Bett, who had the ability to run from box to box and not demand an oxygen mask, had played over 338 games in nine years. But, as he says, 'It was time to go. So I went.'

As fate would decree, it was not long before Willie Miller followed him into the departure lounge. The difference was this was not of his own volition.

CHAPTER 11

The 'Joey Barton' Influence

There's no denying that I've lived in a Wilson Micawber-esque land of delusion for the past few years, praying that something resembling a good job would come my way. By now, I despise just about everything about the Daily Star, *particularly my immediate boss; I believe he is blighting my life with his decision-making and bouts of aberrant behaviour. I'm willing to do anything to alleviate the stress. I explain the circumstances of my health to the Managing Editor and impress upon him that there may be long periods of sickness ahead. Thank God I work for such a caring set of employers! They were caring enough to demote me, if you remember. I look into his eyes and identify feverish activity: I swear he is mentally authorising a compensation package as we speak.*

A few weeks later, that small package comes my way and, with it, the delicious taste of freedom. I'm about to undergo the Mel Gibson experience in Braveheart. *But freedom doesn't mean inertia: mortgage commitments and family needs emphasise that this man must work. Luck decrees that I am offered not one but two jobs. I decline a lucrative offer to become Chief Sports Writer of the* Sunday Mirror – *and accept the invitation to be Sports Editor of the reconstituted* Scottish Daily Mail. *This is more like it: I've always wanted to be a sports editor.*

And now, on 4 February 1995, I'm being a dutiful sports editor by watching a late-night edition of Sportscene. *The rain is battering down outside, but there are also monsoon conditions in my heart. On this day, Aberdeen have lurched to the bottom of the Premier Division with a 3-1 loss to Kilmarnock at Rugby Park. Dougie Donnelly and Co have paid scant attention to what should be a major story. But the instinct that has carried me through over three decades in journalism is telling me that something seismic is about to occur in my home town.*

IAN DONALD, SON OF DICK, was scheduled to feature in this book. I wanted to hear his take on how and why he relieved club legend Willie Miller of his managerial responsibilities on 6 February, 1995. I subsequently talked to him on the telephone and he agreed to meet me in the Ferryhill House hotel one

Friday morning. I duly travelled up to Aberdeen the day prior to this. I wasn't long into my journey when I received a text from Donald. He could not keep our date. There was no suggestion of an alternative meeting. It was as abrupt as Miller's dismissal. I imagined, like *The Killers* song, that he had read my mind and didn't fancy reliving what must have been one of the more traumatic interludes in his life.

There was no such trauma for me that day in 1995, however. I was energised, the power of instinct driving me on. Early on the Monday, I telephoned our chief reporter, Brian Scott, and suggested that he should travel to Aberdeen to witness the Miller demise. Brian's reaction was a confection of confusion and reluctance, and he was probably quite within his rights to be thus inclined. There was no real evidence that the Dons directorship was going to press the ejector button quite so soon. There again, who needs evidence in football? Around lunchtime that day, a finger was applied to that button and Miller became a statistic of failure. He had scarcely placed a foot in the wrong direction during an illustrious playing career, but results, particularly in that season of 94-95, scarcely commended him as a leader in the mould of General McArthur. Aberdeen's immediate destiny was an undignified scuffle in the relegation zone. Bett's allusion to the long-ball game was possibly another factor as to why he had to go. But, on the sunnier side of the street, he had finished second in consecutive Premier League seasons and reached the finals of two Cups in 92-93. Subsequent events would prove that Miller was far from the least efficient of Aberdeen managers.

But, for the moment, allow me to concentrate on signings that showed Miller in the most favourable of lights. In 1992, when he was still savouring the honeymoon period of his leadership, he captured two significant figures, both from Blackburn Rovers: Lee Richardson and Duncan Shearer. Both would become cult heroes with the Pittodrie fans. Richardson gave the Dons a cutting edge in midfield – that's when they weren't bypassing it and infuriating purists like Bett – and Shearer supplied a goal threat from all areas. Here was one man who didn't mind taking on a shot from distance.

Today, Richardson operates in the far more complex area of sports psychology. He works for Lancashire CCC and was recently helping Sam Allardyce trying to forget the England fiasco and extricate Crystal Palace from one of the Premier Division's deepest potholes. The reunion had no longevity, however. After successfully climbing out of the pothole, Allardyce resigned. Back in the 90s, Richardson's professional life was far more straightforward. I call him and ask him to explain the formula for achieving cult hero status at Pittodrie.

'A few things coincided. Obviously, I think Aberdeen fans have a propensity towards that. I appeared to be, if not overtly, then covertly disrespectful towards

Rangers and Celtic and that probably warmed me to them. It was the way I played. For me, the all-round midfield player is someone who can win the ball, play it, score goals and create them. This I strived for, but it's not always easy to attain this two-heads mentality. I think for a good spell of my time there, I probably played some of the best football of my life. Possibly, it was because of the standard. At the time, Rangers and Celtic were as good as most Premier League teams in England, and Aberdeen were just in and around that, although we were a much younger side and therefore less experienced. I think, in terms of cult status, I didn't have some of the baggage that some of my team mates had in terms of growing up and maybe being closet Rangers and Celtic supporters. I mean, I didn't realise that Big Alex (McLeish) was a big Rangers man until years after I'd left, I wish he'd told me at the time. Then there were the referees. I was getting booked for my first intended tackle, never mind a proper tackle. There again, there was the long hair and the Yorkshire accent… '

This theme of Old Firm respect and disrespect is a fascinating one and Richardson is happy to take it on. 'I just knew that we needed to overturn them. I liked Willie and thought he was a good manager. He knew from experience that you had to go down and beat them. I saw that in black and white terms and I certainly didn't have a sense that they were invincible. I'm not saying all my team mates did but, apart from one or two occasions, I felt we definitely didn't do ourselves justice when we played them. That was a frustration. There was definitely a sense for me that some of our players were certainly intimidated by the threat of the challenge ahead in the cup finals. Consequently, their performances were affected. I honestly saw an opportunity and felt that we could beat them, topple them and win the League or the cups, just like they'd done in the Fergie years.'

I tell him I'd attended the 2016 League Cup final. There had been the brilliance of the flag display and the expectation that this would be carried onto the field of play. But that expectation dissolved quickly as Aberdeen players, clearly intimidated, stood off Celtic and were punished with a 3-0 defeat. 'You know, you only need two or three of your colleagues to be below par in a big game and already you're on the back foot. Struggling. Then it takes a mammoth effort from one or two individuals to change that. It would probably be one of the cup finals when I just looked around the dressing room and got the sense that we weren't in the right state of mind. Or up for it. Not quite there. Avoidance is the key term. It's basically a human trait that inhibits and shackles people. It's about the fear of losing rather than the bravery of winning. It stuck in my mind and frustrated me. So yeah, it was probably the same kind of experience that you had.' Avoidance: Richardson's explanation made me wonder whether my verdict on McInnes had been somewhat harsh. Had the Dons players practised avoidance back in November?

Richardson scored against Rangers in the Scottish Cup final, but admits that, as much as he is critical of his colleagues, he didn't play particularly well. 'No, I don't think I did myself justice, so here we have the pot calling the kettle black. But I sense Rangers were ahead of us in experience of these big games, and were able to conserve energy. Our best performance against them, in my time there, was in a league game in February of 1993. We lost 0-1 at Pittodrie. The goalkeeping performance from (Andy) Goram was the best I'd ever seen. I can't specifically remember the saves he made, but I remember the feeling after them. There were figuratively two goalkeepers between the posts. We did everything but score. And Mark Hateley clinched it with a great header from the edge of the box. That was a great opportunity. If we'd beaten them, we'd have been within a couple of points of them and they still had to play Celtic. That was probably my biggest disappointment because we absolutely gave everything. It was one of those games that you'll have seen over the years, where the best team doesn't always win, which was the case that night. But they will argue that they found a way to win.'

There is surely no argument that he rattled teeth and bones in his time. Richardson agrees to some degree, but stresses there were mitigating factors. The admission comes quickly: Aberdeen was by far his worst disciplinary record. But he believes there was a difference in the physicality between the leagues of England and Scotland. Back in his home country, the referees were mindful to be tolerant. Not so in Scotland.

'I remember getting sent off against Rangers. I would argue it wasn't even reckless. I was quick into a challenge that wasn't a challenge. The lad Charlie Miller made a real meal of it – basically, he just dived. It was a really good dive, though. Our shoulders maybe connected. In this day and age, the cameras would have proved me innocent and I would have got away with it after the event. But he should have been booked for diving when, in reality, I got sent off. I definitely felt the referees were pre-emptive. I used to get literally warned (before we began). It was Hugh Dallas, someone like that, who said he had his eye on me. And this was in the first minute of the game – I'd not even done anything. It was judge and jury and pretty biased. I'm not saying I didn't make a bad tackle while in Scotland – of course I did – but I certainly didn't deserve the rap I got.'

Wikipedia describes Richardson as an energetic midfielder. Duncan Shearer goes into rather more detail. 'I knew Lee at Blackburn. I didn't know Aberdeen were interested in him till Willie asked me what I thought. I said, "Well, he's a f***ing header, but a good header. The boy can play football." He was a long-haired, rock and roll kind of guy. I remember the day he signed, he had a tie on – I think it was probably the first f***ing day he'd ever worn one.

It was squint. Willie nudged me. I don't think he wanted to approach him. I was told to go and tell him to straighten his tie as he was going to get his picture taken. It was the way Aberdeen wanted to do things and it was quite right. They wanted to be professional. Lee wouldn't have given a f*** whether his tie was on properly or upside down. But he was a good signing, the fans took to him. It also helps if you go through star Rangers players at Pittodrie. It endears you to the fans. A header? He had that in his game. He was a bit of a Joey Barton type in that he didn't think twice about anyone who needed to be taught a lesson.'

Now, on hearing this appraisal, I wish I had interviewed Richardson after Shearer in order that I could have put to him that he was considered a doppelganger for Joey Barton. I ask him if he feels in any way diminished by Wikipedia's scant description of him. 'It depends on who you speak to. I think most people's recollections of me would be as a ball player who could dig a bit when he had to. I'd like to think I was an all-rounder who, when at my best, could score goals as well. I certainly had energy when I was at my fittest and youngest, but my energy dwindled when I got to 30. I suppose my generation was predisposed to that. It was the way things were back then.'

He is ready to touch on the eighties drinking culture – which he describes as the backend of the play hard, work hard mentality – at his first professional club, Halifax. 'The first thing we did was walk down the corridor to the bar and drink a couple of pints of lager. That was our recovery after a game. Nowadays, they have protein shakes, re-hydration, and all sorts of garments they wear to limit lactic uptake. Therefore a lot of lads are really fit into their mid 30s. Whereas, people of my generation... towards the end of my late twenties, my body was probably starting to creak.'

We have left the subjects of long hair and bone-shaking tackles far behind and have moved on to something that has never occurred to me before: the reason why a team's form can fluctuate dramatically from one game to another. Now, this is the psychologist in Richardson speaking, not the football representative. 'There's a reversal theory, which is the theory of meta-motivation. It's basically about how you're feeling at any one time and is linked to arousal. If you're seeing a player who is over-aroused, you know he's probably got no energy because he can't quite keep himself controlled enough to play the game the way he wants. The idea is our behaviour can change due to three factors: one is external events that can happen, two is frustration, and three is what they call satiation – basically, when you've had enough of something. This is the telic and auto-telic dichotomy. Telic is about focus, achieving targets, being serious. The auto-telic state is just about having fun, being in the moment. It was interesting watching the recent Wayne Rooney thing unfold: people were chastising the guy 'cos he was having a drink in the early hours of the morning. But there's a biological argument in that when you've been in a highly-aroused state for a long time, there's almost a biological mechanism that wants you to relax, chill out and kick back to regain some of that energy that's been expended.'

It's complex stuff and I'm glad I'm not on the end of it whilst lying on a psychologist's couch, but it's also fascinating. What Richards means, in layman's terms, is that a blow-out on the beer has been a useful strategy for many players over the years. It's only when this becomes habitual that it becomes problematic. Would he be able to identify, just by walking along a line of players, those who were mentally strong and those who were weak? I mean, if this were possible, a manager could dispense those without the requisite spirit for battle. Richardson feels that he could, but adds an immediate rider.

'You've got to be careful here with that idea of mental toughness. There's a few problems with it. One of them is there's an implication of a mental weakness on the opposite end. And those words have handicapped and thwarted potentially the benefits of proper psychological analysis and approach at football clubs. It has created a stigma and stigma gets in the way of all sorts of things, including help seeking for mental health issues. So it's a delicate area. Let's go back to arousal. Remember Joe Hart playing for England in the European Championships? Now, if you'd seen him before going out to play that day, you'd have thought this guy is tough; a patriot bursting to play. In actual fact, that was the worst possible state he could have been in for a goalkeeper, who needs to be calm, collected and in an almost observer-style mode.

'But there is a different mental approach and different ideals for different players. I think there's an intensity and an intent in a person's eyes when they are focused on a game. That's something you can see. It's more about their behaviour. Are they absolutely in a quiet place and are they zoned in? Personality does have a large part to play. Extroverts will show more external behaviour that will make you see they're in the right place. Introverts will be less so, appearing to be shut off in a world of their own. That's fine as long as it's right for that person. So, to answer your question, you could walk up a line and see who you think is in the right place, but you'd have to have a bit more of an idea of who they were as individuals to make that connection of where they needed to be. Because some players are good at looking as if they're in the right place when maybe they're not.'

The dressing room, I suggest, is a fascinating place – a place that insists on holding on to its secrets. Richardson agrees and emphasises that the term of co-regulation is familiar to all the best coaches and managers. This is where an individual is able to influence someone else's internal state. 'That's what the best managers have always done. Fergie, for example, will have been a master at creating an environment whereby he would influence his players if they weren't doing it themselves.'

We move to the influence of Willie Miller in the Aberdeen dressing room. Richardson insists that he liked him very much. 'I was one of his signings, so there was a good chance I was one of his favourites. But he could be very intense: that would be to his detriment in other people's eyes. If there was a criticism, he would sometimes overdo the aggressive, demanding, threatening behaviour with certain players. Maybe it didn't always help them at certain times, if I remember rightly.'

Was Richardson there when Miller allegedly pinned McLeish up against a wall? 'No, but if it happened, he may have done it with Alex's blessing. I know of managers who have done that. They do it to make others think, "Shit, if he's getting a bollocking, I'd better pull my finger out." I think it may have been something like that. It's a great tactic – as long as the captain doesn't stand up and chin you back.'

But Richardson's overriding opinion of Miller was very favourable. 'You know there are so many elements to being a manager and a coach and I think in the main he got most of them right. Even Fergie didn't get it all right. I also thought if Willie had ever come south, he could have had a good career, but it seemed he was rooted in Aberdeen. He was certainly someone who tried to influence the state of the players' minds at half-time. Even if we were winning, you couldn't expect a "well done, lads, we've just got to keep this going". He probably did it to keep us on our toes. And I'm pretty sure he picked that up from Fergie. Alex would have influenced Willie as a manager.'

He has pleasant memories of his two years at Pittodrie and that wonderful travelling support. And there's a controversial footnote to our conversation. 'One of the things that has always surprised me is that a consortium has not tried to buy the club, particularly when you think of Scottish football's access into the Champions League. If people can get over the shock of going to Aberdeen, they realise it's a beautiful place with its own airport. Potentially, if someone invested enough money to build a really strong squad, it could challenge the Old Firm and get access to those European funds.'

* *

THE DRAMATIC BACKDROP of the Ochil Hills ensures that Ochilview Park is one of the most scenic football grounds in the country. Nature's rich tapestry was of no concern to Duncan Shearer on 18 February, 1995, however: he was still attempting to adjust to the departure of Willie Miller, the manager who had brought him to the club for £500,000 three years earlier, and the appointment of Roy Aitken. The adjustment experienced a schizophrenic beginning. Goals by Shearer and Billy Dodds had vanquished Rangers in the Premier Division a week prior to this, and the hope was they would carry their form into the Scottish Cup-tie against Stenhousemuir. In the event, it absconded somewhere around Merkland Road: they were vanquished 2-0 by a side that, technically speaking, should not have been able to breathe the same air as them. Predictably, the away dressing room was less lively than your average chapel of rest. 'Then Roy pops his head in the door and says, "Congratulations for being part of the worst result in Aberdeen's history,"' Shearer recalls.

The sarcasm did not go down well with the powerful Highlander, who was already shooting his way into Pittodrie legend. He was disappointed that Aitken had not been in a more explanatory mood, and believed the new manager was thrusting all the blame on the players and not accepting his responsibility. He, after all, dictated how the team should play. 'Roy wanted us to keep playing football, keep passing it. I think it could have been noticed early on that we couldn't play football on a mud heap of a pitch and our style should have been changed. It's all right telling us in the last five minutes to get the ball in the box and create chance after chance, but by then the damage was done. We'd run out of time. I'm sure we got the Monday off. Roy wanted to think about what had happened. I came in on the Monday, anyway, and was doing a bit of stretching. I was having a bit of lunch when he came in and sat beside me. "That cannae happen, Duncan," he said. "Not at a club like this." I had a good heart to heart with him. Once the good pitches came back, we were okay. And, to be fair to him, he did fine. He helped us escape relegation that season. There were a lot of good things happened under Roy.'

Anyone disliking Shearer should take a good look at himself. Here is a man who gives his opinion, perhaps not even the one you wish to hear, but it is delivered straight from broad shoulders. He possesses the kind of social conscience that is to be found in our soup kitchens. You suspect that anyone attempting to cozen him would be put in his place immediately. He has a good sense of humour and modesty is also included in the package. You ask him, for instance, if he is aware of his playing record at Pittodrie and he responds with ironic laughter. 'I'll place my hand on my heart and tell you I haven't got a f***ing clue. Sometimes, I pick up an old programme and scan it, but it goes in one eye and out the other.'

That record, for the record, is impressive for someone who only arrived at Pittodrie when he was 29 years of age. From 1992-97, Shearer played 193 times for Aberdeen, scored 78 goals and profited from seven Scotland caps. He scored twice in his debut against Hibs and discovered that the fans would soon adopt him as one of their own. His social life further endeared him to them. 'Some of the players would go into fancy bars. Not me. I'd always go into bars frequented by Aberdeen fans. It was what I was brought up with. I was never interested in wine bars and suchlike. The thing was I never got dug up in any of these places. When I'd go in, they'd sing and I'd give them a wave. I could be with my mates and someone would buy me a pint. When it was my round, I'd make a point of buying the guy a pint back. And I'd know his name. I learned that from Big McLeish. I'd hear him ask the barmaid what the punter's name was; he'd wait for a few minutes, then shout the boy's name. The boy's chest puffed out. I learned to try and get to know people names, rather than call them Wee Man and Big Man.'

Shearer believed in sporting diversity. As a 17-year-old, he was a right wing back for Lochaber. Football, at that time, did not form part of his dream pattern. Shinty was all. He'd have given his soul for a Cammanach Cup medal in this game for real men. He admits that he dished out a bit of punishment, adding that if you didn't, you'd be trampled upon. 'Of course you took a few knocks – that's why I'm sitting here with false teeth.'

But a year is a lifetime for a young man and, 12 months later, he was playing Highland League football for Clachnacuddin. He went for a week's trial with Aberdeen and Alex Ferguson. He was scheduled to play in a friendly against Arbroath, but the game was called off. The Dons invited him back the next week. But, by then, 'something got lost in the translation. I never went back.'

What he did do was go on to great things in his newly-adopted game. He played for Chelsea, Huddersfield, Swindon and Blackburn, leaving the footprint of goals everywhere he went. Kenny Dalglish paid £750,000 to take him to Ewood Park, where he teamed up with his old Chelsea colleague, David Speedie. 'It was an experience. That was for sure. David was not the kind of boy you'd want to meet on a dark night. Eventually, I got on well with him, but he was an awfully fiery character. And did he not like Dalglish. I remember being pulled by Kenny: he told me he was dropping me and Speedie to the bench. I said there wasn't a problem, so not to worry about it. He said he did worry and mentioned something about that "little shit." He'd obviously told Speedie he was dropping him and got a mouthful from him. But the thing about Speedie was that you always got your 100 per cent with him.'

Blackburn, underwritten by the wealth of Jack Walker, won promotion to the Premier Division and now their spending was destined to burst banks. They bought Alan Shearer for £3.5million and the other Shearer knew that his time in England had come to an end. Aberdeen and Willie Miller were the initial benefactors of the goal machine from Fort William, and in the 92-93 season, they competed in two finals and trailed by nine points to Rangers in the league. Shearer had a variety of partners at Pittodrie and seemed to gel with them all: he began with Mixu Patalleinen, then it was Scott Booth, Eoin Jess, Billy Dodds and laterally Dean Windass. I ask him for his comments regarding the partnerships. He suggests that his favourite was the precocious Jess. And yet there was a special affection for Dodds.

'In our first game, he kept running the channels. He came over and asked me if I ever ran them. "Nope," was my answer. "F***, thanks for telling me," he said. I told him to put the ball in the box and I'd try to get on the end of it. He was soon blowin' out of his arse. Now, the McCoist-Hateley thing was supposed to be telepathic, but I was never a great believer in that. But Eoin was quite clued up to my runs. He had fantastic knowledge of the game and his close control was something else. He wasn't a greedy person and was always looking to thread someone in. I remember him doing the keepie ups in the League Cup semi-final against Rangers. That was 1995 – before we went on to beat Dundee in the final. He was so much on top of Paul Gascoigne in that game that it was scary. Rangers didn't like that. I remember thinking, "Oh, dear." But he was old enough, not a young boy being smart. It was like the Jim Baxter thing at Wembley.'

He is less enthusiastic regarding Scott Booth. 'He was fine. People would doubt Scotty's heart. He got into a situation with his injuries and became too interested in the physiotherapy side of it and how the muscles worked. Everything was a question with him. I always found it better to stay away from the treatment table, because it sucked you in and got a hold of you. Before you know it, you're in there every day, wondering about this and that. Playing with Mixu, though, was great. I loved it. He had a good left foot and could power the ball in the air. He won most balls there. I tended to think we changed our style with Mixu. Instead of getting the ball down and playing it wide to Paul Mason, we started hitting diagonals. If we were struggling, it was always the out ball. They bypassed Jim Bett from the back.'

If Aberdeen were slightly short of success by their own towering standards in the early nineties, they were soon to be accused of excess. In September of 1995, Roy Aitken was allowed to bring Edinburgh-born Paul Bernard in from Oldham. One million pounds exchanged hands. It was and still is the most expensive import by a Scottish club outside the Old Firm. Bernard's record, over six years, was not the kind that anyone would wish to frame on their study wall. He made 122 appearances, including nine as substitute, and scored eight goals. My calculations say that he cost Aberdeen £8,196 per game. That's before his wages were paid. So, what did Aberdeen acquire for this princely sum of money? You may remember the Dick Donald technique as described by Jocky Scott: the chairman inevitably probed his manager, demanding that he justify expenditure on a certain player. I wonder who probed the mind of Roy Aitken.

I ask Lee Richardson for a forthright opinion. He delivers one. 'Paul was a real athlete. A tremendous athlete and I played briefly with him at Oldham.

But, football-wise, I don't think he was blessed with great ability. I think he would have been first to admit that. But he was one of those lads who earned well and finished up being injury-prone, a la Scott Booth. Roy Aitken rang me about him. I couldn't say much more about him other than that he was an athlete. Sometimes people don't get the hint. Paul may have believed his own hype, I don't know. Certainly, he was okay as a footballer, but, no, he wasn't outstanding.'

We go from one strong opinion to another, although, in strict fairness, Duncan Shearer once saw something in the player during a Scotland get-together at Largs. 'He was playing for Scotland Under 21s against our national team. And the boy dominated the game. He was powerful and making passes. I know he had a horrific time with the hamstrings and they couldn't find what the problem was when he came to Pittodrie. He didn't seem to be the player I had seen at Largs.'

Bernard's mammoth fee, allegedly authorised by Ian Donald, probably was one of the integral reasons for the financial landslip that was to blight Pittodrie for years. Bernard, judging by that fee, should have been a hero and taken on the responsibilities of a hero. But, according to Shearer, he even failed in this department.

'I remember one time when things were going badly for us. I was going into training and I remember looking at the crowd which were lined up right down the stand side. They were queuing for tickets. I'm thinking to myself, "Jesus, these people must have taken a couple of hours off their work for this – and we're doing badly." So I park up and walk down, talking to the fans about the game ahead. Then I hears this vroom, vroom noise coming from the Beach End. The noise is going into the car park. It's Paul Bernard and his Ferrari. I'm looking at him and thinking, "We've just paid a million pounds for you and you've hardly kicked a f***ing ball for us. How f***ing insensitive can someone be?"

'Anyway, we get into the changing room. I says, "You know what's happening here, Paul? The team's playing crap and, for f***'s sake, you drive a f***ing Ferrari past all these people who are spending their hard-earned money. Have a f***ing think about it." He says, "I've always wanted to buy that car – I'm entitled to do what I want with my money." I says, "Aye, I suppose you are." And I just walked away. He should have taken responsibility that day. Have a wee think about what things mean. Take your wife's car, but don't be driving past in an expensive sports car. If the guy had been man of the match every week and scoring hat-tricks, it might have been different. But he wasn't.'

Bernard could not provide a panacea for the ills of the Dons, but Aitken had to accept responsibility, too. His reign had begun moderately well with Scottish League Cup success but had deteriorated badly. In November of 1997, it was his turn to take to the highway. The manager's office at Pittodrie, once a seat of comparative safety, turned into a casualty centre. Keith Burkinshaw came in as caretaker, Alex Miller visited for 20 days short of a year, and Paul Hegarty, the former Dundee United stalwart, was there for just under five months. Was this chaos, or what? By this time Stewart Milne had taken over from Donald, Denmark's Ebbe Skovdahl was ready to cross the North Sea and steady the ship. Or that was the plan.

I'm witnessing this carnage from far-off London, but it's not fully registering, for I have my own carnage to address... In that year of 1997, I have been transferred from Glasgow to London to take up the hottest ticket in sports editing – at the Daily Mail. *Staff-wise, it would be nice to retain the status quo and, in my dealings with them, adopt the docility of a spring lamb. But this is simply impossible. During my two years in Scotland, I have seen the way things are run in the South and it's unimpressive, to say the least. Jesus, they didn't seem to be aware that football contracts could change forever with the Bosman ruling. Luckily, I have a freelance in Glasgow who knows chapter and verse of this complicated subject. His name is Graham Hunter and he appears, literally, off the street. His exploits quickly lead to a staff contract. I send him out to Brussels and he blags his way into Jean-Marc's mother's apartment. We have a world exclusive on our hands a few hours later.*

But London is a different animal to Glasgow. The reporters seem more interested in where they will break bread than what will appear in tomorrow's edition. Some wouldn't be able to detect goodwill in a phone call from the Samaritans. Bodies begin to disappear from the Derry Street office and young blood is transfused. It doesn't make me popular, but it makes the paper more energised, efficient and authoritative. And, therefore, makes the Editor, the legendary Paul Dacre, happy. I cannot fail and will not fail. I have experienced the hell and the humiliation of unemployment and alcoholism, so if there has to be sacrifices, then so be it. I just don't want my name embossed on failure.

CHAPTER 12

Close up with Smokin' Ebbe

They say life is short, but my term at the Daily Mail *is even shorter. Three and a half years of frenetic but productive activity and I'm hoisting the white flag of surrender. Only a few months ago, a prior deterioration in my heart muscle necessitated a stay in the London Clinic and a completely new regime of tablets. But more problems seem to have returned. There are pains in my chest, a repeated loss of balance and I feel nauseous much of the time. I'm convinced that my heart is wearing out, just like my brother Michael's.*

Trying to keep the black dog of depression in its kennel is proving difficult. So, why not go and see the doctor? Simple: I'm f***ing terrified of what he might tell me. One day, I take a unilateral decision and tell Paul Dacre that I'm retiring. I note that he makes no attempt to change my mind. Is it my imagination, or have things never been the same between us since I refused to sack a member of staff for writing a story that turned out to be a hoax?

Have I committed a blunder in presenting my resignation? My dear wife certainly says so. I'm in line from a rant from life's distaff side. 'How could you have been so stupid? Why didn't you consult me first? Why didn't you take time off?' I have no logical answer. It just seemed right at the time. But, hey, I'd enjoyed nearly six years in London and Glasgow. We'd rattled more cages than the lion tamers at Bertram Mills' circus: printed controversial stories about the rich and famous football managers and their football clubs. Men like Alex Ferguson, Gerard Houllier and Harry Redknapp have not appreciated our stances. Fergie, in fact, insisted that we were 'slaughtering his team' unfairly. Like many of his obsessive contemporaries, he forgot all the praise and concentrated on any negatives. Houllier, meanwhile, apprehended me at a dinner and suggested that the Mail *didn't like football. 'No, M. Houllier, it's some of the people in it we don't like.'*

I think I've done my bit. The back end of the Daily Mail *is an area of enterprise: it's bold and highly competitive and, more often than not, leads the agenda on pertinent issues. We have a raft of young and exciting reporters. The Observer bitchily refers to them as 'Cooney's Loonies' Some loonies: Graham Hunter, who ultimately became my deputy, has blossomed as a brilliant author, interviewer and authority on Spanish football; Martin Lipton is Deputy Head of Sport at* The Sun; *Ian Ladyman the* Mail's *Football Editor; and John Greechan the Chief Sports Writer at the* Scottish Daily Mail.

Anyway, I bid goodbye to Kensington and retire to my home in Hertfordshire. With my health deteriorating visibly – my face is so pale I could be cast as an extra in a zombie film – I at last discover the courage to see a doctor. When I explain the symptoms, he gazes into his computer and produces an instant diagnosis. He tells me I'm overdosing on a potassium tablet and, at this moment, I'm about three days away from death. He sounds like a hanging judge. In fact, I'm waiting for him to reach out and put a black cloth on his head. But, no, there's a reprieve: stop taking the tablets! Recovery will be slow and perhaps painful, he insists, but recovery is fully expected.

I walk home across Chorleywood Common that day, thoroughly elated on one hand and endlessly depressed on the other. I have given up the most sought-after and best-paid sports editor's job in Fleet Street. And all for nothing. But, hey, I'm going to live and that is surely the most handsome bonus of all. Once I rid myself of the scourge of potassium, no doubt there will be new and exciting avenues to explore. I know Margaret would like to go back to Scotland and this may be the accommodation that restores me to her good books. And there is the additional plus that, in returning to Scotland, I can concentrate once again on my first sporting love: the Dandy Dons. I have neglected them sorely these past few years as I have scampered up the ladder of ambition. Mind you, looking at the disarray they find themselves in, the neglect is almost justified. No matter, this state of affairs is about to be remedied...

BACK IN THE HOME COUNTRY, we found a beautiful home in the delightful seaside town of Crail, in Fife's East Neuk. My health had improved and there was no requirement for the traditional accessories of old age. Who needs a pipe and carpet slippers at the age of 55? No, I wanted to put my boots on and work, even if it was for sweetie money. I applied to BBC Scotland for a job as Sports Editor for their radio programmes. My application arrived too late, or so they claimed. Nevertheless, they said we should talk. We never did. I then wrote to Andrew Jaspan at the *Sunday Herald* and presented my ability for interviewing sports stars. He was far more accommodating, and soon I was occupying centre stage in their innovative sports pages. The Sports Editor, David Dick, and I were in blissful accord. Maybe it was because he hailed from Aberdeen, too. My first interview was Gary Lineker, whom I met one dismal day at Kingsbarns golf course. The interview was a vast improvement on dismal, but it didn't exactly disturb any forests. Former Dunfermline manager Jim Leishman was more my style by taking me 'deep' into the territory of his earlier family life; this was pursued by an educational visit to Hampden and Scotland manager Craig Brown; and finally a controversial one to the notorious ex-boss of Dundee United, Jim McLean. I submitted those three pieces for the 2002 *Sports Journalist of the Year* awards and, f*** my old boots, picked up first prize. There was a rumble of discontent from one particular reporter, pointing out I had only had four interviews from which to pick. Some people will discover fault in anything.

It was time for a trip to my home town and a meeting with the grizzled Dane, Ebbe Skovdahl. The latter was well connected, being the uncle of brothers Brian and Michael Laudrup, and possessed an intriguing CV. He had picked up considerable European experience with Brondby – he was with the Danes on four separate occasions – and a few months with Benfica. The Portugese club was allegedly a political pothole: Skovdahl was considered to be out of his depth, with no rescue team available, in spite of being second in the league and still engaged in national cup and European Cup competitions. Political challenges would lie ahead at Aberdeen. Particularly, you imagine, when Keith Wyness came galloping over the skyline to take up the position of CEO (more of him in the next chapter). But the situation in 1999-2000 season had few affiliations with politics. It was all about a club with perfunctory players, a ballooning overdraft, and a pathetic mentality in the League.

Skovdahl was just positioning his feet under the table when he was presented with the portents of a long, hard season: they went nine games without one victory. Celtic arrived at Pittodrie and pummelled the home side into a 5-0 submission. There were five more consecutive defeats, with the Dons failing to hit the goal register on all five occasions. The humiliation against Celtic was only the beginning. The Dons travelled to Celtic Park and received another battering: 7-0. You suspected even fumigation would not have removed the stench of dressing-room decay: two more games against the Hoops ended in 6-0 and 5-1 defeats. Rangers, meantime, were only too eager to bully the weak and under-nourished: they beat the Dons three times in the League, scoring 13 goals in the process.

Embarrassingly, Aberdeen, in that first season, only avoided having to take part in a Premier play-off because Falkirk's Brockville stadium was not up to SPL requirements. The League and Scottish Cups, for some strange reason, provided succour for the optimists, and two finals were reached. Celtic and Rangers, however, again proved in these matches that the hex Aberdeen once had held over them had been exorcised. The Dons slunk back to base with respective 2-0 and 4-0 defeats. The manager tells me he had warned his players that the ice on which they were skating was of a thin variety. 'It is my duty to tell you that you all have three months to show me if you're in my plans and have a future.'

In the event, most of them had about as much future as fruit flies. Pittodrie duly became a clearing house, with 21 players chased out the door. Skovdahl, having imported quality in Arild Stavrum, Hicham Zerouali and Roberto Bisconti, also favoured encouraging youth. He was quite happy to play young players because they were apt to listen more attentively. 'Once they're beyond puberty, you can't teach them anymore,' he once commented.

Ironically, while results were poor and expectation pinned to the floor, the fans showed a remarkable tolerance towards Skovdahl. Maybe it was because he was a foreigner in a strange land; maybe it was because he was a man of courtesy and dignity. But, as far as I was aware, there had been no suggestions of chasing him out of town, or indeed, hanging him from the nearest available gibbet. Whatever, by the time of my visit, there is the suggestion of a modest light at the end of the tunnel. It might only have had the power of 40 watts and a tendency to flicker as if a power cut could happen any time, but at least there's a light. Now, we address ourselves to the more serious issues. Skovdahl asks me whether I mind him smoking. Of course I don't mind. I begin to hear a philosophy that is in direct contrast to the philosophies I have heard propounded by many managers in football. I wonder whether I have just wandered into a peace rally.

'I'm 56 and I know one thing: if you want a young man's attention, then you don't start giving him a row. If he don't have a Walkman in his ear, then he'll just close his ear. No, if you start a conversation with a youngster, try to tell him some positive things. Remember, it's always possible to find positive things to say about anyone. Then he will open his ears and, later on, you can put your criticism forward in a constructive way and he will listen to that as well. But not if you start by getting right on his back. Of course, I do that sometimes if they don't behave or are out of order. But I prefer to understand why they have to behave that way. I don't often lose my temper. It happens mostly during training. Then, I became – how do you say? – unsympathetic. Yes, when I'm very angry. I am very unsympathetic. And the anger stays longer with me than I would like. I'm a very calm person normally, but everyone has a limit to their patience and I'm not very nice when I'm angry. I swear, not in Danish but in English.'

You imagine a few epithets were emanating from Ebbe when Eoin Jess gave a highly-critical appraisal of the club on Sky television. Skovdahl agrees that he watched the programme but thought, if that was the way the player felt, he should have taken his criticism to either him or the chairman. Jess, in fact, was about to sample justice, Skovdahl-style.

'I was surprised that Eoin should do such a thing. I've always admired his skills and still do. He's very gifted. We were in Glasgow for the Rangers match at the time. I didn't send him home, but took another player to give me a little time to think and do the right thing. In the end, I fielded the other player. Yeah, I acted quickly and ruthlessly. He was only here for a couple of weeks, or a month afterwards (before he left for Bradford City). But I didn't alienate him before he left. First of all, he had been with the club for some time and had played some very good games. He was definitely not an evil or bad person in any way. I think, therefore, it would have been wrong to separate him from his team mates. I was also sure he would not try to do any harm. I thought it important that he tried to stay fit, so he could get another club. But there was no way back. You make a decision and you stick to it.'

I'm beginning to lose the notion about the peace rally. I remember being on holiday in France and meeting a Danish schoolteacher, who walked around all day clutching a giant bottle of Coca Cola which, I swear, was infiltrated by vodka. One day, we were discussing the problems with modern-day youth. He told me he did not believe in corporal punishment. I asked him how he kept order. He took my hand and squeezed it until I yelped with pain. 'That is how you make them be serious,' he smiled through eyes that were bluer and colder than any sea. I'm looking through the cigarette smoke and into the eyes of Ebbe and wondering whether there is a similar potential in him for such covert violence.

Maybe, then, this is not the time to pose an awkward question – one that might see me dispatched from the building in very short order. But, as John McEnroe was fond of saying, if you don't ask, you don't get. I ask him about his drinking habits. I now witness the more steely side of the manager. But there are no histrionics: the measured protest comes from a man who feels he has been sorely wronged. 'Oh, I've heard the rumours; somebody started rumours that I was a big drinker. It is complete rubbish. I don't know why someone should do this. I have a completely normal relationship with things like that. I almost never touch pure alcohol. If I drink, it's a beer or a glass of wine. A vodka drinker? If I have had five glasses of vodka in my lifetime, that's the top of it. And, even then, there's definitely been some orange in them.'

I ask him how he became aware of the rumours. He doesn't flinch. 'The chairman told me. I was surprised, very surprised, because that is definitely a lie. A pure, pure lie. And that hurts me a lot. But I know it's not a good idea to go out and yell about things like that, because you don't know if it will be put forward the right way. What is important to me is that I have a family that knows the truth. I've always looked after my job. I'm driving my car every day which I couldn't do if I had a problem with alcohol. If me and my wife go to a function, of course we take a taxi and have a glass of wine. We leave in a taxi. Quite normal. I have never had problems with alcohol or any other thing, for that matter. The only problem I have is cigarettes. I smoke 20 a day and have done so for many years. I would like to stop it, but I'm definitely not ashamed of it. My parents were smokers and lived to be 80 and 81. You never know, but there seems to be longevity in the family. I don't smoke when the players are present and I would never do so in the coach, or in the dining room. I respect that they're athletes. So, what do I do in the coach? I take a couple of wine gums. Otherwise, nothing.'

Aberdeen have invariably paid their managers handsome salaries. Skovdahl, if my information stands up, was initially paid £300,000 per annum. This was reduced by £100,000 a year. He accepted the cut, partially because of the attrition of the League in that first year. 'It was very tough for me and the chairman as well. What encouraged me was that I never had any of the supporters against me. I do think if that had been the case, I could have gone. I didn't know if they would have the patience. Without any doubt, I could have changed things quicker only if we had a lot of money. I was surprised that they stuck by me, but also delighted. I spent a lot time at the beginning going to the (supporters) clubs and trying to explain how I saw things and what I would try to do. It is gratifying that they seem to like me so much. You can't go on in a job like this if you have everyone against you.'

But there was another factor in his accepting that he was worth £100,000 less. 'Money is not a god in our family, that's for sure. But it gives you some kind of security to make your own decisions. I could have said "no", but for me we were well into the process of changing things and forming a young side. I wouldn't have had a good time with myself if I didn't see how it progressed. I would really like to see what I've started. Of course, I didn't like it, but the fact that they need to cut their expenses was acceptable and you felt you were more or less getting to be part of something. I discussed it with my wife and she said at the end of the day, it was entirely up to me. I like the place. I've had spells where I was quite tired of the whole thing, especially in the first year when every reporter was on our back. But I never even said to my wife that I was going to quit. I do know that I'm a fighter. I've never been a place where I've quit.'

Ebbe Skovdahl was far from being your archetypal football manager. He was open and swore that he never told lies. I believed him. He was human and very likeable. Football was not everything in his existence. Every chance he had in his time at Aberdeen, he and his wife would travel around Scotland, looking at castles and admiring landscapes. In December of 2002, when the club was not making the improvement that was required, he was looking intently at his P45. He'd said he would never quit. They say he resigned. It mattered not. Aberdeen FC were just about to take a quantum leap into the unknown.

CHAPTER 13

David Ginola: Sacre Bleu!

KEITH WYNESS BELONGED TO the new breed of football chief executive in that, unlike his predecessors, he was media-friendly and freely available for comment. Thinking out of the box became his speciality. It allowed him a certain irreverence and an ability to chastise the Old Firm for their desperation to ply their trade in England. Remember this? 'They are like the two old ladies on Sauchiehall Street, lifting their skirts for every league that walks by.'

Thinking out of the box also encouraged this ambitious man to be innovative, daring and enter situations where no other Dons CEO had gone before. Thus, in and around 2002-2003 (my apologies for not being more specific, but the Wyness memory is somewhat blurred on this occasion), he claims he opened signing talks with the agent of French superstar David Ginola. The latter, admittedly, was beginning to creak around the edges of his handsome frame. He was in his mid-30s and had served a myriad of clubs: Toulon, RC Paris, Brest, Paris SG, Newcastle United, Tottenham Hotspur, Aston Villa and Everton. He was nearing the end of his sporting journey, therefore, but Wyness believed there was important business to be completed just before he took the chequered flag: he would attract the crowds, swell impoverished Pittodrie coffers and, just as importantly, lift the spirits of a team that was going nowhere.

Ginola's weekly stipend, according to his agent, would be between £25,000 and £30,000. How would Aberdeen – they were in the process of making swingeing pay cuts and some of whose players were on £900-£1500 a week – be able to afford this? They wouldn't, of course. But Wyness had an alternative plan. It's understood that an approach was made to Total SA, the French multi-national oil and gas giants, and one of the world's top seven oil conglomerates. The North Sea industry was booming at the time and Wyness reckoned that he could tempt the French to underwrite most, if not all, of Ginola's payload. He claims to have met the company's chief executive in an effort to sweet talk him. Perhaps the Gallic CEO had an aversion to saccharine. In the end, any prospective deal fell through the floor. It is unclear as to who was responsible – the oil company, Ginola himself, his agent, or whether Aberdeen directors were afflicted by a case of cold feet. And I apologise for any inability to make things more clear-cut. But, even today, Wyness swears it was a fundamentally viable project. So, let's give him some credit for attempting to pull off such a major coup.

Paradoxically, thinking out of the box sometimes can have horrendous consequences. Here, we return to a rather more painful segment in history for the club and someone's insistence that Steve Paterson should be allowed to rejuvenate the ailing Dons. We must go to the winter break of 2002-2003 and take a snapshot of the team's visit to Portugal play in the Algarve Cup. Paterson had only been in the job for a handful of days.

**

THE SUN WAS SLOWLY, ALMOST reluctantly, asserting itself. The Aberdeen FC coach was positioned outside the hotel, ready to take the players back to the airport for their flight back to Scotland. It had been an exhilarating weekend for them. They had encountered first Wolfsburg and then Ajax in an invitational tournament, and had mixed with men who caressed, rather than kicked, footballs: Stefan Effenburg, Zlatan Ibrahimovic, Wesley Sneijder and Rafael van der Vart. Ronald Koeman was manager of the Dutch giants.

Steve Tosh, the Dons new signing from Falkirk, was enjoying a personal elevation in the football world. He had played in a variety of modest places, but now he was breathing in the oxygen of life at altitude. He took his place on that coach while attempting to convince himself that this was not all part of a fantastic dream. Everyone in the party had been instructed to be ready by 9.15 and everyone, bar one, had complied with the request. There was no sign of the manager. Tosh remembered the Dons party had been drinking in a small and quiet bar in Monte Gordo till about three o'clock earlier that morning. He and his colleague Paul Sheerin had called time on themselves and prepared to return to the hotel. Steve Paterson was standing in what was considered to be his favourite spot in any bar: the corner. His mood was benign if, at the same time, emphatic.

The players asked him if he would care to accompany them back to the hotel. 'No, this place is open for a few hours yet,' he told them. 'His problem was that he couldnae drag himself away,' Tosh recalls. 'He couldnae see the bigger picture. Needless to say, we went back to our rooms. Needless to say again, quarter past nine, we were on the bus. So, too, was Keith Wyness. So everyone was present bar Pele. Dunc (Shearer) had to go back and get him. He dragged him out of his bed and accompanied him down the stairs. He was still steamboats. He got on the bus. It was a giggle because it was the first time the players had seen that. I'd heard about this before, but I thought, "Hey, it happens. We've all done it." But the thing was Steve had made a fool of himself, even more so in front of the Chief Executive.'

The admirable *afcheritage.org* website details the exploits of just about every Aberdeen FC manager over the past 114 years. Alex Miller, in the job for just under a year in the nineties, merits 60-odd lines of copy. Neil Cooper, in joint charge of the team for one match, warrants nine lines. Steve Paterson, by contrast, was in Pittodrie employment for almost 18 months and supervised 82 matches, apart from one crucial one. But there are no words for him, just cold, unimpressive statistics; certainly, no explanation of the fiasco that ensued. Mind you, why would the club wish to compound one of the most excruciating blunders in the history of Scottish football? They took on a man whose louche lifestyle meant that while his team were involved in a Saturday league match, he was in bed trying to neutralise a hang-over; a man who, after he'd been sacked, refused to face the media and left in the boot of a car driven by the security officer, John Morgan.

I still find it difficult to believe, all these years later, that my favourite football team backed themselves into such an indefensible corner. After all, there was abundant evidence of Paterson's somewhat aberrant lifestyle while managing Inverness Caledonian Thistle. No Sherlock Holmes-style magnifying glass would have been required to identify that evidence or indeed spot the seismic flaw in the man's make-up. Nevertheless, in the December of 2002, Steve Paterson was announced as successor to Ebbe Skovdahl.

The deal obviously had to be agreed by the board, but in essence it carried the fingerprints of the Chief Executive. Why was Wyness so keen to sign him? I mean, they must have known it was what insurance companies term 'high risk'. I'd like to speak to him in order that he can deliver his version of events; he's been far from idle since leaving Pittodrie; he's worked for Everton and now is enjoying an executive appointment at Aston Villa. I send him an email asking him to call me. I'm not optimistic of a response. I interviewed him for the *Sunday Herald* away back in the Millennium and I cannot imagine he enjoyed my description of him. I wrote that I had seen men like him before – big, bulky and clad in leotards – leaning over the ropes in wrestling rings, arguing the toss with feverish crowds. He confounds such pessimism, however. The phone rings one Friday evening and my wife informs me that there is a Mr Wyness at the other end. We have an 11-minute conversation, during which he reminds me that 'thinking out of the box' was always one of his specialities. Well, the hiring of Paterson could certainly be applicable to that description. But surely this was against all the diktats of common sense? What kind of due diligence was conducted?

You sense Wyness is not prepared for lengthy orations. 'I suppose it was the regular football diligence of speaking to as many people as we could within the game who knew him or had worked with him.'

But didn't he get any sense that the man had a drink-related history? 'Yes. I think there were stories that came out. But, when I interviewed him, he assured me it was all in the past, that a lot of the stories had been overblown and that he had it under control.'

And I suppose he believed him? 'Yes.'

Who was keener on Paterson, Stewart Milne or himself? 'Probably myself. Stewart obviously had appointed some managers before Steve. Ultimately, the chairman has the final decision, but I felt it was needed to get a young Scottish manager, particularly from the North East of Scotland. Certainly, at that time, we were trying to be a very Scottish-oriented club (David Ginola excepted, of course). A lot of the Tartan Army comes from the North East. Steve, hopefully, was going to fit that role of North East boy made good.'

There wasn't an abundance of finance back then? 'No, we had interviewed more expensive options, but we still felt that Steve was an up and comer.'

When it blew up in his face, how did he feel then? 'It was something I'd never experienced before, or have never experienced since. You still wonder how it all happened. I personally felt let down.'

He was angry, then? 'I think the anger goes quickly. Then it became a case of, "What do we do now?" We had the whole responsibility of the club to look after. Also we had to consider Steve's own position in terms of his health – he had serious issues.'

Was there any temptation to sack him immediately? 'Yes, there was, given that he was a football manager who was unable to manage the team due to drink. We probably could have gone that way if we'd wanted to, but I felt the more human and decent approach was to try and see him through this, see if we could use it as a positive and hopefully guide him onto success. In some ways, you're hoping that he'd repay you for making a big mistake.'

But there was no repayment plan? 'I think it just become too much of an embarrassment for him and he just retreated into his shell. And there was always the problem with Steve that he would never get out of the dug-out; he was never really there motivating people, never seen putting in the energy. He would claim that it just wasn't his style. It soon became apparent that he wasn't motivating the squad in any way.'

I tell Wyness that I've talked to Steve Tosh, who described Paterson's behaviour on the morning of departure from Portugal. Somewhat extraordinarily, he claims. 'That story came back to me, although I could never confirm it. There were photographs from fans of Steve under a table in Edinburgh. Obviously, there was a serious pattern forming. While we offered him help, it appeared he wasn't actually following through on it.'

But Wyness has gone off on another inexplicable tangent. I'm not referring to pictures from Edinburgh, but to an incident that he must have witnessed himself. Surely he can remember that day on the bus? 'I can't. No.'

It is an interview that is not delivering him any pleasure, nor me any great satisfaction. You can draw your own conclusions, but I've certainly drawn mine. For someone occupying the role of Chief Executive to say that he knew nothing of an incident that occurred right in front of him at 9.15am is, well, wholly unsatisfactory. The more likely theory is that Wyness chose to ignore the matter because he began to realise what he'd engineered. There again, if the club had acted there and then, they might not have paved the way for the ultimate fiasco. There is no evidence of any disciplinary action. And Shearer, the assistant manager who had so much with which to contend, doesn't remember the incident with any clarity. But he is quick to acknowledge that if Tosh says it occurred, then it must have occurred.

I'm sticking with this intriguing guy in this chapter. I sense it'll be worth my while. He is an impressive character. Born in Kirkcaldy, he is candid enough to admit that his football loyalties are shared. He is essentially a Raith Rovers fan, but formed an appreciation society in his youth with the Dons because his uncle hailed from the Granite City. Then there is the Rangers affiliation. This was down to Graeme Souness: 'He was my hero. He was charismatic. Those flashing eyes; the way he controlled a game.'

Tosh remembers playing for Arbroath against Rangers and having his picture taken in a light blue jersey. He cringes when he thinks of it, for this association has landed him in confrontation. He takes you back to his early days playing for the Dons; even then, he had shown that he was prepared to give everything and more for the red jersey. So, he is in the toilet of a city-centre pub and someone comes in and asks if he can take a picture. Another man enters the toilet and insists, 'You're no wanting a picture of him – he's a f***ing Hun!'

Tosh is told he doesn't deserve to wear the red jersey. He asks the man how he arrives at this conclusion. 'Oh, we all know you've got a Rangers tattoo.'

Hereabouts, there is an attempt at a conciliatory response. 'Listen, I havenae got any tattoos and I'll strip down till I'm naked just to show you.'

The man is not for turning. 'Do whatever you want. I know you've got a tattoo and that's enough!'

This story is retold in the breakfast room of the Dutch Mill on a Saturday morning. Tosh has stopped off here on his way to Dundee to watch his son play football. 'The man's words will stay with me forever,' he says.

You suspect that he will never forget his short career with Aberdeen, either. He recalls his excitement at having signed for Scotland's third team and that he was the easiest guy in the world to deal with. But soon the edge was being filed away from the excitement. He discovered a weird situation. Where was the sense of camaraderie that he had left at Falkirk? 'Some of the players were very arrogant for a team that had achieved nothing. They were very young, new to the game and were part of a club that was struggling. But they played as if they weren't part of the struggle. Some of the better ones – your Russell Andersons and Kevin McNaughtons – went on and succeeded. Some of the poorer ones didn't. But you see how certain people fall out of the game and there's a reason. At certain clubs, they are protected. But as soon as they step away from that protection, they get found out.'

Aberdeen had an established way of doing things. There was a layer cake and those sitting on top of that cake were smothered in the cream of privilege. 'The first-team boys would get showered, changed, and then go into the canteen. You walked straight to the front of the queue, past the youth team guys, past staff from others departments, and you got served. You then went and sat at the table. I didn't buy into that. You're not telling me that the finance manager should stand aside as I walk to the front of the queue? So I created a situation by taking my turn and by going and sitting beside two girls from the ticket office. I wanted to create a situation where, ultimately, we'd want to win on a Saturday, but win as a team. And the team isnae just the 11 boys on the park.'

But there were other problems, one that were not so easily corrected. Most of them revolved around the new manager. 'Stevie wasn't protected to a certain degree. He was made to buy a house which he never ever stayed in. I know for a fact that if I had been in their position, as managing director or sporting director, I would have told him he had two choices. He either stayed in that house and focused on Aberdeen, or he resigned. That would have saved the hassle of the drink. Steve wasn't a recluse, but he liked to be away from the limelight and didn't want everybody intruding on his day to day life. So, we'd be at the training park even before he'd got into the club. You're talking about 10 o'clock. That didnae look good. We were like Raggedly Arsed Rovers. We'd be doing our warm-up, and then Stevie would come out, discuss things with Duncan Shearer and Osher Williams. We'd be doing needless drills just to fill in time before they could get things set up. I didn't find it professional. Look, I enjoyed playing for Stevie and I'm certainly not bad-mouthing him, or Dunc, or Osher. But it didn't surprise me, down the line, after working for certain other managers, that we weren't successful at that particular time. I felt sorry for Stevie. But, at the same time, I've said it to his face; he should have done things different. He should have been more in control. Me? Listen, I'd kick my ain granny if I thought I was getting a bonus at 4.45 on a Saturday. Aberdeen didn't have enough players like that at that time. A lot was down to the fact that we weren't a professional outfit.'

> *22 February 2003: I have re-invented myself as a travelling fan and find Dundee is a favourite destination, what with its two teams. Of course, the short journey from Crail is another bonus. But, today, there is no windfall. The Dons are dislocated. This is nothing like the team that commanded centre stage in my dreams all those years ago. Dundee, on the other hand, attack with pace and intent and our hopes of developing a Centenary season Scottish Cup run are flattened by Steve Lovell and Nacho Novo. I like the look of Lovell, who is rangy and pacey, and Novo has the capabilities of a buzz-bomb. But there are others in dark blue like Nemsadze, Caballero and Khizanishvili who are gliding through this game as if they were on roller skates. We had better get our roller skates on.*

> *21 January 2004 – I am joined by a friend of well over 50 years on the Scottish Cup journey to the City of Discovery. Shirras Cantlay is a solicitor in St Andrews and we meet up occasionally to share our love of the Dons. We used to travel to the games together and now there is additional poignancy because he has his son Greig with him. The baton belonging to a true fanatic has been handled effortlessly down. We stand in the packed visitors' end and hope for the best, while preparing for the worst. Steve Paterson has already disgraced himself against this same team – by not even turning up. He needs to atone in this replay. He does. We win 3-2 and the old times are back: we're hugging each other and daring our lungs to explode. We're old men now, but old men find it's easy to rejuvenate in this game of passion.*

Back in the Dutch Mill, we have arrived at the moment when Steve Paterson's passion for football seemed to disappear, if not actually dissolve completely. On 15 March, 2003, Aberdeen had a home game against Dundee. Paterson had been attending a function in the Beach Ballroom the previous evening, but it had only been a rehearsal for an extra-time drinking binge. He had also been out on the Thursday and the warm-up signs were present and correct. They visited a wine bar after the function but quickly transferred to O'Donohue's to have a Guinness nightcap. After one drink, Shearer walked away and left Paterson to his own devices. 'I believe he finished up in a house about two in the morning, where I believe he drank another bottle of wine…' The rest belongs to history.

Now, I want to know how the players felt when they were presented with a managerial no-show. Tosh provides the answer. 'Rumours were rife that he'd been up the town on the Friday night. So, when he hadn't been seen and they were trying to fob it off as a dodgy stomach, the bright lads in the group weren't believing it. I remember asking Dunc and was probably told to mind my own f***ing business. But I didnae like it. I thought it was so unprofessional. I thought: "Wait a minute – I'm here – he should be here, I don't give a f*** if he comes in here, half gone. Give a speech, then I don't give a f*** if he wants to go and sit in a box. That's okay. Just be here. He's our figurehead."'

Tosh spoke to Shearer during the warm-up and this time there was transparency. That didn't make it good news. Paterson was back in his flat and that's where he would stay. Tosh remembers, 'Me being me, I started to rally the troops. I told them to forget about this – we've got a f***ing game to play here, it's no' going to be cancelled because Steve Paterson isnae here. So let's get this over and done with and try to get a positive result. Let's dae it for him, even though he's made a fool of himself, not to mention a fool of us. I didn't let it affect my game – I was probably as poor as ever. We drew 3-3 that day. The aftermath was always going to be horrific.'

The players were instructed not to talk about it and, if anyone asked, play the dummy card by saying that Paterson had been suffering from a bug. 'I hated that, 'cos it was not ma fault that he wisnae here. It's hard because you have family and friends and I wisnae keeping it from them. But this city's a village – everybody knew. I hope Stevie appreciates this opinion. He let doon everyone who worked for him that day – I'm not trying to build it into a Hollywood thing. But he should have gone home at two in the morning, slept till midday, got up, had a cold shower and turned up for his work. Like we did. But a bit of credit from me. He didnae deny what had happened. I think at the start he was annoyed that he never got the support he deserved, but it wisnae the first time: he'd done it in Inverness; he'd done it in Portugal. Mind you, fitba players keep thing to themselves: you dinnae go to all and sundry. I'm doing this because Stevie's out of the big-time game and we're telling truth in your book. Like, he wisnae coming to every game like that; he wisnae coming into training like that. He messed a good thing up. But, hey, we've all messed up. I'm divorced now because I messed up. It's something I'm no' proud of and I guarantee Stevie's no' proud of it, either. There are consequences for your actions. They (Aberdeen) done well not to bullet him straight away. I think Human Resources were playing their cards right.'

Tosh was not alone in his intolerance of the spurious line that was handed out about Paterson's absence. The man who had delivered it, Duncan Shearer, still recoils when he remembers it. 'You know, I loved working with Steve. I miss standing beside him and having a drink, but it just got too much. I always knew when to go home. He didn't. He was the last man standing. First in, last out. Out of all the time I had to cover for him, to make me go in front of the cameras and tell lies to people. That was the biggest thing in my football career and I f***ing hated doing it. Those lies. You bastard. I've never really forgiven him and I don't suppose I ever will. As for the job, well, I really wanted to make it work. I'm not saying he never gave it his all, but I think he realised quite quickly it was too big for him. He never talked to me about his fears, never said it was too much.'

Shearer reveals that Paterson has never apologised to him. 'That's all he needed to do for the effort we'd made and moving our families to Aberdeen. But alcoholics are like that: they're selfish people. Everything is everybody else's fault, bar theirs. I made a point recently of listening to a radio programme which had Steve on it. He was manager of a junior team called Dufftown. He sounded like a man who had changed his ways. The next thing I heard he was sending out texts about two o'clock on a Sunday morning, slagging off the team. That tells me there's no change there.'

I return to Tosh, wondering whether he has a solution to the due diligence conundrum. Without hesitation, he confirms the theory that it wouldn't have been difficult for them to discover how Paterson lived his life. The problem, he suggests, was Dundee United. 'They found themselves vying against United for his services and said to themselves that they were going to get this guy regardless. I really do think that's how they played it. United, remember, then took Ian McCall, who was alleged to be a bit of a loose cannon. Ian was a very intelligent man who was vocal and would have been quite happy to tell you what he thought of you. He stood up to Graeme Souness at Rangers. I think Aberdeen thought at the time, "Out of the two loose cannons, which one are we going to take? Oh, we'll take the quiet, silent one and hope he doesn't hit the drink as much 'cos he's through here in Aberdeen." It was very naïve.'

If they had been naïve in appointing Paterson and allowing his lifestyle to go unchecked, Aberdeen learned how to be smarter in the summer of 2004. The season ended in some disarray, with five consecutive defeats. The reign of Steve Paterson subsequently ended – without the introduction of any additional melodrama, it should be noted – in the close season. Tosh and Russell Anderson heard the news when they were on holiday in the Algarve. Emotions tumbled through their heads: disappointment, excitement, intrigue, annoyance. 'Certain players have emotions, others are emotionless,' says Tosh.

'There's the "ah, well, he's a prick anyway" mentality. But I believe, even with the drinking issue, as much as 49 per cent of the sacking was results based. And that's casting aspersions on me, because I'm one of that team he's picking. Ultimately, he's picking the team that's getting beat, but if you're playing, you cannae be happy if someone's losing his job. If you are, then in my book you're a spineless, heartless bastard. That's the players I don't like. I didn't want them to get rid of him. It hurt me when they did. But we all knew it was inevitable what was going to happen. Certain names (for the next manager) were being bandied about back then. Eric Black's was one. From me and Russell's perspective, we liked that. There were other ones talked about, but then, suddenly, the brownest man in the world joined the fitba club.'

CHAPTER 14

The Rollercoaster Man

With Jimmy Calderwood as manager, there are no alternatives. You are obliged to climb aboard a rollercoaster and peer at events through your fingers. One minute all is well; the next bedlam breaks out. But, unless you are devoid of soul, it's really exciting for the most part. Unlike some of my contemporaries, I'm a fan of the man. I mean, on an October night in 2004, we go to Celtic Park and stun most of the 57,000 fans with a last-minute winner by John Stewart, reputedly the best finisher at Pittodrie. My seat in the main grandstand, right in the middle of a rabid Celtic support, means it's essential to celebrate internally rather than externally. Four days later, celebration is the furthest thing from my mind: we're humped, 5-0, by Rangers. It's said that Calderwood's affiliation towards the Gers makes the defeat easier. But this is only heresay.

Two years later, a friend and I are at Tannadice for a Scottish Cup-tie. Two first-half goals from David Fernandez mean we are enveloped by a blanket of stygian gloom. My friend is so incensed with our display that he charges to the front of the grandstand and berates Calderwood, who's standing directly beneath us. But we should know the script by now. The Dons come out with bayonets fixed in the second half and two goals from Stevie Crawford and a late effort by Barry Nicholson gives us victory. Our delight is such that we almost miss the stramash that breaks out in the technical area between Calderwood, Sandy Clark (our side) and Billy Dodds and Tony Docherty (Dundee United). Call it an acrimonious interlude. Up here, we're now laughing like drains.

But, if I'm to pick out the ultimate moment from the Calderwood Collection, it would be the night of 20 December, 2007. I'm now living in Skelmorlie, on the Ayrshire coast, My friend and I are perched high in the upper section of the Richard Donald stand as the Dons decimate fc Copenhagen, 4-0, to reach the last 32 of the UEFA Cup. The tactics, that night, are quite brilliant, Lee Miller being played in a withdrawn role and Jamie Smith up front. He scores two brilliant goals. I am so hoarse it seems someone has attacked my throat with Grade A sandpaper. Shame about the domestic cup competitions, of course.

It's all about heaven and hell: Calderwood is equipped to take you to both destinations.

My interview with Jimmy Calderwood is due to be conducted in a discreet corner of Glasgow's Pond Hotel. It begins, however, ahead of schedule and somewhat unconventionally, as we walk across the rain-blighted car park. Suddenly, out of nowhere, comes a conversation killer that is delivered without any discernible emotion. The 62-year-old confesses that he is suffering from Early Onset Alzheimer's. You tend to forget the elements on occasions like these. Our walk is temporarily suspended: he is searching my face for a response that is inevitably inadequate. 'Aw, Jimmy, I'm so sorry…' He seems suffused with relief, as opposed to my sense of shock. Doesn't the Big A violate people's minds and strip them of their senses and dignity? Here is a pragmatic guy who has always insisted on scattering any ghosts daring to infiltrate his world. I imagine there is zero chance of his banishing this particularly threatening spectre. The depression closing in on me is reminiscent of a North Sea haar.

This meeting is taking place on 3 August, 2017, and therefore a fortnight before this closely-guarded secret is transferred into tabloid headlines. By then, Calderwood, on the advice of the PR company tasked with handling the announcement, will be emancipated from all the predictable hullabaloo of breaking news; he'll be flying to South Africa, anxious to prostrate his body on some sun-kissed beach. 'I'm expecting it will mean clarity for different people. I don't want a cock-up. If it's to be done, it should be done properly. I just hope it helps somebody somewhere. So there'll be the press conference thing and meanwhile I'll be celebrating on the plane.'

Can there be any celebration in someone who has contracted Alzheimer's? He interprets the look on my face. 'I mean… apart from this, there's nothing wrong with me. I'm as fit as a fiddle.'

Calderwood will never be a candidate for sainthood, as evidenced by events in his private life. Only two years ago, he left his wife of 41 years and set up home with another woman. The *Scottish Sun* registered him as a love rat, but even love rats have rights. I recognise that he has placed his trust in me and therefore nothing is going to break that trust. Much of my career has been influenced by instinct, and instinct has taken me here today. I initially based this chapter of my book on nine-year-old cuttings from the Sunday Herald, but I realise I am short-changing him and his importance to the story of Aberdeen FC. A re-write is imperative. But at no time did I think the re-write would include such personal devastation.

We settle in a quiet corner of the hotel bar. Here, my depression gradually ebbs, courtesy of a companion who grows more upbeat by the minute.

Calderwood orders a Coke, explaining that the days of serious drinking are some way behind him now. I put to him what I imagine is a difficult question: if he were lying on a psychologist's couch and was asked to explain his life, what would he say? He dismisses any difficulty. 'Ach, you're talking about the illness. It's taken me three or four months to make the decision (about bringing it into the public domain). I've had it for three or four years. Don't get me wrong – I'm no' having any hassle with it. I take one tablet a day and that's me. I'm in the gym regularly, running about like an idiot. Otherwise, I'm on the bike.'

I ask him if memory lapses encouraged him go to the doctor's in the first instance. It appears so. 'I had to know. I've always been nosey. Once I know about things, I can handle them. Sometimes, I have my bad days, but no' often. Maybe I get a headache about once or twice a week. But, listen, ma life hasn't stopped. Me and Yvonne (his partner) we've been all over the world these last few months.'

Hereabouts, I'm remembering our 2009 interview up in Aberdeen after Stewart Milne sacked a manager whose team admittedly toiled in Cup competitions but twice penetrated the frontiers of Europe. That day, Calderwood was already occupying the role of malcontent. The taste of football honey had gone – now he was sampling the bile of unemployment for the first time in his life. And his words told you everything. He said back then, 'It has been a different world in ma house these last couple of weeks. I'm not a house husband. Oh, no, murder polis! I said to myself, "I'll need to get out of here, or else, with all this arguing with my wife, we'll end up in a divorce court."'

Those words were uncannily prescient. The sombre backdrop of the divorce court loomed. However, to his credit, here in the Pond Hotel, Calderwood refuses to abrogate responsibility for the marriage failure. 'It was ma fault entirely and I still feel bad about it, but life goes on. I'm no' one for regrets. Ma three daughters, ma sister and ma son disowned me, but there was no going back, People say it was something to do with ma illness – it wasn't. I make a decision and that's it – right or wrong. But I tell you, life with Yvonne has been f***in' brilliant!'

His partner of two years was with him on the day of diagnosis. Calderwood gives an involuntary shudder. 'Yes, that was a hard one. At that moment in time, it was the end of the world. I'm sure I cried for a wee while but, after that, I accepted it. I'm no' one for brooding. I think I've had a great life and I hope there's a long… as I say, I always look for people I've still tae get. F***in' enemies. I've still got to catch them all.'

A smile returns to a normally deeply-tanned face that today carries only a faint imprint of a Scottish summer. The smile proves that if his memory is not in pristine condition, the fighting spirit is gloriously intact. There has been enough focus on this man's private life, however. I came here, purportedly, for an interview about football. And it's this vicarious game that should now be addressed. Eight years on from his departure, Calderwood is still in love with Aberdeen FC and it's an attachment that will never be severed. So, we take occupation of the memory module for a replay of his exit. He recalls he was driven to chairman Stewart Milne's house by Director of Football Willie Miller; this was a few days before the Dons beat Hibs and secured a UEFA Cup situation. Naively, he believed it was to discuss plans for the following season. 'I got sacked in Stewartie's dining room. Him and Willie were sittin' at the big table - the chairman didnae know whit tae dae. But I did. By this time, I'd sussed it out.

'I said, "Chairman, I know what you're f***in' gaun tae dae. I can't believe you."

'He said, "How much do I owe you?"

'I replied, "Stick the money up your arse!"'

Milne and Co, notorious for sporadic outbreaks of boardroom buffoonery, did not comply with Calderwood's precipitous demand. They settled their debt (believed to be almost £400,000) within days. I recall writing that if the players were as adept with the final ball as the directors were with severance deals, they'd be up there at sporting altitude with Real Madrid. Calderwood, meanwhile, aggrieved as he was by his sacking, kept it secret from everyone until the Hibs game was over and the staff 'jolly' - the annual reward for services rendered - had begun at Pittodrie. He challenged Miller to make the announcement: it turned into the supreme party pooper. Many of the female staff members were in tears. Sue Calderwood, meanwhile, excoriated Chief Executive Duncan Fraser, telling him he'd made the biggest mistake of his life. Future events demonstrated that she was in Nostradamus territory with that prediction. But Calderwood's personal upset was about to intensify when he heard the name of his successor. 'I was ragin' with Mark McGhee taking over. In my opinion, he was a f***in' clown. He was so arrogant. The boys f***in' hated him. And, don't get me wrong, they were a great bunch of lads; hard trainers, every one. I was very close to them. It was a really happy club.'

Calderwood, like most of us, is unable to subdue his idiosyncrasies: the devil inside him insists on him cremating his face and body when the sun shines. That same devil encourages him to massage his testicles when he believes (wrongly) no one is looking. It's a scenario that was ruthlessly parodied by Jonathan Watson in Only An Excuse. But, place these quirks to one side, shed a natural inclination toward bias and ask yourselves this question: is he a good football manager? Or, perhaps more realistically, was he a good football manager? There appears to be an unequivocal answer: people who know what they are about think very highly of the man (Andrew Considine, for instance, gives him a glowing reference later in this book). And yet this cruel and often sporting world of ours seemed to declare Calderwood to be a non person. He managed, briefly, both Kilmarnock and Ross County after leaving Aberdeen, saving them from relegation. And he scuffled, again briefly, over in his beloved Holland with Go Ahead Eagles and De Graafschap. He has remained in the wilderness, then, for ostensibly six years and even a co-option to the board of Cowdenbeath has not rescued him from that fate. Could it be that his name is prominent on the blacklist of someone with influence?

But, if that is true, Calderwood's troubles were to be found closer to home in that a sizeable proportion of the Dons support was vehemently ranged against him. They ridiculed the colour of his face and called him Tango Man and, even all these years later, they seize every opportunity to deride and dismantle his image. Is it simply because this man hails from Glasgow and nailed his colours to the mast of Rangers at an early age? Steve Tosh thinks it is just that simple. You will note that I interviewed Tosh some months ago. 'Why he gets all this stick is because he's a Hun. So was Jimmy Nicholl. I'd worked with Jimmy Nick: he'd signed me for Raith Rovers in 1998. God, I was at a time in my life where, if I could find a way of daen somethin' stupid, I'd dae it. But, at the same time, I liked Jimmy. He made me captain of my hometown club and it made my dad and me very proud. So, when the two Jimmys came up here to Aberdeen, things really changed. It was fun but it was also serious and professional. The best thing Jimmy C did for AFC was he was going to ensure that they became a force again. And they did. We got back hope. It was the cup results, losing to Queen's Park and Queen of the South that did for him. It was also, I think, Jimmy being Jimmy. I found him endearing, funny, arrogant, and abrupt at times, but I really liked working for him. Along with Gordon Chisholm, he's the best manager I've worked with.

'I just felt that when things went wrong, (he felt) it was the players' fault. When things went right, it was his doing. I think you can get away with a lot, but sometimes you've just got to stick your hands up. I felt as it went on, a lot of the players started to feel that way about him. But, honestly, talk about tactics - the man was astute. He was professional, diligent and a joy to work for. I'm disappointed he's no' in the game now. He's just dwindled away. His reputation seems to have gone against him for no particular reason. No mistake, he was the best thing that happened to Aberdeen.'

Tosh's thought process gives an insight into the reasons for Calderwood's downfall. 'Jimmy, being intelligent and bright, thought if he could make us successful again, he'd look good and then he'd move down South (to England) or to his chosen club, Rangers. He basically made people aware of that as well. That didnae help him up here. He didnae do it the way Derek McInnes has done it. Listen, if the Rangers job became available again, Derek's name would be bandied about again - if they could afford to pay what Stewart Milne would want for him. Jimmy came out and said all this. Derek wouldnae have done that. But Jimmy took the club to the next level and he did it in a very good way.'

Two games at Parkhead resonate in Tosh's mind, one under Steve Paterson, the other with Calderwood. He recalls that Celtic had gone 77 games unbeaten at home despite the fact that their visitors had included teams from the highest echelons of football: Barcelona, Liverpool, Juventus and AC Milan. He remembers Aberdeen travelled down with possibly the 'worst team you've seen in your life.' Aberdeen, at the time, were renowned for getting skelpings at Parkhead under the leadership of Ebbe Skovdahl. 'We turned up and I swear our supporters wouldnae have known the names of some of the players that night. We went 1-0 doon, inevitably, to Henrik Larsson. I then decided I was going to change the game by coming off. I cannae really come off 'cos there's kids on the bench. But I do come off and Stevie pits on Bryan Prunty. He scores in the second half and David Zdrilic makes it 2-1 with the last kick of the ball. Raggedly Arsed Rovers had triumphed. We go into the players' room afterwards and Neil Lennon, gentleman that he is, gave us a couple of crates of beer for going back up the road. We took the crates on, but got them taken off us. Because of what Stevie had done, we werenae allowed a drink on the bus. I think Keith Wyness enforced the ban.'

A year later, Aberdeen were back under the leadership of Calderwood and won 3-2. Tosh reveals that the game ended on a negative note. He'd gone down to the Aberdeen section and thrown his strip to the fans. He was taken out of the dressing room by the police and told he was lucky not to be arrested for inciting a riot. Apparently, when he'd lobbed the strip into the crowd, there had been a stramash to claim ownership. Tosh responded with humour, saying he was surprised the fans didn't throw the strip back at him. The police killed such humour by pointing out that a wee boy had been caught in the crush. 'I turned up at Pittodrie a week later and there was a man standing with my strip – and his kid. Thank goodness he was fine. The good thing about that night was we did get to drink: win or lose, on the booze.'

The difference between the two managers (Paterson and Calderwood) was respect and discipline. 'When the two Jimmys came in, they earned the respect straight away because of what they said and how things were done. You were left in no doubt as to who was running the show. With Stevie, I think it was an Inverness thing; he allowed the players a bit more freedom in decision making. When Calderwood became manager, we went to Holland for pre-season training. At meal times, you didn't leave the table until Jimmy said you could go back to your room. Stevie would give you a bit more freedom. You finished your tea and disappeared. A lot of times, though, footballers need to be treated like kids. You need to have them regimented. If you were five minutes late for one of Stevie's meetings, you'd probably get the piss ripped out of you rather than anything else. Five minutes late for Jimmy's meetings, you wouldn't play.'

But Calderwood had other methods of keeping the clock ticking. He'd seen some of his counterparts lobbing cups of hot tea at players and others, in the throes of apoplexy, basically spitting at team members. So he introduced a new tactic. 'Jimmy would leave things for about two or three minutes at half time,' Tosh recalls. 'It was the first time I'd seen anything like this. But he would let the players vent their frustration on their colleagues, maybe about not picking up someone. Then he'd come in and would actually tell them who was at fault. He wasn't coming in, ranting, because players are not listening at that time. He was letting them calm down and getting their blood pressure down to a certain level. Commonsense. It's how it's done now. But it wasn't done so much back then.'

After leaving Aberdeen in fourth place and consequently in line for another tilt at European competition, Calderwood was sacked. The man who invariably sounded the bugle for all-out attack was gone. The bugle, on this occasion, had played the last post. But now, back with Calderwood in Glasgow, this is not a time for gloom. I want to know more about the great nights: the 4-0 humbling of FC Copenhagen, the 2-2 draw with Bayern Munich. The Coke-sipping man beside me is pleased to oblige. 'We used to do a lot of tactics – and I was lucky that I'd been in Europe and knew a lot of people who could help me. We had two or three under 19s against Bayern at home. Sone Aluko was brilliant. The full back he was up against was subbed and, believe me, he was glad to get aff that night. Bayern were struttin' aboot a wee bit and we got right in aboot them and they werenae likin' it. I remember Ottmar Hitzfeld, their manager, was f***in' ragin'. Copenhagen was just one of those nights. They didn't turn up at all, thinkin' it as going to be too easy. I put Jamie Smith up front that night, with Lee Miller withdrawn. Jamie was clever; he had pace and vision. Very introverted, mind; head often buried in a heavy book. "Whit are ye reading' noo?" I'd ask. He wisnae introverted that night...'

Pace was the defining image of Calderwood teams. Barry Nicholson didn't possess the after-burners, but he survived because of an astute football brain. Darren Mackie offered the distinction. The often-derided striker had a first touch that often materialised into a second, maybe third, touch, but he had speed in abundance. 'Darren still takes some stick. Disgraceful, in my opinion. He didnae give a shit, mind: he was as hard as nails and would kick his granny, man. No-one liked playin' against him. He was a hardy bastard and an evil bastard.'

I've got to ask Calderwood about Ricky Foster. There is no hesitation. 'The times I had to tell him, "Listen, you're the luckiest guy alive to be here. But you're here because you're lightnin'. That's savin' you. Otherwise, you probably wouldnae even get in the reserves." He'd come back. "That's a bit strong, gaffer." I replied, "Fozzy, in every dressing room, there's a mirror. Look in the f***in' mirror and he'll tell ye!" He thought he was the best man on the park. I'd say to him, "Fozzy, stop f***in' dreamin', this is as high as you get. I've got you here. Don't make a c*** of it!"

'All the boys ripped him apart. "Fozzy, what have you got to moan about today?" Jimmy Nicholl and Sandy Clark used to wind him up, telling him he should be playin' in the centre of defence. I'd be hidin' listenin' to it all. He'd say, "I f***in' know that!" I'd jump out. "Fozzy, shut up! You might no' even get intae the team the way you're goin'!" The thing is he had an arrogance that was misplaced. You know I told him that I might have had somethin' to do with him goin' to Rangers. I'd told Walter (Smith) that he never shut up and thought everythin' he said was right. "But all your boys are slow, Walter. He's goin' to cost hardly anythin'; and he's lightnin'!" Know what? He done brilliant for them.'

To all intents and purposes, Calderwood is back on his beloved turf and his face is a poster for enthusiasm. So, the logic is that I have to ruin the mood. Surely there were failures – didn't Steve Lovell disappoint him? 'Oh, f***. Big time. A very strange boy; very deep. He had tae be home all the time. The first day he was at Aberdeen, we were going to Holland for a pre-season game. We were in that country for 20 minutes when he came in and told me he had to go back to Dundee. I told him we had a game that night. "Aye," he says, "but I've got to go home." And that's where I sent him. But I told him he'd be peyin' it himself. I wasn't peyin' and neither was the chairman. Stevie? No, not my kind of person.'

The mood, however, remains buoyant. I ask him about that nickname: Tango Man. The sound of laughter surrounds me. 'It was quite funny, actually. They (the fans) werenae wrong, were they?' What about the Dons fans who disparaged him for his lifelong affiliation to Rangers? 'Well, they had a poll about me with the supporters and if I remember, it was 60-40 in my favour. That wasn't bad, was it? This is no' bein' big-headed, but I'd be surprised if you asked my players how we set up, how we trained and how they laughed – there wouldnae be many that would say it wisnae brilliant.'

As I run him home; he tells me that this 'wee guy from Govan' has been around the world about ten times and it hasn't cost him a halfpenny. 'I've played and managed in great stadiums and played for great managers. Sir Alf (Ramsey) at Birmingham, for instance. F***in' brilliant he was and he f***in' loved me; the only thing was he put me at right back. I f***in' hated it!'

We arrive at our destination. I watch Calderwood as he heads for a small semi-detached house in Glasgow's West End. I've been in the company of a condemned man for over 90 minutes and yet he has invigorated me. But, remember, knowing him is committing yourself to a ride on a rollercoaster. The news of Calderwood's condition broke before he left for South Africa. It was announced at a press conference in Glasgow.

CHAPTER 15

From Hero to Zero

SHOULD events go according to plan, history will be swept aside when the wrecking ball keeps its appointment with Pittodrie Stadium sometime soon. But, before the old fortress finally surrenders to what is defined as progress, you would almost believe it is anxious to inflict pain on all those who traduce its tradition. And thus we arrive on the doorstep of Mark McGhee and a narrative that is almost dystopian in nature. Once upon another time, McGhee was accorded hero status in the Granite City; he was one of the giants of a glorious night in Gothenburg. An abject 18-month spell as Aberdeen manager – including an early admission that he lamented missing out on the Celtic job – and an inexplicable failure to apologise for a 9-0 defeat by Celtic changed that dynamic forever. Somehow, he's managed to achieve in the Granite City what might once have been considered impossible: pariah status. There can be no doubt that, on the evening of February 15 2017, with his Motherwell team being vanquished 7-2 by a rejuvenated Aberdeen, the Glaswegian shredded his credibility as a leader of men, his antics being more embarrassing than the inadequacies of his team. A pointless argument with the fourth match official ended in a policeman escorting him to the Pittodrie stand, whereupon, immediately in front of his former chairman, Stewart Milne, he revived his conflict with a baying home support – a support he once claimed had spat on him.

If you're seeking fairness, the abuse he received that night possibly did not qualify as being acceptable. There again, McGhee's reaction was even more unacceptable. On hearing himself dismissed as a 'f***ing clown', he suddenly found himself disturbed by a mobile phone camera. He suggested that his privacy was being invaded, forgetting in the moment perhaps that football grounds are not big on privacy clauses, and that he, as an errant manager, was occupying the supporters' territory rather than the other way round. He ended this phase of his evening with a snarl at the offending camera and an adaptation of a popular Glaswegian epithet: 'Get that tae f***!' Ironically, that sentiment is one many Aberdeen fans would wish to impose on McGhee. You imagine it would trouble them not if they failed to see him again. Why has a man of his undoubted intelligence and ability allowed this ugly feud to develop?

You could confuse yourself whilst attempting to configure McGhee. He can be the personification of charm, an agreeable companion who has a fund of stories to keep you amused. There is another side to him, however, and it is not an attractive one: this one mainlines on hubris and arrogance, and the occasional disregard for life's courtesies. At times, in his company, you are the most important man in the world and therefore the focus of his undivided attention – until someone more important comes along. I first met him at the Football Writers' Player of the Year dinner, at London's Royal Lancaster. I was Head of Sport at the *Daily Mail* at the time. He was unemployed, but this did nothing to reduce his notion of himself. He spent a few minutes detailing how he had 'cemented' Alex Ferguson the day after Aberdeen had beaten Real Madrid in the European Cup Winners' Cup. The argument began apparently as Fergie objected to the way McGhee was holding the trophy. The player allegedly dragged his manager back to the dressing room area before they were separated. For all the braggadocio, he was stimulating company.

As a result of our meeting, I invited him to the Café Royal for a sportsmen's dinner – an expensive event attended by a host of formidable names. This time, however, there was little time for discourse and I spent most of the evening regarding the empty chair beside me. McGhee was still unemployed and desperate to end this depressing cycle of being absent from the cutting edge of football. To this end, he repeatedly excused himself from the table, to take mobile phone calls from a potential employer in Theo Paphitis, the then Millwall chairman. There were other times when he didn't even bother excusing himself, but I put this down to his understandable excitement. It proved justifiable excitement: they eventually reached a verbal agreement that evening. We repaired later to a club in Shaftesbury Avenue, ostensibly to celebrate this imminent appointment, but, on this occasion, most of what he had to say was obliterated by the band. We talked again on the telephone after I had retired and was writing freelance articles for the *Sunday Herald*. By this time he was Millwall manager and, being a dutiful manager, was about to review the merits of another team. He arrived at Brentford an hour early and we talked for about 30 minutes. It's important to remember that this was the third conversation we had shared. And so we come to a lovely autumnal day in 2011.

I'm on an express train from London to Brighton and currently entering my old stamping ground of Sussex, where I stayed as the sixties became the seventies. I'm on my way to interview McGhee for the website which Jim Black and I run. I'm surprised that he has agreed to the interview in the first place, as I wrote a somewhat unflattering newspaper piece about him only recently. I ring him and tell him we're closing in on Brighton. He tells me he'll pick me up at the station. A few minutes later, he phones and says that he is now unable to pick me up. He asks if I know Brighton. I do, as it happens. At least, I did 40 years ago. 'Well,' he says, 'proceed to your right when you exit the station and walk down the hill. You'll come to a sex shop. Wait around there and I'll be there as quickly as I can.'

The message is understood, but there are initial misgivings. Sex shop? At my age? Hand on heart, I wouldn't even know what one looks like. Anyway, I arrive in Brighton and follow the instructions, but fail to identify any sex shop. There is a guy sweeping the pavements. I ask him for directions. A knowing gleam comes into his eyes. He obviously thinks he recognises a dirty, old man when he sees one, and tells me there is a choice if I just walk further down the hill: there are two! I do as I'm advised, but I am apprehensive. Now, Brighton is a cosmopolitan place, replete with many people from the media world. Suppose someone sees me hovering on the pavements between two sex shops? I could scarcely say I'm lost and am looking for an ironmongers, could I? All sorts of unpleasant thoughts are rumbling around my suspicious mind. Is there any chance that I'm being set up here by a vengeful manager? Just as the beads of sweat are forming on my brow, I spy the jaunty figure of McGhee striding towards me. Here's how I remember it. Incidentally, the recorded interview never makes it to the website. The clattering of coffee cups and the chatter of shoppers makes it far more suitable for newspaper use.

WHILST he contemplates the isolation of unemployment, Mark McGhee is practising his German just in case Deutschland requires his coaching skills. But his views on the city of Aberdeen – not to mention the chairman of its football club, its players and fans – could never be misinterpreted in any language. You won't find them in the local tourist board brochure, that's for sure.

Here's a taster: 'I'm sitting here not because I'm a bad manager but because I made a bad decision. I will never, unless it's in a professional capacity, look in the direction of Aberdeen again. Any association I had with them ended the day I walked out.'

I tell him he has my admiration for agreeing to meet me. His reply is almost insulting. 'First of all, I never saw it (the article). But I wouldn't have been interested. Whatever you wrote and whatever you were saying, you were probably wrong anyway. Seriously.'

The temptation is to ignore the arrogance and examine the reasons behind that remark. Now, McGhee likes to present himself as the kind of guy who wouldn't squeal even if you applied hobnail boots to his backside. But surely there's vulnerability somewhere? Anyway, the sparring has begun in earnest as we sip morning coffees in the trendy Lanes district. I tell him I always endeavour to be objective. This brings a slight concession. He asks me to recall the gist of my article.

Where should I begin? I had suggested he was the pariah of Pittodrie and claimed that he was aloof and showed no interest in the players. It was claimed that his assistant, Scott Leitch, was a bully. And Sone Aluko, allegedly, had suffered rough justice. Was I wrong?

'So you wrote that without speaking to me? It's all nonsense. I had Sone's mother up from London, sat her down and went through the whole thing. Listen, he f***ed off to Nigeria without even telling the club when we were at a crucial part of the season. So, as a board, we sat down and decided we'd get him back. Sone Aluko and I have no issues. In fact, I recently tried to help him get to Sheffield Wednesday. It's a f***ing scandal!'

I'm not quite sure what is scandalising McGhee at this moment. But let's return to the fact that he's here in the first place. He doesn't appear to be a bearer of grudges. 'Friends of mine have said to me that I should remember for longer, but it's just not in me. Maybe it's a weakness and other people can use that to their advantage, if you like. But I just don't think that way. I move on quickly.'

Here is a newspaper reporter's golden opportunity. Has he succeeded in moving on from the embarrassing memory of his most recent preferment? McGhee points out that he doesn't really want to talk about Aberdeen and you can understand that reluctance. Who would want to be reminded of unmitigated disaster? He replaced the popular Jimmy Calderwood in June of 2010, and was gone in early December of the next year, having won only 17 games out of 62.

But, hey, it would be like talking to Liam Fox and failing to raise the subject of travelling companions (this was a reference to the politician forming a controversial friendship with a certain Adam Werritty). Inevitably, then, we return to the dissonant theme of Pittodrie. And, in spite of what he says about not holding grudges, you can smell the resentment.

Pursuing the maxim that leadership comes from the top, let's begin with Stewart Milne. Can McGhee talk about the chairman's role at the club? Sure he can. His eyes look for the heavens. 'Within the club, there is no strong influence: there's nobody whose character is strong enough to preside over everybody. I think, in many ways, it does have to come from the chairman. I have to say to him that he has to be seen around the football club. Stewart is down there a couple of times a week at boardroom meetings. He gets into his car and goes. He never walks through the offices or asks people how they're doing. Within the club, he has to be the influence. He's the man. Maybe he just underestimates that. Maybe he doesn't understand that.'

The hitherto invulnerable 54-year-old is now betraying his vulnerability. 'I wasn't comfortable (at Aberdeen). Five minutes after I was at Motherwell, I had Betty, the secretary, being like a mum to me. I had people looking after me and out for me. John Boyle introduced me to his friends in Glasgow, who were then making sure I had the right place to live. I was invited round (to their houses) because they knew my partner Maria was doon the road (in Brighton). I was just made to feel instantly welcome and accepted. You felt that everybody there wanted to make you the best you could be; they wanted you to succeed.

'I didn't feel that at Aberdeen. In fact, from a players' point of view, there was some sort of resentment towards me – a resentment I didn't understand. I imagined I was coming home, but it wasn't like that at all. I needed to jazz the place up: it needed two million volts. The girl on the desk couldnae look me straight in the eye: there were wee cliques. It needed to change.'

McGhee offered solutions for change – solutions that would have cost the club in the region of a million pounds – but Milne allegedly ignored them. Surely, his European Cup Winners' Cup medal provided him with some currency with the fans? 'The new generation of Aberdeen supporters couldn't give a monkey's about Mark McGhee and the Gothenburg Greats. I could have been somebody they'd never heard of walking in the door. The past was of no relevance whatsoever.

'It made me feel very isolated. For the first time in my career, I felt it was me, Scott Leitch and Colin Meldrum against the world. There was absolutely no empathy. Whereas at Motherwell, they were falling over themselves to be nice. When my baby Archie was born, they were all bringing in presents. I go back there now and they all want to see pictures of him. I go to Millwall and the new chairman seeks me out. I go to Brighton (another former club he managed). I've got a relationship with these people. But none at Aberdeen.'

Let's return to the players. McGhee, you suspect, would love to talk in specifics about guys whom he believes have been there too long. Instead, he generalises. 'At Motherwell they embraced 4-3-3 and all the other things I wanted to do with them. I went to Aberdeen and it was like talking a foreign language. There was non co-operation in terms of getting a system going, and the training was, well... "Training on a Sunday? We don't train on Sundays."'

What about the allegations of bullying? 'Don't get me wrong: there were times when I had to reel in Leitchy because he's one of those boys who gets emotional and angry. It was in danger of spilling over into something that couldnae be. But it was about them, not Leitchy. We got feedback that they were going to the sponsors with stories. But, f***'s sake, Fergie (Alex Ferguson) used to throw things at us. These charges are embarrassing.'

McGhee's sigh comes from deep in the diaphragm. 'You get people who enthuse a room. You know them and catch their enthusiasm. Coisty's (Ally McCoist) one. Then you get other people who suck the life out of a room. Aberdeen is full of people who are drainers. Until it's cleared out and there's a freshness about it, it's not going to get any better. And no-one, not even Craig Brown, who's a good manager, can do anything until they change that.'

But McGhee knew all there was to know about Aberdeen before he joined them? Surely he did his homework? He looks embarrassed here. 'If I made a mistake, I never dealt with Stewart Milne up until the point I was at the club. Remember, this was a club I held dear to my heart and because of my trust, I thought they held me dear. I thought I didn't need to do the due diligence. I thought I'd go up there and sweep them away. So I didn't go into either the implications of the exact state of affairs and how good or bad the squad actually was. So, yeah, I should have thought twice before taking the job. But there you go: you live and learn.'

Today, Aberdeen go to Celtic. McGhee took his Aberdeen there almost a year ago and were slaughtered 9-0. You imagine the horror of it is still being distilled in his head... It has not put him off working again, however.

'I've been brushing up my German a bit, trying to stay modern. The engine is still running. The other week I was at seven games in eight days, looking at what's new in the game until such times as somebody decides to take a punt with Mark McGhee again. My feet didn't touch the ground when I left Pittodrie. But I wasn't in mourning or anything. I would have applied for a job the day after I left had the right one been available.'

You don't really qualify as a sports reporter until you have had your ears battered by recrimination. The vitriol arrives in many forms. Graham Rix, for example, was in the running to become manager of Partick Thistle when I interviewed him for the Sunday Herald. *He chose the direct route of a Sunday morning phone call to my home, complaining bitterly about a headline that identified him as a sex offender. I sympathised greatly with him, but pointed out that I didn't write the headlines. That was the end of any relationship we shared. Terry Cassidy, once the managing director of Celtic, elected to send a fax after he inferred in my newspaper (the* Daily Star*) that his then manager, Billy McNeill, should practise his technique for the high jump. The fax went something like this: 'After your article, you are still welcome at Celtic Park, albeit less welcome than anyone else in this world!'*

When the McGhee piece is printed, there is a slight delay before hell is unleashed. I receive a call from BBC *Radio Scotland asking me to contribute to their evening programme and answer allegations made by McGhee. They play me their interview with him. The man who would not squeal if someone applied hobnailed boots to his backside has made a tactical change. He is squealing like mad, claiming that much of the article is based on off-the-record comments. 'This guy, who I didn't know from Adam, seduced me over a cup of cappuccino.'*

I am angry on two fronts. There is the imputation that I have done him like some kipper. Listen, this is the ultimate and rather pathetic refuge of football people all over the world. The power of the printed word can be awesome and has the ability to make people lose their nerve. They then claim misquotation or that they said things that were strictly private. But my ego – which is not even in the same division as McGhee's – is also offended by his other statement. So, he does not recognise me from Adam? Has this man no shame? I respond vigorously, resisting an attempt by the presenter of the show to interrupt me. 'Listen,' I begin, 'Mark lives down in Brighton and I fear the seagulls have been pecking at his brain.' I mention our much-interrupted evening in London, the one he has conveniently forgotten. I suggest that I have interviewed sportsmen from all over the world, without ever once being accused of using off-the-record material. I was never going to break that record with someone like Mark McGhee.

Now, all these years later, I reflect on this man's aberrational moments at Pittodrie and admit there is a small temptation to gloat. These moments were propelled by his own energy; no-one demanded that he should behave like an idiot. Instead, I feel a small measure of compassion for him. I look back on that interview in Brighton and can hear his defence against my line of questioning (this was material I had not used in the *Sunday Herald*). Had he been ferociously ambitious? 'I think there was a time when I was encouraged to take a certain route, chase a certain ambition along a certain path. But it didnae get me anywhere. I'm on record as saying that along the way I made bad decisions. I'm sitting here not because I'm a bad manager but because I made bad decisions in terms of jobs I took and didnae take. When I left Reading, Sir Alex advised me strongly that I shouldn't go, that I should not take the Leicester job. That even he, Bobby Robson and everybody else together couldn't have kept Leicester up. He felt it would be detrimental to my progress. My argument was that if I went to Leicester and got them straight back up, then it would undo any damage associated by going down. It would even probably strengthen my position. So, although he was strongly against it, I still made the decision to go. At that stage, I felt I had gone the course with Reading. Now, with hindsight, that was clearly the wrong decision.

'One of the important things that Alex said to me early on, if not the most important thing, was about decision making. Unless you're prepared to make strong decisions, then you shouldn't be in it. Whether that came naturally to me, I'm no' really convinced it did or it does. But I knew I had to do it. So all along the way I've been prepared to kind of stonewall it, if you like. Particularly early on. So leaving Leicester and going to Wolves, for instance, was totally against my gut feeling. I'd become convinced it was right for my career path. Therefore I shut off any sentiment I had for Martin George, the chairman, whom I liked, and my family, which I was dragging all over England. Or for the supporters, or the players that I had brought to Leicester. I had to shut that out and just go for it. But, beyond that, I realised I couldnae dae that any longer; that it wasn't right.'

Seeking to build on this rare admission of humility, I asked him if self-confidence had always been his signature tune. The answer came wrapped in more humility. 'You're obliged to demonstrate a certain amount of self-confidence. Now, how much of that is real and how much is what I've just described I don't know. Not sure. Certainly not all of it is real. I'm as human and vulnerable as anyone. As I'm sure, underneath the skin, Alex is as well. But you still have to ride it out, because of the job that we do. Supporters expect it, players expect it, you've got to show a certain confidence.'

Some of you reading this may remember the good McGhee, the guy who would have chased an empty crisp packet for the cause of Aberdeen. He was never the most gifted of footballers, but the vitality and the effort could never be denied. You suspected he never needed to think too much about it. When he embarked on the more difficult profession of football management, he initially applied a match to the heather, but the fire brigade was not occupied for too long. His failure to lift Wolves into the promised land of the Premier Division had three detrimental effects. First he incurred the wrath of the owner, Sir Jack Hayward, who insisted he would no longer act as the 'golden tit', supplying his manager's financial requirements. Then, worse, his relationship with Ferguson deteriorated until it became almost non-existent. Many experts suspected that the axing of Darren Ferguson, Fergie's son, was responsible for this. Thirdly, his sacking signalled his descent into managerial mediocrity.

You only need to look at the litany of clubs – Reading, Leicester, Wolves, Millwall, Brighton, Motherwell, Aberdeen, Bristol Rovers and Motherwell again – to know that Mark McGhee has fallen disastrously short of his ambitions. He will watch the television and see others who may not even have as much managerial talent as himself and know that he should have done so much better. The thought, I'm sure, must torment him at every juncture. He admitted that day in Brighton that a man must learn from his decisions. It appears that Mark McGhee recognises it, but fails to act on it.

CHAPTER 16

The Whiskering of Joe Harper

Memories are like floodwaters in that they are well nigh impossible to contain. They arrive, spontaneously and irresistibly, in all shapes and forms: brilliant ones, fond ones, appropriate and inappropriate ones, embarrassing ones, wholly unpalatable ones. On a warm day in August of 2009, I'm subjecting myself to flashbacks of the less favourable nature, and therefore experiencing a tortuous 1975 afternoon at Hampden, covering the Scottish League Cup final for Radio Forth. Life at that juncture was presenting itself in a serious hue. I was a former sports journalist – suitably disgraced – newly married with a ready-made family, and staring into the remorseless features of unemployment. A lifeline presented itself with Saturday shifts on Radio Forth, preparing the sports bulletins for the newscasters. They then asked me to cover the Old Firm extravaganza between Celtic and Rangers, reporting live to the George Farm Show. *Due to a set of circumstances which might well have been described as difficult, my radio debut evolved into a disaster. It culminated in me spluttering a handful of inconsequential words before drying up completely, putting the telephone down on a plaintive George Farm ('where are you, Bryan?'), and racing for the Hampden exit door as fast as my legs would allow. Radio Forth were forgiving to such an extent that they offered me a job despite the fiasco. But I was spooked as far as radio was concerned. Even unemployment could not persuade me to change my mind. My confidence had been dismantled in a few torrid minutes. Never again. Ever.*

Of course, you should never trade in such negativity. More than three decades later, I have overcome this rather unnatural phobia about the airwaves. I've completed three series of programmes for BBC *Radio Scotland, picked up a Sony bronze award for one of them, and now I'm embarking on another series. My initial interviewee on* Stuff of Legends *is Eddie Turnbull, the inimitable, irascible legend of Scottish football. I am only slightly less tense than I was on that fateful day at Hampden. Eddie and I have 'previous'. We met in a dark and dingy office at Easter Road in the year of 1974. He had just signed another striker in Joe Harper for Hibs (to my calculations, that made four or five potential centre forwards on the club's books). I asked him whether he'd find difficulty in accommodating everyone. His response was not far from being robust: he indicated that if I was intent on asking questions like that, then I'd had better choose my exit... door or window!*

Some weeks later, I met up with him again, this time at his former club, Aberdeen. He had just placed one of those aforesaid strikers, Alan Gordon, on the transfer list. The player had claimed that the fee being sought was prohibitive and I duly recorded his angst in my newspaper. So, there I was, standing in the Pittodrie foyer, where Turnbull was being interrogated by a reporter called Stewart Weir. Patently distracted, the manager kept looking over at me. A storm was about to break and it had Eddie's name attached to it. I was unable, however, to forecast its ferocity.

'Excuse me, sir,' said Eddie, 'but is your name Cooney?'

'Yes, that's right...'

'Bryan Cooney?'

'Right again.'

'Bryan Cooney, of The Sun*?'*

I felt I may inadvertently have stumbled into a recording of 20 *Questions. 'Three correct answers wins a prize,' I replied, far too flippant for even my own liking.*

'Well, you're a c***, then! A f***ing c***! Don't you f***ing come near Easter Road again!'

**

THERE ARE INSTANCES IN THIS old life where the past insists on blighting the present. Feuds have been engaged for far less. This, I'm delighted to report, was not the case with Eddie Turnbull. If I had upset his equilibrium on those occasions back in the seventies, he'd regained his balance when we met at his Edinburgh home in 2009. He exhibited no trace of rancour. Here, I was the one asking the questions, and this now rather energetic and entertaining octogenarian seemed anxious to answer them to the best of his ability. We talked about the Famous Five of Hibs, plus his successful management of that club and the ultimately unsuccessful attempt to keep George Best away from alcohol. But he reserved some of his most enlightening memories for his six years at Aberdeen. Here are some excerpts from the recording:

COONEY: Did you have much to do with Willie Young?

TURNBULL: I took him to Pittodrie. I took three of them from Edinburgh, but Big Willie was the only one who made it. His father was a sergeant in the police.

COONEY: He was a character.

TURNBULL: I felt sorry for Jimmy (Bonthrone). He couldnae handle him – he was too soft. But he was a great foil for me, was Jimmy.

COONEY: 'Cos he picked up the pieces, didn't he?

TURNBULL: Exactly.

COONEY: Willie's a good lad. He's down near Newark, I believe. Runs stables.

TURNBULL: He was lucky – he married a good girl. He changed his ways. Or she made him change them.

COONEY: Let's test your memory, Eddie. You'd taken the managerial road to Aberdeen. That's 1965. I've always wondered about it – is this where the initial foundations for the later success of Aberdeen were laid?

TURNBULL: Undoubtedly. I say that without any fear of contradiction.

COONEY: Because it's all laid at Fergie's door...

TURNBULL: If I hadnae gone there, Aberdeen would not be a football club today. They would be extinct. Now that's a big statement. But when I got there, I thought what have I come to? What have I done here? There were about 30 players and they were at the bottom of the league and on the road to being relegated. They had all these players and I had to assess them. I joined in February and we had very few games for us to stay up. I thought: 'In the name of fortune, what have I got to do?' I had to get sorted out the ones who were no' bad and got to make them believe that they were better players than they actually were – to get us out of this situation.

Do you know who the first game was? Rangers at Pittodrie. I remember, I was still (living) in Glasgow and I was going back there that night. There was only one train going to Glasgow. It was the same train as Rangers were going back on. Scott Symon was their gaffer. I met him at the station. 'Come on,' he says, 'come in the dining car.' We'd beaten them 2-0! But, after I'd taken the job, I thought: 'Right: I'm going to get this club sorted out.' And I did. Bobby Calder was a great wee man. He was a scout as such in those days. Half of Glasgow knew Bobby. He worked in the railways and all railwaymen, including porters, knew him. They'd say to him, 'Hey, Bobby, there's a good lad playing for so and so... Have a look at him.' So do you know what I used to dae? I used to tell Bobby to get a train carriage full of laddies and bring them up here. Glasgow boys. The Glasgow boys were wide. They were sharp. This was my philosophy. If there were two guys running across the road and there was a tramcar coming, the wee Glasgow guy would get there ahead of the Edinburgh one. That's how I used to think. That's what we used to do – get a load of laddies up from Glasgow and we'd put them up. I had this great Aberdeen supporter, Mr Esslemont, who had a hotel and a huge place at the back. We'd put camp beds down and the laddies would sleep there. They'd come down to training and on the Friday I'd go up to the hotel and give them all a fiver to spend for the weekend. They wouldn't have called the king their uncle, these laddies. That's how I used to operate.

COONEY: There was a certain acerbic side to you.

TURNBULL: Pardon?

COONEY: An acerbic side. Some people used to reckon you were a cross between Lucifer and Attila the Hun, and you were certainly on the front foot with directors, players and members of my profession. Would that be fair to say?

TURNBULL: Yes. Yes.

COONEY: You don't mind the assertion?

TURNBULL: No, no.

COONEY: Didn't one unfortunate director once take his dog to training?

TURNBULL: Yes.

COONEY: And what did you do?

TURNBULL: You don't want me to repeat it, do you?

COONEY: As much as can be properly broadcast.

TURNBULL: We were training and everybody had to concentrate. And I'm working on a fault that happened during this particular game. The next thing is this dog runs across (the pitch). And I hear someone shouting, 'Fifi! Fifi!' I says, 'I'll effin' Fifi you!' Oh, I went crazy. Someone says this was Mr Spain's dog. I says, 'Well, Mr Spain should have his dog on a lead. I don't want anyone interrupting me when I'm working.' Fifi: oh, I used to have this image of being hard, but the players will tell you I was a very fair person. I'd want them to have confidence in me. This I could do. I'd have them in the palm of my hand.

COONEY: Tell me, did you once whisker Joe Harper?

TURNBULL: Yeah.

COONEY: What was this for?

(We have arrived at the infamous sand lorry incident, where two members of the club commandeered a council vehicle and drove around the city)

TURNBULL: I signed Joey for Aberdeen. He was the king, as you well know. He liked to go out and mess about. Him and Ernie McGarr got a hold of a Corporation lorry of some description. I used to tell the players that there was one street in Aberdeen. Now when you walk along Union Street, you perhaps don't know anybody, but there's a big percentage of the people in Union Street know you. There's no place that you can hide. So I told them, 'Don't you ever let Aberdeen Football Club down.' Wee Joey could be cheeky at times, so I says, 'I'll effin' cheeky you, Joey.' So that was it.

COONEY: So you hit him?

TURNBULL: Yeah. And hard. And he rattled up against some furniture, you know. I shouldn't have done it – I know that. But that's life. He could have said, 'Right, I don't want to play for you.' But what did he do? He scored a hat-trick in his next game. You know, he come to me one day – he'd been involved in some accident with a door. He was living in digs. 'Boss', he says, 'there's a glass door when you get in the house...' It was broken. He had stitches. I says, 'Who are you tryin' to kid? You were drunk.' We were playing in a European game; we'd just got them into Europe. I says, 'Stitches, or no stitches, you're going out on that park!' Of course I spoke to the doctor and he says, 'Eddie – you're taking a chance.' I says, 'Okay, I'll take that chance.' He went out and scored two goals.

COONEY: Tell me about your relationship with Jock Stein, of Celtic. It was one scarcely made in heaven.

TURNBULL: The first time I met him was when he was a player – he was, how it's described in horse racing, a cart horse. He was a centre half and centre halves in those days were big and cumbersome. Anyhow, I played against him many times. But, do you remember when Willie Allison had a golf outing every year? I was at Queen's Park at the time. You know they are amateurs. Anyway, I'm out there with Peter Buchanan and Niall Hopper and of course Celtic and Rangers and all the other professional clubs were there. Big Stein comes up and says, 'Ah, here's Ned, here's the amateur – Ned doesn't need to be paid.' I never had a lot of time for Stein. I was never scared of him. No way. Eventually, I got on quite well with him.

But when I went to Aberdeen, playing Celtic, they'd gone 20-odd games unbeaten. (Playing-wise) I had a load of crap; young laddies. Up come Celtic. Most of them would be Lisbon Lions. Jim Craig, Gemmell, Simpson in goal, McNeill, Johnstone, all that lot. But we beat them. Do you know the directors' box? He (Stein) was on his side, I was on mine. When the game was finished, I was down sharp. You know Stein had a bad foot and he used to clip, clop, clip, clop, so I hears this as I go along the hallway to the dressing room. I thought, 'Slow down.' So I slows down. I waited till he came up. I says, 'How d'ye like it, big man? Hey, I'm no' scared of you, Stein. Or your counterpart at Ibrox, Waddell. You don't bother me, you two.'

But eventually, things smoothed out. I worked for him for a while with the Scotland side. Eventually, I got on all right with him. But he had no time for coaching, nor did Waddell at Rangers. They wouldn't allow any of their players to go to coaching courses. I was an avid coaching person. I loved coaching. I felt this was the start of a new era in British football. But they never allowed one player to go to the coaching course. Then, one day, there was a wee boy called

Davie Wilson, remember the wee left winger? He was the first Old Firm player to come to the course 'cos Stein and Waddell didn't believe in it. Yet the head coach in Italy at the time was the defensive man. Helenio Herrera. The *Scottish Daily Express* paid the fares of Stein and Waddell to go over to Italy and spend a week watching training. You check back the records. You'll find that's fact. Waddell didn't believe in coaching, 'cos he couldn't coach.

COONEY: That was a good reason not to believe in it. So, you were the pathfinder in that...

TURNBULL: Yeah, I was. But there was also Willie Ormond. Willie and I were great mates when we played (for Hibs). Willie actually introduced me to coaching. Back then it was held down in the Dumfries area. He went down and when he came back, he said, 'Ned, you'd love this. It's up your street.' He was right. I went down to Largs and passed my test.

The word 'legend' is applied, at times injudiciously, in today's world, but Eddie Turnbull possessed all the ingredients necessary to belong to popular myth. And I was grateful for just having the chance to meet him away from the battlefield. We had tumbled into conflict twice. Yet, that day in August, a former opponent had become a good companion. His eyes were twinkling as I left his home: he had delivered with aplomb and, by God, he knew it. 'It's been worth your time coming through, eh?' he chuckled. It certainly had. Eddie was a man who knew his worth and he was not shy in delivering estimations of it.

Two years later, on May 9 2011, I had occasion to revisit Edinburgh. Turnbull had died, aged 88. His funeral was held at the Mansfield Traquair. Like many of the matches in his career, there was a full house. The players who had served him at Hibs and Aberdeen were there as the football world said farewell to the great innovator. Martin Buchan delivered a eulogy on behalf of Aberdeen FC. They played over the public address system a short excerpt from my BBC Scotland interview. Within me, there was a ripple of emotion. When the Proclaimers sang 'Sunshine Over Leith', that ripple upgraded to a tsunami. But that in many ways was quite appropriate. Eddie Turnbull was a tsunami all on his own.

CHAPTER 17

No More Good Cop

I love interviews with footballers, those of a forensic nature rather than those that skim along the surface of reality and deliver platitudes. Football clubs, of course, have press officers and directors of communication and it is their job to squash controversy and encourage platitudes. But are they enhancing our television viewing or newspaper reading? Of course they're not: they become as boring as football matches that are played predominantly in midfield and end in the sterility of 0-0 draws. Hopefully, you'll find that these interviews, from my work on the Sunday Herald, *take you beyond the stereotypical. The first was published in October of 2009.*

YOU suspect only a laundry mat could provide the requisite capacity to process the dirty linen shared by Aberdeen legends Willie Miller and Joe Harper.

Harper – King of the Beach End when he was mobile; an enthusiastic proponent of blunt speaking now that he isn't – highlights their lack of relationship. 'It's my belief Willie doesn't have a friend in the world. He walks about the town like a lone soul. When he was a team-mate, I'd have run over broken glass for him, but I wouldn't have gone for a drink with him at night. I think that's the best way to sum it up. We'll never be friends. We speak, we say hello, but he'd never stop and have a five-minute conversation with me, and, to be fair, neither would I. As a matter of fact, I've been standing in the wee reception area at Pittodrie, talking to the girls, and he'll go straight past me and up the stairs. That doesn't bother me, though. In many respects, I feel the same about Willie as I do about Fergie. The fact is I couldn't give a shit about either of them.'

It's five years this month since Joe Harper directed himself towards such singular thinking. At the time, he'd suffered a stroke at an after-dinner speaking engagement in Fife. A few days later, his two daughters, Laura and Joanna, and former wife Fiona visited him in hospital. Just then, his son Ross telephoned him from France. The nurse asked Harper if she should bring the phone to his bed. The response was typical. No, he would rise and travel the short distance by Zimmer frame. When he reached the telephone after an epic struggle, he heard his son crying. So he began crying, and the girls joined in. Right then, Harper made a conscious decision to take a grip of a situation that was spiralling out of emotional control. That stroke perhaps made him the man he is today: an unrepentant man.

We shall return to his acidic association with Alex Ferguson much later. Right now, at our meeting in an Aberdeen hotel, the past makes way for the present: football is replete with absurdities and anomalies, and the Dons apparently have a share of the freehold on these. At this troubled club, still forlornly attempting to escape the shadow of Ferguson, Miller (797 appearances) is the Director of Football and paid £160,000 a year for that honour. Harper (199 goals), in contrast, is a match-day host and remunerated in comparative buttons to entertain the punters.

Understandably, 'meeters and greeters' are a reluctant breed when talking on the record about club matters, especially the deficiencies of their paymasters. Harper is the exception. Just over two weeks ago he described the Dons players as 'bottlers' for their abject surrender to Dundee in the Co-operative Insurance Cup, and despatched arrows towards chairman Stewart Milne and Miller. Those arrows were not autographed by Cupid. I suggest that the club might have pointed him towards the exit door for what might have been interpreted as an excessive outburst, but then remember this is the wee tough guy from Greenock whose prison cells were inevitably empty. Was he intimidated by Neanderthal centre halves? Was he ever! He'd slap their testicles, stand on toes and break noses if the mood took him.

While I'm considering the tricks of this violent trade, he is considering the implications of that outburst. 'It wouldn't have been a very clever thing for them to do, would it? Can you imagine what they would have done in the paper? "Aberdeen legend gets sacked for saying his piece." Not, mind, that it would worry me. I mean, they don't pay me enough to worry about that sort of thing. I know I could go somewhere else on a Saturday that would pay me a lot more. And that's with a Highland League club! I don't do it for the money, though. I do it because I like Aberdeen. I love entertaining people in my lounge. I was always wanting to score goals and entertain. I know a lot of times I wisnae the best player. For instance, Davie Robb worked his socks off many times and probably deserved the bonus more than I did. But I would be the one who'd stick it in the net with a minute to go to get us that bonus.'

Certainly, entertainment was forever Harper's forte. Still is. A small boy recently told him his hero was Darren Mackie. Harper replied that it was right to have heroes. 'Are you as good as Darren Mackie?' the lad asked. 'I think so, son,' teased Joey, 'but you've got to remember I'm 61!'

We're back with his evangelistic streak. 'That's where you get this hero sta-tus from, and I've carried that on all my life, even when football gave up on me and I gave up on football. I've always spoken to people. When sitting in restau-rants, I've put my fork and knife down and signed autographs, given them five or ten minutes of my time and left them happy. There are other people in this game, and you probably know who I'm talking about, who are the exact oppo-site. They can't be bothered.'

Is this, you wonder, a reference to Miller? Harper responds with silence and a non-committal smile. But it's a warm smile, unlike the one captured the other week when a showdown meeting between the men was scrambled at Pittodrie. The meeting was expertly monitored by the local paper, the *Evening Express*, for whom they are both columnists, but was seen by more objective elements as an attempt to mollify Harper before he crucified the club and its panjandrum any further. As if…

In the event, these heroes in red posed almost nose to nose for the photog-rapher. This stunted act of accord was significantly absent a year previously at a fans' forum organised by the same newspaper. Friction erupted between the two when Harper asked, fairly logically, if Miller should not start knocking on the doors of the oil companies' executives in order to bring in some much-needed revenue to an impoverished club.

With Miller claiming it wasn't his job to chap doors, this led to a tense exchange of semantics. The event was filmed and fed to *You Tube*. What viewers didn't see was the aftermath when their confrontation allegedly became almost too silly for semantics. Harper rejoins the story.

'Willie said, "Why don't you tell the fans about the time you stole the sand lorry?" In fact, we (Harper, Ernie McGarr and Derek Mackay; so, there was a third sand boy) didn't steal it but commandeered it while we were bladdered. We ended up throwing a bit of sand over cars. Details were in my autobiogra-phy last year. I said to him, "What's that got to do with it?"'

In spite of this latest meeting, at which Miller reportedly showed signs of humility, the men are scarcely scheduling an exchange of Christmas cards. Harper's questions remain unanswered: why was Mark McGhee brought in only to find his inheritance was tantamount to managerial pauperdom? Why were hundreds of thousands of pounds spent on the severance money for Jimmy Calderwood and Co when it could have bought three or four good quality players? Why was Calderwood sacked at that juncture? Maybe even more per-sonally: how do Miller and those other highly-paid subordinates of chairman Stewart Milne spend their days as the club totters from one fiasco to another? And when is the feel-good factor destined to return? Many club watchers are of the belief that Harper could be applying for his state pension before any answers are forthcoming.

'Listen, when we did that forum, I wasn't wanting to crucify Willie Miller. I was simply wanting answers. And one of the questions that had to be answered was why doesn't he go out and knock people's doors. With respect, I would want Willie Miller the legend at my door, not a sales girl. So what does he do for 160 grand a year? Hey, he got a £100,000 bonus for the year they got to the last 32 of Europe and to two semi-finals. Now I don't even class that as success. In fairness, I've always been the good cop in the newspaper, with Stewart McKimmie the bad one. But, to be honest, after the Dundee game I just couldn't f***ing put up with it any more. I just says to myself, "That's it. I'd better have a go at these people and see if we get any reaction."'

That reaction was a 0-0 draw at Rangers and then a 1-1 draw at Kilmarnock. But the festering sores will be paraded inside Pittodrie next Saturday, whether or not they are evident to the eye. As the club prepares to entertain Hearts, just imagine the factors involved. You can imagine directorial anger at Harper still lingering, and some players still sulking at one of their own turning on them so viscerally. The fans, meanwhile, who won't be party to this fascinating subtext, doubtless will be stumping up their twenty sovs to witness the kind of inexactitudes they could watch on local council playing fields. Harper? You cannot imagine his beauty sleep will be in any way compromised by the thought of impending confrontation. 'I don't think any of the players would come up and abuse me. I don't think any of them are brave enough. Obviously, my saying that they're bottlers has got to them, but if my saying that gets them doing what they did against Rangers, well…

'But, hey, don't let anyone kid you on: the Rangers game was shite! Aberdeen were shite! They could still have got beaten four or five nil. All it did was cover the cracks.'

Now that he has recovered from his illness, Harper seems partially free of fissures, too. Fighting an ongoing battle with his weight and also the fact that football has rendered his legs and knees obsolete where strenuous exercise is concerned, he performs 150 sit-ups in the morning, and another 150 in the evening. He swims, plays golf if he can find a buggy, drinks sparingly and shares a wonderful relationship with his second wife, Sheila. But, crucially, he is holding onto life. That life, he tells us with a smile, is Fergie free. He and Ferguson became enemies almost as soon as the latter joined Aberdeen as manager in 1978. Harper believes that jealousy in an earlier incarnation was a contributory factor. They first met as players on a Scotland world tour, when the 17-year-old scored ten goals in three matches and had the media forgetting Fergie and instead salivating over his replacement.

Harper was not impressed with his playing ability. 'He was all about wee steps and elbows. He didn't have any skill. When he came to Pittodrie, I'd scored 31 goals and 33 goals in those last two seasons, and yet he still kept saying to me, "You'll no' be here next season." He was desperate to get rid of me. As I says to him, "Listen, I didnae call myself The King. That was the fans." We'd had a row one day and his finger started getting closer and closer. I just grabbed it, bent it a bit and gave him it back. I said, "That's bad manners. I was brought up with good manners." The next day, I opened the door to the long corridor at Pittodrie and he'd opened a door at the other end. It was like the Gunfight at the OK Corral. As we walked towards each other, I'm thinking to myself, "Should I stiffen him?" He walked past and said, "I hope you're in a good mood today." I never even answered him. I just kept going. So, really, that was the start of it. There was never going to be any sweetness after that.'

Time has not removed the jagged edge of Harper's opinion. 'So when I see him now, I just ignore him. I have no interest in him and don't care what he does with his life. We had a Gothenburg night at the Aberdeen Conference Centre; Fergie had been at the top table and had ignored me when he came in, which was fine with me. At the end of the night, I was standing with these people; I've got my back to him and I hear him saying, "That's me away. Right, Wee Man, I'll see you later." I just stood there facing those people. Two of them said, "Your mate's calling you." I said I knew. And they're all laughing. That must have got right up his nose. Hey, the first time I was going back to Pittodrie after I'd left was for a European game. I was taking my two kids. I phoned up and asked to buy tickets. They asked me how many vouchers I had. I says, "Pardon?" Barbara says she was told to ask me about the vouchers. I told her to forget it. No, Fergie doesn't come into my reckoning. Great football manager, yeah, but he's not moved on as a person. He puts on a good show, like he comes up to Govan and does the Boys' Brigade thing. But I do that every day of my life in Aberdeen. Things for charity, things for sick children. I'm starting a race tomorrow morning in aid of a heart foundation. Our great manager Eddie Turnbull brought us up that way when we were young guys. He insisted we always appreciate others.

'I often think of the kids in children's hospitals who are probably going to die and did die on us. Bobby Clark, Davie Robb, Drew Jarvie and I always went in on our way home and give them programmes from the Saturday. There was this girl who was paralysed. The best way to put it was she was in one of those steam machines, with just her neck and head that showed. We bombarded her with scarves and programmes. One day she says, "Sorry, but I've got to tell you something… I'm no' interested in fitba!" So we asked her what she was interested in and she told us she loved Elvis Presley. We went away round the town and bought up everything concerning Elvis, so that she could just look at her hero. That lassie died.'

Harper's eyes are noticeably wet. 'Then there was this young boy who appeared fine every time we went to see him. He was always cheery and a real Aberdeen fan. Then, one day we went in and he wasn't there. One of the nurses said he was away home. "That's great," we chorused. "Not really," she said, "he's away home to die." A fortnight later we got a letter from his mum and dad just thanking us. I mean, thanking us. What had it cost us? Half-an-hour of our time, that's all.'

The 'laundry mat' must close. The 61-year-old man who's unafraid to wash dirty linen in public is leaving to prepare for his weekly radio show. *Up Front with Joe Harper*, as ever, promises to be a listening experience.

∗ ∗

This interview with former Dons favourite Dean Windass was conducted in October of 2007...
WHILE the 1995 version of Dean Windass was attempting to establish his credentials at Aberdeen, there was a distinct dichotomy in his life. The day-time was fine, the football no problem. Night-time, when he was full of beer and belligerence, was a different proposition. It terrified him. On these occasions, the past came back to punish him and transport him to illogical outposts. How, after all, does a young man forget nature's ugly statistics, such as a father's infidelity and the inevitable demolition of his parents' marriage? How does he shelve the memory of seeing his mother cry every day for three years? Does he simply dismiss her attempted suicide as an inescapable vicissitude?

Maybe, as the song suggests, he should look on the bright side of life, but there is no bright side here in the Granite City while he is chasing the beer monster. The wife and kids are in bed – he would never consider harming them – but Windass is taking his anger out on the mortgage; punching holes in walls and doors of his home. There is so much chaos. How can it be stopped?

God, these memories stink. The anger is a bile in his throat that threatens sickness. But how does he stop thinking about being turned out into the street by a surrogate step-father? Or his desperate under-age drinking culture that began in his early teens. And, don't forget the bed wetting that accompanied the binges. It's still there. Sure, according to the voting register, he is a man, but he's a man who pees in his pyjamas after a night on the beer; how does he cope with that little indignity?

There does not seem to be a contradiction in the life of the 2007 version of Dean Windass. Admittedly, he looks tough enough to punch holes in not just one house but a whole estate (one of my former colleagues wrote that he was the epitome of how one imagined a press ganger to look). Not to worry. The 2007 version has effected a peace deal between himself and the hostile world. It's as if he's called in the UN and sanctions have been passed against the demons. Whatever, night-time is no longer a call-centre for terror. Windass has shut down on violence in the home. There are no imprints of his fist on walls or doors; no soiled bed clothes, either. Day-time? As ever, that's champion. He is 38 and still playing football to a high standard with Hull City in the Coca Cola Championship. Having served managerial masters like Bryan Robson, Steve McClaren and Neil Warnock, and played for Bradford City, Middlesborough and Sheffield United, he's still scoring goals. He's taken his coaching badges yet he insists he will play until he is 40. He is portrayed as a character, and therefore provides a veritable dartboard for the arrows of the opposing fans. They call him, rather simply, a fat bastard. Provocative stuff, eh? Not when you've spent years in the stinking fox-hole of your own imagination. No, when insulted nowadays, Windass smiles and playfully shows his belly to his persecutors. Their scorn is more than music to his ears, it's a concerto. It means he is still important enough to figure in their calculations. He can hurt them. He's still a player.

Straight to the point, he asks how long the interview is going to take and seems somewhat exasperated when you tell him it will be at least 20 minutes. You suspect it is inadvisable to exasperate Windass. Nevertheless, we'll go carefully hereabouts and concentrate on less inflammatory matters for starters. Like the issue over his weight. Words are not wasted. 'It's got to the stage that when they stop calling me a fat bastard, I'll start worrying,' he insists. 'Then I'll know I can't be playing f***ing well! To be honest, it just spurs me on some more. I have a laugh with the crowd. When you walk into the pub and meet someone you haven't seen for ages, the first thing they say is, "You're not fat, are you?" No, I'm not, but television puts weight on. I'm 13 stone. I've always been chunky. Wayne Rooney's my sort of build. He's not fat, either. That's just the way you're built, you can't f***ing help that. But I eat the right foods. I'm not the quickest, but I've always been up there with the runners pre-season.

'The thing about McClaren was that you had to be under 10 per cent body fat, and I was. The trouble came when I put my kit on, I'd look a fat bastard. I couldn't do f***ing owt about it. I've had loads of supporters come up to me and say, "f***ing hell, yeah, we hate you but we wish you played for our team." That's the way I like it. No, the one thing that really pisses me off in this life is people talking about my weight. I probably look a bit lumpy on the pitch, but listen, when I'm naked in the bedroom and having sex with my wife, she says I've got the best body in the world!'

Okay, that's broken the ice quicker than climate change. Let's make progress towards the jugular and talk about the past which used to come at Windass in remorseless waves. Let's talk about this cruel sea of remembrance and how he turned its tide. Let's talk about the book he has written – Deano. The anatomy of a disturbed childhood is there in plain and simple language in this rather remarkable book. So you start on a home life that started to fracture when he spotted his beloved father with another woman. The cosy, familial world fell apart when he was 13. As he lay in his bed alongside his dad, he was informed of an impending divorce. Predictably, he burst into tears. How did he cope with all that? He is brisk and matter of fact, and the impression given is that he has already taken the shovel out once to dig up his life and he may not be too keen on resorting to this form of manual labour again.

'Look,' he says, 'it happens to lots of people. There's thousands of kids whose parents have split up.'

Not too many are able to write about it, or would want to write about it in such graphic terms, you point out. 'No, maybe not. But I didn't purposely go out to hurt anybody or upset anybody. I just got asked the questions and I answered them as honestly as I could. Hey, I had a decent upbringing as a kid, but then things started going a bit pear-shaped when me mum and dad split up. It wasn't very nice. Mentally, it hurt me a little bit. It affected my life. I could have gone either one way or the other. Fortunately, I went the right way.'

So, regarding the intolerable behaviour in Aberdeen, what saved him from taking the cinder track? 'Well, one day you wake up and know you can't carry on like this. First and foremost, you have to consider your wife and your kids. You've taken on the responsibility for having them, now you've got to face up to that responsibility. My football was going very well at Aberdeen, and I was scoring a lot of goals. Away from the park, though, I didn't know how to do it, but I wanted to punish people for what had happened in my earlier life. Strange. I was never aggressive towards anybody. I was never in nightclubs, wanting to punch somebody because they looked at me funny. The only time I got that way was when I got home and seethed about things by myself. Having had those few extra pints, it was then that I sat and thought. I was punishing my wife and myself, really.'

Help, however, was so close there wasn't even a corner to turn. Windass's wife, Helen, an athlete, trained every day with the Aberdeen fitness coach, Stewart Hogg. She mentioned her husband's extraordinary behaviour to him and he suggested a meeting with an Edinburgh psychologist called Richard Cox. Windass, initially, was not very keen on opening a file marked private and confidential.

'It's hard when you have got to go and tell a total stranger how much your personal life is affecting you, but it was the best decision I'd ever taken in my

life. At first, I suppose I got a bit paranoid by thinking, "Do I have to go and
see a shrink?" But it wasn't like I imagined. Richard just sat me down in front
of him and said, "Tell me what you think your problem is." I opened up to him
and shed a few tears. It was the best thing I ever did. The problem was I lived a
strange existence because I had never opened up to anybody. I wasn't telling anybody about things that had gone on. When I was going out having a drink with
the lads or my wife, this thing was always in the back of my mind. After I had
expressed all these feelings properly to Richard, everything was fine after that.

'This was early doors at Aberdeen, but I had the problem when I was a
young kid and had started drinking heavily. I was punching walls at Hull when I
was a kid. But I didn't have the back-up until I went to Aberdeen. By then, I was
sort of questioning myself and wondering, "Am I going mad?" Sometimes you
wondered why you needed to go and see this man. But Stewart said, "Nobody
will know about it. Whatever you say to him will be confidential." Even Stewart
didn't know what I said to Richard. He didn't ask me and I never told him.

'Eventually, the solution was simple. I didn't even need to stop drinking.
Richard told me I didn't have a problem with the beer, but advised me just to
tone it down a bit. And that's what I did. I haven't had that problem since. The
anger is gone. I still go out, have a laugh with the lads and a few drinks, but my
wife doesn't worry about me going out any more, like she used to at Aberdeen.
The bed weeing is also a thing of the past. Touch wood, I haven't wet the bed
for 12 years. So obviously what Richard said to me worked.'

You suspect Windass wants this strand of the interview to end. That's
implicit in what he next says. He tells you he has never read the book. Obviously, he knew what he had put in it, but he'd never actually picked it up and
read it. 'And I never would now. I've put it to bed. That's my past. I don't want
to go back there no more. I've got through it, I've moved on and I've done well.
And now I want to go on and progress even further, play as long as I can, and
then hopefully go into coaching and management. And, after this interview with
you, I'll never speak about it again. People will read it, so what's the point of
asking me about it? As I say, that's the end of that life and I move on.'

So, Windass being Windass, you do as he suggests and explore the other terri-
tories in his existence. His proclivity for battle, for instance. You consult his record
– on one memorable occasion for the Dons he picked up three red cards against
Dundee United –and note that he doesn't exactly scatter at the sound of gunfire.

You imagine your reward is a smile that is so small that it is under-nourished. 'Listen, it's not big and it's not clever to fight, is it? I'm a family man, but
when I go to work I do my job and do it to the best of my ability. I've never
walked away from anything. I received death threats when I got sent off against
Bournemouth last season. Now that was genuinely worrying. But the one thing

you learn from life is that you don't let people affect you. Everybody don't like Dean Windass; there's a lot of people who do and a lot who don't. But those who don't like me don't bother me. Like having the satisfaction about having f***ing proved them wrong. If people walk up to me and call me a twat, then fair enough, I'm a twat. I ain't bothered. I don't go around calling people. If I've got a problem to say to anyone, I'll do it to their face.'

Had the football experience at Aberdeen been good for him? 'Yeah, it was the best move I made in me life. I needed to get away from Hull and further my career. It was a massive move at the time. I never wanted to leave Aberdeen. It was circumstances, with the man who bought me, Roy Aitken, getting sacked and Alex Miller coming in and not really fancying me. But I tell you it was the best two and a half years of my life. I enjoyed my football, my wife liked living in Aberdeen, I had loads of friends outside football and we still keep in touch. I still go up every year and have a drink with me mates. Every summer. I really enjoyed the place, loved living there. I didn't want to go, but it was time to go.'

And what about those three red cards? 'Hey, it wasn't really three reds. I got one, and then I got done for swearing at the referee and punching the corner flag. I got a massive ban for it. It's not something I am proud of. I let Roy down. I knew he was under pressure. I was too fired up for it and paid the price. That probably cost me my Aberdeen career. But you do silly things in your life and I'll probably do more silly things.'

The 2007 version of Dean Windass has given me not 20 but 32 minutes of his time. Considering what went on in his past life and the fact that he has a lot of catching up to do, it is very precious time.

* *

This last interview, with popular Icelander Kari Arnason, was conducted in February 2012.

KARI ARNASON'S INTERPRETATION of paradise was spending two years on America's West Coast, where the concentration was on wine, women and Pink Floyd song.

Attending Gonzaga University and studying for a business degree, he and four other aspirational hedonists shared a house in which reality was rarely confronted. A mirror image of Jason Biggs comes graphically to mind hereabouts.

An exaggeration? Not according to Kari. 'Yeah, we're talking American Pie here. When you look at the films they make about college life in America, it's actually like that. So, yeah, I have lived the life. No regrets.'

Regrettably, it's time to bid bye, bye to American Pie and say hello to Pittodrie potpourri. Almost a decade later, Kari Arnason occupies the unforgiving world of professional football and is the subject of an intriguing political battle that is rippling through the corridors of Aberdeen FC.

To summarise: the Dons have travelled to their fiscal extremities to accommodate his desires. They've offered him £2,400 a week – a salary only previously enjoyed by Paul Hartley and Zander Diamond – plus a living allowance and the gold dust of a three-year contract.

Now we know Arnason has rejected this deal. We also know that those delegated to influence his fortunes, in their naivety, published wage demands of £5,000 a week, together with his curricula vitae, on the Internet (the brochure, apparently, has now been removed).

What is not known, until now, is that an innovative plan has been formulated (I understand it to be manager Craig Brown's brainchild) to have the player sponsored for approximately £2,000 a week by one of the many locally-based companies – those, it should be pointed out, that continue to defy the trend of the country's economy.

The targets? One of the oil conglomerates, perhaps. Then, perhaps even more logically, there's Aberdeen Asset Management. Apart from having two directors on the football club board (Martin Gilbert and Hugh Little), the financial behemoth already has an extensive sponsorship portfolio, including golfers such as Colin Montgomerie. Arnason would fulfil an ambassadorial role for the proposed benefactor.

You might think such enterprise would be applauded, for there is precious little of it available in this raw corner of the North-East. However, it is claimed some members of the boardroom are offering robust resistance to the suggestion. Apparently, they fear this would set a precedent and engender disharmony in the dressing room.

But is it realistic in this age to dedicate yourself to the theory that all men are equal? And wouldn't it provide an incentive for other squad members? What would prevent them seeking individual sponsorship if their ability merited it?

So let's discuss this Arnason meritocracy in more detail. Brown views him as an all-purpose player who has the ability to score spectacular goals and make defenders quiver with his ability to throw the ball farther than many can kick it. He also sees someone who takes his fitness very seriously. 'I try to have a good training regime,' Arnason concedes. 'When you're not naturally the quickest, you've got to do something extra. Drink? Yeah, I like a glass of red wine, but I'm not by any means what the British would call a heavy drinker.'

The manager predicts a long career for his employee. He says the midfielder will eventually take a logical step backwards to centre half, where he has the capability to play until he's 40; he will become, in essence, another Davie Weir. This confidence surprises Arnason, but not for long. 'I'm not sure if I can, but if he thinks it, who am I to argue? I think he knows a little more about football than I do.'

An application of psychology brings him nicely to the boil before each game. 'Is there a better player than you in that other team?' Brown whispers in his ear. 'If there is, I've yet to see him. You should be the master of this midfield!' The mantra doubtless will be repeated in the Fir Park dressing room today when Aberdeen travel to Motherwell to attempt to further their Scottish Cup ambitions.

Whatever the outcome of this afternoon's proceedings, you can sympathise with Brown's pursuit of external finance. Aberdeen, during his stewardship, have begun to deliver an impression of progress. They dare not regress now because the supporters are still sceptical of the club's ambition and, as evidenced by their dwindling numbers, are not willing to forgive the horrendous past any time soon.

In Arnason, they have not only a cult hero but a player who thrives on long odds. 'I honestly believe you can go into any game and win it. You just got to be organised and then you can beat any team in the world.'

Once upon a glorious time, of course, that last statement could have applied to the Dons but no longer, not in this year of 2012 when the club clings to every penny as if it were a lifebelt in a Force Ten gale. Arnason feels the time is right for them to speculate, even if not on him. 'Can they be restored to their former greatness? Yeah, I think the time is now, actually. Rangers are in administration and Celtic are not as good as they were a few years ago, so the time is now for Aberdeen to try and gamble a bit, without going into admin.

'They've got a great manager – he's an old fox – and we've actually got a great squad. We've been unlucky with injuries. We need a little bit extra. If they could secure that, I definitely think we'd be up there.'

Arnason, of course, is familiar with the iniquities of administration. He spent eight unpaid months at Plymouth and was sacked when he refused to sign a document that allegedly promised to levy additional fiscal hardship upon him. He even had an even more impecunious colleague living with him for some time. 'There was no goodwill. It was an absolute disgrace. Administration means that your life becomes ruled by hope.'

He pauses but quickly rejoins the argument. 'There is a black side to football. People generalise about footballers. Sure, the Premier League is glamorous in that you live in a massive mansion and drive about 18 cars – if that is your cup of tea. Personally, it don't interest me. You could say I'm not materialistic, but it's probably that I can't afford what people would call a proper car. I drive a Mini Cooper S and I love it.'

If he has his transport sorted out, what about that unsigned contract? 'The thing is I've said all along to Aberdeen that I haven't said I'm not going to sign. I'm just not going to sign the contract in front of me at the moment. In my mind, there's still a negotiation there. I don't know if Aberdeen are on the same page regarding that.

'But the things said in the media have been blown way out of proportion. It's been quite frustrating. I've been thinking about it a lot lately and it's been quite a burden on me, 'cos obviously you care what the fans think. I only hope they don't think I'm a greedy bastard.'

Those looking for negativity concerning the man do not require explicit directions: like all gifted players, there is a whiff of arrogance about Arnason. Even people close to him claim he has an occasional tendency to look down on lesser mortals: they vouch that he can be a bit supercilious at times. If there is contempt in him, it is not obvious to me. But it's apparent that there's also a free spirit lurking within him, harking back to his days when American Pie was in the oven. 'Listen, if you take yourself too seriously, you're going to end up with an ulcer. So the thing is to keep it as light as can be.'

That may be so, but he is certainly capable of being controversial. 'My brother used to support Liverpool,' he says. 'I liked certain players and disliked others. I liked those who don't have the natural physical attributes. For example, you will remember Jan Molby. He was a fat player, but he was absolutely brilliant. Players like that appeal to me, not those like Ronaldo, who can run 100 metres in under ten seconds.'

A cursory study of Arnason's roots tells you he was born in Gothenburg, host city to Aberdeen's memorable European Cup Winners' Cup triumph over Real Madrid. But you'd better be prepared to run like Ussain Bolt if you call him Swedish. 'No, I'm not,' he snaps. 'Never say that. I'm as Icelandic as they come. My parents are Icelandic. It was just that my old man (he's a doctor practising rheumatology) was studying in Gothenburg at the time.'

He delivers his definition of being Icelandic with similar despatch. 'It's just being proud of my heritage. In the core, it is a working class people. The credit crunch put a bad light on Iceland: there was a lot of corruption and what (some) people were doing was horrible. But it's a hard-working nation and, in the tradition of my parents and grandparents, you just get on with it. I like to think I'm carrying on the tradition.'

Today, you've glimpsed the complicated life of Kari Arnason. Whether that life continues in Aberdeen remains to be seen. But one thing is incontestable: there were no such complications when Kari helped himself to a slice of American Pie.

CHAPTER 18

Griffiths No More

MANY PEOPLE BELIEVE that our beautiful game of football is devoid of any moral compass, but I'm about to relate a story that somewhat destabilises that theory. I present the case history of Craig Brown, Leigh Griffiths and Aberdeen Football Club. In the summer of 2011, Griffiths was a Wolves player who had been purchased for £150,000 from Dundee a few months earlier. The then leader of the Wolves pack, Mick McCarthy, had made minimal use of his talents and was seeking to loan him out. The preference was that he stayed in England, but it appeared that the managers in that country, perhaps mindful of the baggage occupying the Griffiths carousel, were inclined to ignore that preference (I shall expand on this matter in a moment). The only alternative was that the striker returned to Scotland – although this was an eventuality that allegedly filled McCarthy with apprehension. Apparently, he didn't favour his employee going anywhere near the honey pot of his native Edinburgh, where friends and temptation had an unfortunate habit of coalescing.

Back then, Darren Jackson was fulfilling the role of a diligent football agent, and thus was tasked with securing for his client a new and welcoming, if temporary, environment. Aberdeen presented the perfect solution. Their management team comprised Craig Brown and Archie Knox, a couple of guys in the business of actively discouraging inappropriate behaviour or indeed any departure from professionalism. Jackson duly contacted his former Scotland manager, who was still attempting to insert the words 'Aberdeen FC' and 'respectability' into one coherent sentence after the ill-fated Mark McGhee reign. Griffiths was more than anxious to come north, according to Jackson. Normally, anyone placing temptation such as this in front of Brown would be liable to have his hand amputated. But caution monopolised the mind of the old fox. The antenna that had guided him through years of successful international management began to quiver uncontrollably.

We should properly contextualise matters hereabouts. Jackson's attempt to sell the Griffiths brand equated to a thirteenth Labour of Hercules. his player might have been able to kick a ball harder, more accurately and ingeniously than most of his Scottish contemporaries, but his reputation as a social maverick had gone viral within the rather incestuous confines of the game. Thus, he had found himself seared by the branding iron of consequence. He was a professional footballer by name, but his behaviour defined him equally as a part-time love god (by then, he had two children by different mothers – and more were on the way). If this were not enough, there was a hair-trigger temperament to consider. There remained a disturbing irreverence in his attitude towards his seniors.

We return to Brown and temptation. He was vulnerable to it at that moment, for he was seeking a potent goal-scorer (this was prior to the discovery of gold in Niall McGinn) who could provide that spark that is vital to any team concentrating on blind ambition. He asked his closest colleague for guidance in the matter and Knox's enthusiasm almost bowled him over. Knox, of course, was someone who didn't know or understand the true meaning of trepidation. However, the prudence that had accompanied Brown's survival in the killing fields of football kicked in; second and perhaps third opinions would be sought. He turned to his goalkeeping coach, Jim Leighton, who had experience of Griffiths at international level, and his part-time forwards coach, Jocky Scott, who'd been the player's manager at Dundee.

Leighton almost shuddered as he related one particular anecdote: Griffiths' rambunctious past was about to confront him. Trying to give the striker the benefit of a wisdom derived from 91 Scotland caps (including 45 clean sheets) and halcyon periods at both Aberdeen and Manchester United, Leighton claimed he'd attempted to impart one particular pearl concerning one-on-one situations. He advised Griffiths to renounce the daredevil option, and instead to put the ball across the goalie rather than attempt to beat him at his near post. The striker's alleged response didn't encourage further equable dialogue. 'You shut the f*** up! You're (just) the goalkeeping coach!' Legends tend to frown on imputations such as this. Leighton confided that had it not been for a hamstring injury he was carrying at the time, he would have returned this insolent pup to the boarding kennels. 'I'd have smashed him,' he reportedly said.

Whatever, the manager found himself impaled on the horns of a dilemma. Griffiths, impudence aside, would have guaranteed him goals. Alternatively, what impact would it have on a club that he was patiently reconstructing? The dressing room was scarcely an admirable template: Paul Hartley had allegedly described it to be the worst in his living memory.

Step forward, Jocky Scott; he had even more expert knowledge than Leighton. As Dundee manager, he'd signed Griffiths from Livingston in 2009. Remembering his various lively consultations with the player, he normally favoured describing Griffiths as 'difficult'. But a far more definitive appraisal emerged as he chatted with the Dons' not Dons boss. His opening gambit was spectacular enough: touching Griffiths with a bargepole might even be considered unacceptable, he suggested. Brown, reasoning that high principles are not always appropriate when the devil drives, threw the dice one more time: he asked Scott if he believed he and Archie Knox could manage him. The response was emphatic. 'Nobody could manage that bastard!'

Brown, a man of countless disciplines, reluctantly decided that Griffiths was not the man for either him or team spirit. Sod's Law was invoked thereafter. The player subsequently signed a loan deal for Colin Calderwood at Hibs and, nine months later, he scored the winning goal against the Dons in the semi-final of the Scottish Cup. By then he was under the stewardship of Dubliner Pat Fenlon. There remains a commendable honesty in Brown. 'If Leigh had been in our side in the semi, we'd have been in the final. So that puts me in the wrong, then. Still, life is all about having certain standards. If you don't have them, you're nothing.'

Late on a Friday afternoon in Aberdeen, I'm listening to the raison d'être of this remarkable septuagenarian. He has invited me to his luxury apartment at Kepplestone. He may be retired from the battlefield of management, but he's now a non-executive director at Aberdeen and so his race is not run yet. He acts in an (unpaid) ambassadorial role for the club. Tonight, he is talking at an event at Aberdeen's only five-star hotel and he still has some preparatory work to put in. I'm wondering whether I may have appeared at an inconvenient moment, but he dismisses my fears. He is not the sort of man to break promises.

He's taken survival something close to black belt status, although there has been some important help given along the way. When he finally gained managerial autonomy with Scotland, he was called by SNP politician Margo MacDonald; they knew each other from their schooldays, both having attended Hamilton Academy. She said there was something she needed to tell him in person, emphasising, 'Get yer arse roon tae my office.' Brown did as he was bid and Margo was soon as bold as her politics. 'I've been listening tae ye since ye got that job. The punters don't like you being polite. Ye need to be far more gallus! That's what the fans want.'

The advice was inculcated and acted upon. Invariably, the politician in him played the part of white-collar respectability in front of the public, but 'gallus' was a profitable alternative when the occasion demanded. 'Sub-consciously, I became less measured in what I said. You cannot succeed in football unless you have an inner core of hardness.' This inner core escorted Scotland to the Euro 96 in England and the 1998 World Cup in France, feats that none of his successors have succeeded in emulating. His benign features, redolent of a peace-loving man, were at odds with reality. At one point, Stewart Hillis, the Scotland doctor, stressed that the players were afraid of him. He couched it in the uncompromising terms of Margo MacDonald. 'You've got some tongue. They're shitting themselves!'

You suspect there were several moments of incontinence as Brown impressed himself on his players. There were no second chances. Even big names found themselves bombed if they didn't fit Brown's facsimile of professionalism. Gough was a prime example. 'I didn't pick him and he knew why. Both Walter Smith and David Murray knew why, but I never publicised it, despite Gerry McNee asking me (to do it) every weekend. But I don't talk badly about anybody like that: I was offered £60,000 by the Daily Record if I told the full story regarding Richard Gough. In the end, I got £20,000 from the Daily Express. No revelation about RG, though. I simply said in my book: 'He's not the kind of man with whom I'd like to run a quick single.'

When he finally arrived at Pittodrie, having stopped off at Preston and Motherwell (he held several advisory appointments in between), Brown was importing years of vast experience. He'd seen the Dons at close quarters in January earlier that year and left unimpressed. 'We'd taken Motherwell up here and beaten them 3-0. We were putting young boys on at the end to give them a bonus. Archie was mad with me. "Whit are you puttin' them on for? We might lose a goal." Brown smirked. "What, against this team? We'll never lose a goal." So, when the offer came in I was wondering why we would want to go to Aberdeen. We had a far better team at Motherwell. But we came because Fergie phoned us. I think Stewart Milne had got in touch with him. He rang me in the car. "They tell me there's a chance you're going to Aberdeen. What a fantastic club it is; the potential is unlimited." I said I wasn't going. He suggested I reconsider. I said I'd seen their team and I didn't fancy it.'

The Fergie endorsement stayed in Brown's mind, however, and a bitter dispute with Leeann Dempster, the Motherwell chief executive, merited it further consideration. He rang Aberdeen and asked if he could change his mind. The Dons directors travelled to Glasgow for a meeting the next day, but there was another obstacle to hurdle. Archie Knox was friendly with the man who'd been deposited in the Aberdeen out tray: Mark McGhee. They'd worked together at Millwall. He told Brown, 'I cannae go there without speaking to Mark. It'll look as if we've stabbed him in the back.'

Brown admired the honourable stance – normally, you'd find honour in football only slightly more often than a sighting of the Yeti. But, ultimately, there was nothing to concern him. McGhee gave Knox his blessing and, suddenly, Aberdeen had a new managerial coupling. They travelled to Tynecastle to watch their new team in action, but despaired at the lack of action from their new side. They lost 5-0 to Hearts and were propping up the SPL. Brown observed to his colleague: 'This lot need a rocket up their arse'.

No one was required to travel as far as Cape Canaveral for the launch of that rocket. The Brown-Knox tag team went to work, sorting out a dressing room notorious for cliques and careless whispers. The side wrestled 13 points out of a possible 18. The remedial guys saw to it that the rejuvenation process for a depressed team was under way. But the fiscal delinquency of the nineties was tantamount to having a herd of elephants in the room; there was no remedy for cost-cutting. The overdraft was spiralling on a weekly basis and every penny became important. So, important players were sold at every opportunity and high earners encouraged to run down their contracts. Chris Maguire, Zander Diamond, Sone Aluko, Richard Foster, Jack Grimmer and Paul Hartley left in 2011; Kari Arnason and Fraser Fyvie followed a year later. They had taken in £2million to appease the banks, but the consequence was that form began to dip alarmingly once again.

And yet, after a season and a half of fighting against the ramifications of debt, that crazy parabola began to swing upwards again. One sunny October day in 2012, Aberdeen travelled to Rugby Park during an unbeaten run which would last for 13 games and take them to Premier League prominence. I found myself spoilt for options, with one eye fixed on a delicious Killie Pie, the other on the possibility of not only a renaissance but the emergence of a legitimate star. Really, it was no contest; I was obliged to concentrate fully on some of the most engaging football I'd witnessed for ages. With the pugnacious Ryan Fraser going past defenders as if they were statues, it was apparent that wing wizardry was back in vogue. The statues occasionally came to life and kicked him, but there was a wonderful resilience about Fraser; he would simply dust himself down and go again. However, this was not the only game in town. Niall McGinn, once of Celtic and the subsequent alternative to Griffiths, had a glorious habit of ghosting into significant central positions in attack. He scored that day in a 3-1 win, but then he scored as often as not. That season, he would claim 21 goals in 40 appearances. The dynamism of Jonny Hayes had still to be factored in, so I left Rugby Park surfing the waves of optimism.

Now, it should be said that not everyone in the city had approved of Brown's appointment. In fact, he seemed to polarise supporters' opinions. The younger elements, dismayed by his seniority, irreverently christened him Pa Broon. Theirs was no country for old men, they insisted. Others took the criticism to another level, claiming that he was too negative in his approach and consequently responsible for too many drawn games. Some, like myself, saw it in a different perspective. For my money, he introduced much-needed backbone to Pittodrie and imported some of the most influential players to arrive in the North East for many years and all without spending a penny on transfer fees: McGinn, Hayes, Arnason and Mark Reynolds. He also brought the leadership qualities of Russell Anderson back from Derby for another spell. Therefore, a tighter and more disciplined ship, one with a conspicuous absence of mutiny, was sailing towards friendlier waters. It was time for me to test those waters: I was the first national newspaper journalist permitted to speak to Ryan Fraser.

It's 30 October 2012 and Craig Brown invites me into a newly-painted home dressing room before my interview with the boy destined for the stars. During my working life, I've been in the manager's room and the boardroom, but this is something else: I'm fraternising with red and white gloss and, of course, history. Fraser is next: he represents the present and the future. He is reminiscent of Pat Nevin; he's brave, doesn't dive and is two-footed; crosses better with his left foot, shoots better with his right. What more could a manager desire? More than two and a half years ago the youngster had been presented with a two-year contract for sweetie money. Or, in his case, pizza money. The youngster was then offered another year, but he was so desperate to sign that there wasn't even an agent in sight. All he wanted to do was play football for Aberdeen. Now, he's probably pulling in around £500 a week basic, but this will be doubled, maybe almost trebled with bonuses and appearance money. I'm wondering: will he be as keen to sign when he is presented with his new contract? Chief executive Duncan Fraser is handling negotiations.

Our young hero reveals that his father is an electrician in the oil business and consequently he has spent seven years in the Middle East before returning to Blighty and becoming involved in football. He's never heard of Charlie Cooke, but offsetting this is the fact that he's a nice, self-deprecatory kid who hates seeing himself on the tv. He's unnatural – head disappearing into shoulders and mini legs going like crazy. There are compensatory factors, of course. 'I just do what my feet tell me. If it comes off, great. If it doesn't, well, I'll just try again.' I tell him it looks great from where I'm sitting. The kid is living the dream. 'Life is not full of problems for me. The best bit, apart from the football, is getting a Domino's pizza on a Tuesday.'

I ask him if he is a loyal person. He tells me he hopes he is. I point out to him that Fraser Fyvie and Jack Grimmer have relocated recently. Is he likely to stay around learning, or will ambition take him elsewhere? 'No,' he stresses. 'I've still got a lot of things to learn as a young footballer. I can't just say I've played a handful of games and that I've made it. I can't think like that. I've nowhere near made it. There are so many things I could do better, which Archie and the gaffer can show me.'

Sadly, Brown and Knox were not going to be given the chance to further that education. On December 7 2012, the ball game was declared a bogey. Aberdeen FC experienced the type of mutinous moment they dreaded more than most. Ryan Fraser, now advised by the Platinum Group from Dublin, rejected the offer of a new contract. His initial eagerness to play for his hometown team had apparently evaporated. It was said he held a vision that was predicated not so much on how he could learn but how much he could earn. England certainly beckoned him with guarantees of wealth. He would earn thousands of pounds per week down south instead of the comparative Pittodrie pittance. Some fans were highly critical of his desire to move, citing greed, but let's bring reality into the equation here. How many of those fans would have turned down a pay rise of something like three or four hundred per cent? Not many, I wager. So, almost six weeks later, Fraser moved to Eddie Howe's Bournemouth, then an extremely ambitious League One club, for the relatively modest fee of £350,000. He was 18 years of age and had made 23 appearances for the club.

It was alleged that former Aberdeen striker Steve Lovell, Eddie Howe's brother in law, had alerted Bournemouth to the emergence of a 'smashing young player' and had picked up a finder's fee for it. In my book, no-one needed to be a talent scout to predict a great future for Fraser. Anyone could have seen through a black-out blindfold that there was a vast potential in this 5ft 4in frame. This is what mystifies me about Aberdeen's part in affairs: Willie Miller, as Director of Football, handed him a two-year contract and followed it up with a one-year deal. Why had the term not been made longer, say for three years? This, at least, would have given the club more protection when they were negotiating a fee. You might argue that this is pure speculation on my part, given the propensity of young footballers of failing to match their potential. I would remind you that speculation leads to accumulation. Sometimes you've got to gamble. But, of even more relevance, what were the vital clauses in the contract between the two clubs? Had Aberdeen asked for extra money when the player was capped for Scotland? Or, when he had played a certain amount of games for Bournemouth? And, even more crucially, what would Aberdeen receive if, say, the player was sold on to a bigger club for multi-millions? All will be revealed when I talk to Duncan Fraser: I have put in a request for an interview.

I do not have long to wait. One morning, the phone rings and the chief executive is at the other end of the line. He tells me he is perfectly happy to walk me through the whole episode. 'It's no' something we've discussed (in public). There was a lot of criticism at the time; we tend to close ranks in terms of that, but let me be very candid with you.'

Now, I love the sound of the word 'candid'. Transparency is at hand. Hallelujah! The story unfolds: Ryan Fraser signed on initially in July 10 2010. Willie Miller could see the spark in him. Around March of 2012, Miller, Brown and Duncan Fraser were reviewing which of the youngsters would be given another contract. It was decided that young Ryan, or Rysie, as he was known, would be given one year only. Why only a year? It was claimed he had a bit to go; a bit to prove. Perhaps the spark had vanished – it happens with young men. 'Craig would have played him three or four times in a year and a half. I think he had a dip in the second year. It came down to the fact that they offered him a one-year deal when they could have offered him longer. But there were some doubts. I can't tell you what they were, but those guys saw him every week.'

That contract was signed in May. He was given a very small increase, as he'd only been involved in five games. Importantly, the vital spark duly re-appeared less than three months later. Fraser was one of a bunch of kids who impressed in pre-season friendlies in Germany. That form was taken into the league campaign; you imagine by now the Dons' executive was experiencing frissons of unease.

'Rysie had an incredibly good spell and played 21 games in total that season. I remember, in a few games, he took a helluva pounding – there were really physical games against Inverness and Hibs – and he was getting treatment that people got maybe 20-odd years ago.'

Around late September, early October, contract offers were made to seven youngsters: Jamie Smith, Jamie Masson, Jordan Brown, Joe Shaughnessy, Declan McManus, Nicky Lowe and Fraser. 'We made it clear to them the terms were very similar, the only variation being the length of the contract. Some had one, two or three-year deals. All the lads signed pretty quickly, except Ryan. A month later, he indicated that he had an agent, the Platinum Group, and their expectation was at the top end of our club earning-wise. When you're bringing through a young player and he's only had a few games at the top level, that's not a process that's going to work. We had a couple of meetings, face to face, and made two or three offers that would have increased his wages by up to four times. It would also have given him a guaranteed 50 per cent increase over the next few years. But the beginning of December, the agent made it clear he just wanted to go down south. It wasn't about money; it was more that he wanted to live down south. He was injured at that time.'

Duncan Fraser says Aberdeen were disappointed, but I'd imagine the word 'devastated' would be a more appropriate description. The player was now free to go in the early summer of 2013. Because he was under 23 years of age, he would become the subject of cross-border compensation. In other words, the bigger the club, the more money for Aberdeen. But to which footballing behemoth would he go? Bournemouth, then in League One, declared an interest in him in January. This was infiltrating lead-balloon territory with some Pittodrie folk. Duncan Fraser recalls, 'Now at the time, people were suggesting, "Bournemouth? It's not possible." I thought that was brutally unfair, for something struck me at the back of my head.'

This was the realisation that the manager, Eddie Howe, was young and already showing signs of vast potential and the owner, Russian businessman Maxim Demin, had pockets that went right down to his knees. The concern, however, was that if Aberdeen held on to the player until his contract was up, the compensation they would get was in the region of £165,000 to £170,000. But Bournemouth were serious players and they didn't want to wait until summer – they wanted him in January. The road was clear for negotiation and a fee of £300,000 was agreed upon, with a further £50,000 any time they were promoted. So, Aberdeen accrued £350,000 instead of £170,000 which, I suppose, was something. But Fraser points me to what he describes as the 'sting in the tale that nobody picked up on. We recognised that he could be a star. What I wanted to avoid at all costs was him going down there and becoming a top-class player and us ending up, even though we'd doubled our money, with ostensibly nothing. So, there's a clause in his contract that says that Aberdeen FC are entitled to 20 per cent of the proceeds for any further sale. If the manager's (Eddie Howe's) judgment of £8million is correct, we'd be entitled to just under £1.6million. So, add that to the £350,000 we got, it's just shy of £2million. We've never had a £2million player in our lives. Was that a good deal for us? It was the only deal we could do.

'Now, you know the money that goes around down there: one day, Rysie may go to a huge club and both us and Bournemouth will have benefited. My desire at all times was to protect Aberdeen. There was no way he was going to commit to us. There were no add-ons as far as international caps were concerned. You're talking about a grand here and a grand there for caps. Our central desire was that if he developed into a top-class player, we would make the money with a percentage sell-on. At the end of the day, if we'd kept him to the end of the season for another 18 weeks, we'd have got £170,000. How would that have looked? I went to Stewart Milne at the time telling him what we'd done. He thought it was excellent, considering the circumstances. You get things right and you get things wrong. I think deep down we operate in a pretty good way. I'm just delighted he's gone down there and made a name for himself. We'd all rather he'd played a hundred games for us, but, you know what, he broke into our team and it just shows you what's possible. I've watched him recently. He was always a stocky, strong player, but he's bulked up incredibly and he still has that pace to burn. Sometimes, when they bulk up, they lose that pace. He hasn't. He deserves all the praise in the world.'

I'm most grateful to Duncan Fraser for removing the mystery, but I'm surprised, if not astounded, that it has remained a mystery for so long. I ask him why they weren't more transparent about it at the time. He says he can't remember, but what he does remember is one really critical article that he describes as 'very, very unfair.' The panacea to all this unfairness would have been a bit of explanation – something, for some unknown reason, that doesn't come easily to Aberdeen. So, taking into consideration the protection that a further transfer might offer, who was to blame for the exit of Ryan Fraser? Duncan Fraser, obviously, is not about to claim responsibility. My money, for what it's worth, is on Miller. The latter's accountability did not go beyond the youth set-up, so he had all the time in the world to assess the young man.

That transfer to Bournemouth in the January window more or less subverted the Brown master plan. It left him desolate because he knew it would undo much of the progress he had made, particularly when you factored in an injury list that would have been more appropriate in a hospital accident and emergency waiting room. 'The loss of Fraser was the biggest loss of all,' Brown admits. 'In the middle of that November, we were second in the league, just behind Celtic. There was a photograph in the newspaper: I was Manager of the Month, Niall McGinn Player of the Month and Fraser Young Player of the Month. It was January when we sold Ryan but, at that point, we'd lost Jack, Osbourne, Clark Robertson and Andy Considine through injury. And that was it. Willie Miller said to me when they were giving Ryan a contract, they told him to take his dad in with him. Ryan had said just to give him the contract and he would sign it. He just wanted to play for Aberdeen and didn't negotiate the money at all. When that contract was up for renewal, I told him to stay at Aberdeen and that he'd get into the Scotland team and end up at Manchester United, Arsenal or Liverpool. Archie and I knew the right people and told him we'd start at the top if at any time he wanted to leave. I'd phone Alex Ferguson and see if he wanted him; if not Archie would get on to Brian Kidd at Manchester City. If that was not on, I'd contact Rafa Benitez at Chelsea and Arsene Wenger at Arsenal. In other words, we'd assist at every juncture to get him the best club and the best deal. But, obviously, he saw the short-term pot of gold.' (Fraser is now believed to be on £40,000 a week).

Brown recalls, 'It was a disappointment for us that we had to take so little for him.'

The Aberdeen manager was becoming familiar with disappointment. In the summer of 2012, he had taken 6ft 3in Icelandic midfielder/defender Arnason from Plymouth Argyle, on freedom of contract. Arnason, apparently, had been destined for Hearts, but had somehow altered his mindset after a trip with the club to Italy. The next thing he was appearing for Aberdeen in a friendly against Inverurie Locos and laying on four or five goals. Brown was smitten by his ability. 'He was outstanding for us. Real class. Made a pass, composed and he could strike a ball. He was a big, arrogant boy, but I liked him. My experience over the years was that the bigger the star, the easier they were to handle. I used to say to some of the mouthy ones, "you've had three shites at Hampden and you think you're a player." Arnason was very respectful.'

And valuable to Aberdeen, it should be added. A year later, contract negotiations began. Arnason was on two grand a week. His agent, former Don David Winnie, intimated that he needed five grand to stay – a figure Brown dismisses out of hand. 'If we'd given him an extra 500 quid a week, I think we could have got him to stay.'

Intriguingly, Brown wanted someone to sponsor the Icelander. Shades of David Ginola and Keith Wyness here. Colin Manson, then chief executive of Xodus, said his company would be willing to underwrite Arnason and Mark Reynolds for up to £100,000 a year. Stewart Milne, however, pointed out that however much they appreciated the offer, it was fraught with implications, in that if either player had been dropped, there was the possibility of an indignant phone call from the sponsor. Brown recognised the flaw in such an arrangement. Arnason decamped for Rotherham, where he earned a weekly £4,500, plus another grand of appearance money. After three years at Millmoor and 116 appearances, he was sold to Malmo FF for £600,000. He is now, of course, back at Pittodrie.

So the frustrations of Brown and Knox multiplied. 'We'd brought in ex-internationals in Gary Naysmith and Gavin Rae, but injury bedevilled these guys. We were trying to get a dressing room with a bit of character. We were just about there, but you were desperately looking for a spark. Aberdeen did it by getting Charlie Nicholas. We looked and looked, but we hadn't the money to buy that extra spark.'

The enigmatic talent of New Zealand striker Rory Fallon appeared on the horizon. He was also at Plymouth and had been recommended by former Don Chris Clark. He had this lackadaisical, ambling style which suggested he might not have given off a spark if someone had handed him a box of Swan Vestas, but Clark emphasised that if you could make him angry, you'd find a player in him. Unfortunately, save for a couple of classically-executed goals, including the Scottish Cup semi-final against Hibs, no-one seemed to provoke him enough. Former Open golf champion Paul Lawrie, an ardent Dons fan, sent a mischievous text to the manager saying, 'If Fallon is towing his caravan around Pittodrie, I won't be there today.'

And then there was the ultimate enigma: Josh Magennis, the goalkeeper turned striker. Brown recalls, 'The boys used to take the Mickey out of big Josh. He was so ingenuous, a big, daft laddie. One game, just to emphasise how bad he'd been, I said to him, 'By the way, that was shite! Get your agent to get you the hell out of here!' He came in on the Sunday and asked when I wanted to see his agent. I was only making a point. Listen, believe me, there was a player in that guy. He became Michael O'Neill's go-to striker with Northern Ireland.'

Aberdeen reached three semi-finals during the Brown years and lost all three. On two occasions they met a very good Celtic team, pretty much as good (if not better) than the present one. Those were the days of Fraser Foster in goal, Victor Wanyama, Gary Hooper, Kris Commons, et al. But the 2-1 loss to Hibs at Hampden still lingers like a foul odour. Goals by Gary O'Connor and Leigh Griffiths were too much for Fallon's single strike. 'That's the one that really rankles with me about my time at Aberdeen,' Brown recalls. 'O'Connor was offside and we were unlucky. We got back into the game when Rory scored and were in the ascendancy. But then Wee Griffiths did us. It was ironic that the man we didn't take because of issues scored the winner. We'd have won the Cup if we'd taken him. A terrific talent, but he'd have had to compromise (if he'd joined Aberdeen). Mind you he didn't hold it against me. I was on the top table when he was Player of the Year and he was as courteous as anything, referring to me as Mr Brown.'

Brown describes the period as 'challenging. But it was also enjoyable, and the goodwill was incredible. We didn't win a League Cup, like Derek did, and we didn't get second in the league, but there were times when we had good runs.' And his appreciation of his old cohort Knox deepened. He recalls a time when they shared a flat in Preston. Brown informed his friend that he was about to get this small, artificial Christmas tree out of the cupboard. Knox told him not to bother. Brown wanted the know the problem. Knox told him that his wife Janice had died on Christmas Eve and therefore he didn't celebrate Christmas.

'I thought at the time. "Shut your mouth, Brown." That situation went on for years. Then, one year, I saw Archie with Christmas presents for his grandchildren. He was beginning to get over the death and beginning to acknowledge the festive season. You know, Archie deserves the utmost credit: he visited his wife every day when she was in the hospice and I think she was in it for four years. When he was assistant at Rangers and they were playing in Europe, he'd visit her and then fly out independent of the team. He was simply devoted to her cause. He's been a very good friend to me and, just think, all the men he's supposed to have killed are still alive. He's not fearsome; okay, he shouts a lot, but you don't need to be worried about him. Mind you, Walter Smith once said, "It's easy managing players – it's hard managing Archie."'

A certain doctor at Albyn Hospital would validate that remark. Knox had experienced debilitating back pain for some time, and arrangements were made for him to undergo an operation on one Saturday during the playing season. Aberdeen was down at Kilmarnock that day. But when Knox entered the private hospital, he learned that a different surgeon would be carrying out the procedure. The new man informed him that they would be pressed for time, as they only had the operating theatre until 4 o'clock. Knox, in his gown and prepped for surgery, was bullish. 'Tight for time? Ye cannae be tight for time for an operation, for God's sake!'

The surgeon asked him to delineate, between one and ten, the kind of pain he was experiencing. Knox's response was maybe between four or five.

The surgeon frowned. 'Well, I don't think I can better that.'

He possibly wasn't prepared for the response from the Aberdeen assistant manager. 'Well, what the f*** am I doing here? Could you no' have found that out beforehand?'

Knox dressed, left the hospital, and phoned Brown. 'I'm out.'

Brown was perplexed. 'How can you be out?'

Knox laid it on the line. 'The operation didn't go ahead.'

The pair were inevitably on the same page at the centre of Aberdeen operations as they tried to lift their team and slaughter the odds. But, on this particular occasion, they were in different books, never mind the same page. They were playing Hearts and they were in Jim Jefferies' Tynecastle office, together with Jefferies' assistant, Billy Brown. While the teams were doing their warm-ups, Sky Television came along and asked if the managers would care to do trackside interviews. As Brown and Jefferies were walking along the corridor, they began to discuss Zander Diamond, at that time with Aberdeen. Jefferies confided that as Diamond was out of contract, they would be making him an offer. Brown responded by saying that Aberdeen didn't have the money to make him a similar offer, but they would be trying their best to put a package together. At the same time, back in the office, the team sheets were produced. Billy Brown remarked, 'I see Diamond's no' playing'. Archie replied, 'Thank f*** for that!'

Diamond was set to have a medical. Strangely enough, he failed. Brown turned on his colleague and said, 'You've scuppered the deal! Billy Brown must have told Jefferies [what you said].'

Brown has reservations about this tale being included in my book. I tell him it's one of the football stories that deserves to be told. Besides, humour is a prerequisite in any book. He adds, 'I asked Jim why he fancied signing Zander. Romanov was running Hearts at the time. Jim told me the chairman was anxious to get him because he liked his name. Anyway, Zander ended up at Northampton and was excellent for them when they won the league.'

The incidents that occur off the field of play have always been a source of intrigue. Events staged in the dressing room, the dug-out, the technical area and, of course, that troublesome tunnel are sometimes far more fascinating than the match itself. The football fan is invariably denied the delicious detail of it all, however. A vote for transparency means we're going to focus on a particular incident that involves all four areas and provides so much information about the call to Pittodrie arms of Brown and Knox. Now, like me, they hail from a generation that is dramatically distanced from youth. Brown recalls he and his colleague stepping out of their car in Glasgow, and a passer-by remarking, 'Oh, it's Jack and Victor from Still Game.' Appearances, in this instance, are wildly deceptive. Jack and Victor they are not. More like Burke and Hare, some would attest.

And so we alight on 11 February, 2012 and a Premier League match against Hibs at Easter Road: Brown and Knox are still trying to resuscitate the 'patient' after Mark McGhee's attempt at surgery has gone disastrously wrong. They need compliance from the players, rather than resistance; respect rather than disrespect. Both men are ardent admirers of Ryan Jack. They regard him as a durable guy from Aberdeen who refuses to be bullied by any foe; it's important he keeps sending out messages of defiance. The score is locked at 0-0 and seems likely to stay that way. Suddenly, the tannoy system declares that the crowd is just over 10,000 and thanks the Aberdeen fans for their attendance. Jack, at that moment, tries to nick the ball from Eric Stevenson, but this is one challenge he's destined to lose. Stevenson whacks him and Jack falls down. Knox is incensed: he feels that his player has surrendered too easily. Anger ripples through his voice. 'You're a fanny!'

Jacko, indignant and embarrassed, fires back. 'F***in' shut up!'

Those words do not come across with the same clarity and volume of the sound address system. They are uttered almost sotto voce and are, perhaps understandable, in the heat of conflict. Brown doesn't arrive at a similar interpretation. He has always demanded discipline. You don't supervise the Scotland football team for 15 years (seven as assistant, eight as manager) without the spine of discipline running through not only your own teams but your own body. It requires guts, of course, to announce that you're never going to pick Richard Gough for Scotland again; to challenge major personalities like Mo Johnston, Frank McAvennie and Ally McCoist. But, on this occasion, Brown is disconcerted. In all his years in football, he has never heard a player talking back to a member of staff in such a disrespectful way.

Whereas cowboys are renowned for reaching for their guns, Brown utilises the only weapon he has at his disposal. He orders one of his colleagues to produce the substitutes' board. 'Get that bastard off!' he screams.

Wee Davie, the man with the board, urges a rethink. 'You've got your three subs on already, Craig.'

That voice of practicality mollifies Brown but only marginally. He is still raging. But common sense has now joined the debate and he knows if he were to pursue this unorthodoxy and Aberdeen lost a goal, he would be letting those travelling fans down. He also recognises that this would direct disapproval his way. He begins thinking ahead: there are other ways to discipline Ryan Jack. The game finishes at a status quo. Aware of potential retribution from Knox, Brown enters the tunnel and orders the player to stay behind with him as the other team members disappear into the dressing room. There's no time for the preliminaries of shadow boxing. Jack's horoscope is about to be read. 'You are a f***ing disgrace! We're going to play Queen of the South in a Cup replay on Tuesday; don't even look for your name on that team sheet, 'cos it'll no' be there.'

Brown remembers he did everything but tell Jack to go and apologise to Knox. 'If I'd said it, he'd have done it. But then Archie would have said this was only because I'd told him to. But this was the only time in my experience at Aberdeen that something had happened you could call indiscipline. I'd been dealing with big-name players all my life and never had heard anything like that. They were all respectful. Anyway, I kept him back in that tunnel and kept dreaming up things to say. So, when we eventually went into the dressing room, it was absolutely quiet. Archie was sitting at a table, growling. So, I started talking to the whole team. I don't know how I managed it, but I must have spoken for 15-20 minutes. Eventually, I told them I'd kept them too long and said, "Let's get the f*** out of here!" They were desperate to get into the shower and werenae wanting to listen to all this shite I was coming out with.'

The Brown monologue was conducted for a purpose: he needed to remove the heat from the situation between his deputy and Jack. Normally, Knox would emphasise a few points after the manager had spoken. But not on this occasion: it was too late for another verbal contribution. Knox was not exactly ecstatic. 'Ya bastard! I wanted to talk.'

Jack was speedily disabused of the notion that the Brown bombast was simply transitory. The team duly travelled to Dumfries on the Tuesday – without him – and a late goal from Andrew Considine gave the Dons a 2-1 victory. The outburst had proved fiscally damaging. 'I suppose he dropped the best part of a grand,' says Brown. 'I could have fined him, but I didn't believe in fining players because there are other ways to deal with him. Dropping a player is effective. It all worked out, anyway. Ryan apologised to Archie and the story was over. He's a competitive player and a fiery character. The other day he was fighting one of the Celtic players at the end of the game.' Now, of course, Jack is fighting for the other half of the Old Firm.

The football management business is transitory and callous. One minute you're in demand and the clubs are begging you to join them; the next they are impatient to see you gone. Brown believes that, given another year, the Aberdeen team of his wildest dreams would have been assembled. It was not to be. The Dons wanted new blood in the manager's office and 'Jack and Victor' were sacrificed for the newer and younger models of Derek McInnes and Tony Docherty. Brown remains magnanimous. 'They've done exceptionally well and have turned out to be inspired appointments.'

CHAPTER 19

The scout wants a Jag!

THE STORY OF ANDY RITCHIE and Aberdeen FC has not registered in the pages of our national newspapers. This does nothing to subtract from its merit. Ritchie, you may remember, was a former Celtic and Morton striker and a mercurial one at that. His form recognised no middle ground and thus fell into the category of either sensational or uninspiring, dependant on the way his bed had been vacated that morning. There was no such contradiction in 1979, of course, when he won the Scotland Player of the Year and saw a £1million transfer tag dangling from his curly head. Years later, after having retired at 28, frustrated beyond belief not only with his unpredictable alter ego but also with his parsimonious paymasters at Cappielow, he turned his attention to talent spotting. He achieved more consistency hereabouts. Initially working alongside Davie Hay, he became an exemplar of the scouting game when Fergus McCann's Celtic cavalcade was gaining an impressive momentum in the nineties. His gift for picking out players with healthy residual values meant that the Glaswegians were many millions of pounds in profit by the time he had left Parkhead. The names of the men he assisted in bringing to Glasgow's East End are worth recalling: Pierre van Hooijdonk, Paolo di Canio, Jorge Cadete, Mark Viduka, Paul Lambert and Craig Burley. For the record, in sharp contrast to those who were signing on for handsome salaries, Ritchie divulges that his remuneration package was confined to the bargain basement area of £15,000 a year. Plus expenses, of course, and Club Class air travel.

He once invited McCann to discuss the curious fiscal situation, pointing out that if Celtic had bought frugally, they also sold expensively. His cogent argument was that he should have been in receipt of a token cut of the spoils. He might as well have attempted to run backwards up Ben Nevis. McCann reportedly proposed a rather meritorious counter argument. He said he'd be prepared to give the scout a percentage of any sell-on fees if things went well, provided Ritchie was prepared to take a financial hit if matters worked to the club's detriment. To be fair to McCann, on the subject of parsimony, he might at that moment have been considering the casebook of striker Harald Brattbakk, whose 12 goals in 44 league appearances was adjudged an insufficient return for the £3million outlay to Rosenberg. Brattbakk's residual value, therefore, could be correctly described as risible. Now, Ritchie had always been a gambler, but there are some wagers that even a cavalier spirit finds unsustainable. 'I should have taken the offer,' he recalls, 'But the fact is I didn't have two pennies to rub together at the time. My kids were relatively young and I could see myself having to sell the wee hoose I owned to pay Mr McCann back. And I knew if it was in the contract, he would hold me to it. So that was that.

'Hey, there is no exact science about the scouting game: I used to sign players and hope to hell that they'd hit the ground running. Viduka – £3million, for instance. Now, that was a lot of money for Celtic to spend. The deal had been on and off more times than a whore's knickers. I mean, he came and signed and then pissed off back to Australia. There were lots of problems. Three million had been deposited in a Swiss bank for the Croatian. My arse was playing Land of Hope and Glory because I knew if this continued we'd never get our money back. So, aye, I was beginning to think it was a wise move not to accept Mr McCann's residual offer. Mind you, when Viduka came back from Australia, he played in a cup game at inauspicious Cappielow. I was feeling quite nervous on the way doon in the car, but he scored a wonder goal that night – one that Andy Ritchie would have been delighted with. I didn't feel so bad after that.'

We leave one unsatisfactory situation and move on to another and, in doing so, alight in the now familiar territory of paradox. In 2012, Ritchie accepted an offer from Craig Brown to become Aberdeen's scout, with a remit to seek attractive deals in England. This would provide no glamorous lifestyle, with extended stays in luxurious hotels, like he had with Celtic; no opportunity to wine and dine contacts. This would be a job stripped of any varnish: ahead of him lay the prospect of long, cold, sleepless hours, driving through the night; plus, no doubt, moments of untold drama and frustration. The price tag for such a situation made Celtic's stipend seem generous: £5,000 a year. Ritchie was undeterred. He wanted to return to employment. He also wanted a club car.

In fact, none of these imagined situations arose. Eight months on, Derek McInnes took over as manager from Brown and the scout was binned. In that time, he had not even scratched the surface of his remit. The fact was he had recommended only one player to his masters – Scott Allan – and this was on the day of his sacking. He had attended only two or three games, none of them, significantly, in England. At one point, his line manager, the then Dons chief scout, Craig Robertson, had asked him to run his practised eye over a player in Scottish League One. A demoralised Ritchie admits that he never moved from his fireside that Saturday, preferring instead to watch Jeff Stelling and the gang on Sky Sport. He was being realistic rather than disobedient. He had seen the player himself and two phone calls from his contacts reinforced his view that he did not meet Premier Division criteria. This appraisal seemed to be vindicated subsequently when the man in question was transferred to a lower division. But this is scarcely the point. What I wish to know is why in the name of heaven such a situation occurred? Why was Ritchie demoralised? And why did it go so disastrously wrong for a guy of such a scouting pedigree?

I'm sitting in a subdued corner of a café in Glasgow's Princes Square where most, if not all, of the answers are supplied. I have a vested interest in this: Ritchie is an old friend whom, incidentally, I recommended to Craig Brown in the first place. Not that they really needed any introductions. They met when the sixties were working themselves into a frenzy of liberation and floral decadence. Ritchie was 12 and a free-spirited and often recalcitrant pupil at Belvidere primary school in Bellshill. Brown became his teacher and suddenly the difficult pupil became an invariably dedicated pupil who began to pick up awards and prizes. Teacher knew best in this instance, says Ritchie. 'The fact that Mr Brown also ran the fitba team also helped, but he had an influence on me apart from that. I remember thinking it was important to impress him. Here was a man of principle and intelligence. A handsome, popular man who had an aura about him. He cut a dapper figure, which was quite unusual for Bellshill. As I remember, he was quick to smile when things pleased him. Did I get the belt from him? Aye, many times and I probably deserved every one of them. Oh, he could rap a bit of leather on you, aye. I remember him coming to the house a few times when I wisnae behaving myself, to let my mother and father know. He was somebody who cared. To be a teacher, you need to be somebody who cares. And he cared all right. I think he's held that caring part right through his life. It's important to him. So, all this made an impression on a 12-year-old when he was at primary school and also on a 58-year-old man when he was unemployed.'

Brown and Ritchie were soon reunited under the Dons banner, after an initial bout of horse trading. The Aberdeen boss, in hospital having a hip replacement, offered £100 a week over the telephone; Ritchie tentatively suggested a 50 quid improvement on that but insisted that they'd talk about it when the older man was on his feet again. But he accepted it later when it was explained to him that money was at a premium at Pittodrie. A plan was hatched: England was to be targeted: bargains were to be sought. Brown acknowledged that his former pupil had a wealth of contacts down south, having also scouted for Aston Villa and Derby. So Ritchie professed himself to being enthusiastic and, in terms of scouting, ambitious. 'Craig was a good, honest man and I so desperately wanted to do right by him.' All that was required to make the situation complete was a car. Simple. Well, maybe this was not so simple. The phone rang in Ritchie's mother's house one day. It was a guy who worked for Chief Executive Duncan

Fraser. He asked for Ritchie's National Insurance number and also wanted to talk about expenses for the car. 'I told him I was looking out my front door and thinking that the Jaguar out there wouldn't go very far on 30p a mile. Actually, it may have been 25p a mile.'

I'm about to sip the latte that has arrived at my elbow. I change my mind and ask a question instead. 'So, you told him you drove a Jaguar?' Ritchie chuckles heartily. 'Yes, I did. But, hey, I was kidding him on. Bellshill humour. Have you ever heard of a football scout driving a Jag? Not in this part of the world, that's for sure. In fact, I drive a Vauxhall Insignia. But the point I made was not a joke: I told him that I would not, repeat not, be driving all over England in my car, for so little a mile. So if they could provide a car, I would go everywhere and come up to Aberdeen for meetings as often as they liked. The guy had obviously gone back to Duncan Fraser and told him that as he drove a Jaguar, I wanted a Jaguar.'

Ritchie's flippant remark appears to have been converted into fact. The alarm bells were clanging in the executive corridors of Pittodrie. Aberdeen FC now believed that their prospective employee was demanding a limousine with which to negotiate the motorways of England.

We are now at the heart of this unlikely story and those lattes are getting cold. After his chat with the man from Human Resources, Ritchie was summoned to the North East to speak to Mr Fraser. Craig Robertson was present at the meeting. There was no mention of a club car, Jaguar or otherwise, but Ritchie remained silent. He understood that Brown was having problems putting the deal together and had no wish to cause him any further hassle. 'I felt the meeting with Fraser was quite frosty. I'm still waiting for a handshake to confirm the appointment. It wasn't hostile but it was a less than warming welcome. I was not expecting him to rush over and throw his arms around me, but one or two niceties would have been nice. It would also have been good to have heard, "Welcome to Aberdeen." Maybe that's old fashioned, but I'm an old fashioned kind of guy. I used to like the city. And I loved going up there to play fitba. I scored my first ever goal for Celtic at Pittodrie on a wet Wednesday night. I enjoyed the place, the crowd, the travel, the excitement of being there and playing against a big club with big players. Suffice to say there was a soft spot there for Aberdeen.'

In direct reference to that infamous tweet by Ryan Christie, Ritchie adds, mischievously, 'I wisnae going in on the back of people calling Aberdeen sheep-shagging bastards.'

I suggest that maybe the club thought they were signing an upstart who had ideas above his station. Ritchie is in no way disturbed by this rather impudent inference. 'It could well have been. But maybe their information was misconstrued somewhere along the line. I'm surmising here, but maybe there was a bit of mischief. I've got to assume that he (Fraser) didn't want to dae the deal in the first place and that's why the coldness was there. As for the car, consider this: if you had any common sense whatsoever, what they hell would they want to give me a Jaguar for? It just disnae make sense. No, they expected me to use my own. Besides, Craig Robertson had a firm's car, although to my knowledge he rarely made it out of Fife.' It should be noted, at this point, remembering Ritchie's stipend, that Robertson, his line manager, was on the somewhat princelier sum of £24,999 per annum.

In Ritchie's eyes, even although it was scarcely the ideal way to start a relationship, he was not surprised when the plans and schemes hatched with Brown did not come to fruition. Ritchie suspects that Craig Robertson might have felt uneasy over his appointment. 'Maybe he thought they were going to get rid of him. It's something that happens in this game – a new manager will bring in their ain' people if they can. Maybe, though, Andy Ritchie found himself in the wrong place at the wrong time. It was the story of my life.'

His dismissal would have been even more abrupt had not Ritchie failed to assemble his wits. He came home one night to find that Derek McInnes had been on the phone. 'I knew that meant he wanted to sack me, but I also knew that if he wanted to do it, he'd have to do it to my face. I told my mum that I'd be away at 7am the next morning. And I was, straight up the road to Aberdeen – in my own car, of course. When I arrived, Tony Docherty nearly wet himself. We both knew what was about to happen. He said they were going to training. I said I'd get a cup of tea, have a wander down to the beach, have a fag and watch the world go by. Then I'd be back and see Derek after training. I said to Docherty that it's never nice to lose a job, but that I'd come in here and breeze out again as if it didn't matter to me. And that's what happened. Only it did matter. I had hopes, high hopes, and was looking forward to working with Craig and Archie Knox. But that had all gone. When I eventually saw McInnes, he said he had nothing against me but said that this guy Russ Richardson was going to do the job down in Preston. I suppose I was with him for about half an hour. There was no emotion from either of us.'

There remains, however, a small measure of regret on Ritchie's part. Aberdeen's scouting tradition was built initially on the concrete foundations of Bobby Calder and Jimmy Carswell. Ritchie believed that he might have provided an additional consignment of cement had it not been for the misconception of what club car he was seeking. 'Look, I wisnae asking for first-class air travel all around the world – I was asking for something that would be beneficial all around, considering I was going to haul my backside all over England. Plus the fact that a company car would have made everything legitimate. Let's face it, if it had been my ain' motor, I could have claimed I'd driven 500 miles while sitting in the hoose. This way, everything could have been monitored, and my car wouldn't have suffered the fatigue of motorway driving. I expected a lot more because it was Aberdeen and was disappointed that it didnae work out better for everyone. It's not as if I don't like Aberdeen now, but I'll admit I don't have the warm feeling of the past.'

We're forgetting something, of course. We return to the intriguing subject of Scott Allan. Ironically, as Ritchie was preparing to exit Pittodrie for the last time, he brought up the player's name with Tony Docherty. 'I mentioned that Allan was at Portsmouth on loan from West Brom and that he might be good for Aberdeen. Tony, apparently, had known Allan in his time at Dundee United – he indicated that he wouldn't touch him with a bargepole.'

Ritchie, however, refuses to even criticise Docherty for what might have been an oversight. 'Hey, we all have opinions. I wouldn't have signed Calvin Zola for Cowdenbeath, but it's easy to be critical of other people's signings. And you can be so wrong about players. I remember being signed by Celtic as a 15-year-old and playing for the Hoops against the All Greens at Barrowfield. I was 6ft 1in and playing at centre half. Big Jock Stein came over to us and asked me my name and where I came from. I told him. "So you're a six-footer from Bellshill and they think you're going to be a centre half." He says to the guy running the team to put me in the middle of the park. At the end, he said: "You cannae run, you cannae tackle, you cannae heider the ball – and you're a f***ing coward! Who telt ye you were going to be a centre half?" I thought my career was finished at 15. I wisnae a coward, but Big Jock wisnae far away with his interpretation of me. He was right on the first three counts. Was he right in the long run? I'd say "no" but then I'm biased. But, hey, a good scout is everything. How successful would Brian Clough have been without Peter Taylor? How successful would Aberdeen have been without Bobby Calder and Jimmy Carswell? Success has many fathers: failure is a bastard. So, if you go out and sign two or three players and they're great, everyone wants a bit of the credit. If you sign a dud, naebody wants to know: it's your fault. You've got to be able to decipher what's right and what's not. I think I had that ability, but it was not to be at Aberdeen.'

Now, given my involvement in the story, it would be wrong of me to describe McInnes's actions as precipitate – managers do like to have their own people around them in a cocoon – but you might have thought that Ritchie's experience and success in the import business would have awarded him a stay of execution. You should also be aware that the experience I talk about has been used at an international level. Until recently, Ritchie was watching players and opponents for Scotland manager Gordon Strachan.

It's time for something stronger than lattes. But, just before we leave the opulence of Princes Square, Ritchie, who works for BBC *Radio Scotland* on occasion, has both of us laughing again. One for the road constitutes a couple of Celtic stories and another, inevitably, about Aberdeen.

'Wee Fergus called me to his office. I expected to be held over hot coals for certain signings, whatever. But he asked me about a foreign expense form and why I had ordered Chicken Kiev instead of plain chicken. I telt him I liked the taste of Chicken Kiev. The trouble was it was more expensive by about 12 Swiss francs; the meeting lasted about 35 minutes. Here we were spending millions of pounds on fitba players, yet here he was arguing about the loss of 12 Swiss francs. Conversely, I was once summoned to Tommy Burns' office to be asked why I'd booked into a guest house in Blackpool. I told him I liked that B & B, and that it was only around the corner from the football ground. I was told when I represented Celtic, I should book into a five-star hotel, or something comparable. But that sums up this crazy game of football.

'And try this one for size. I met a guy recently who does scouting for an English club. "What about that Aberdeen mob?" he says. He told me that he came across two guys scouting for the club – two guys at the same game at Easter Road: Tam O'Neill and Nobby Clark. He added that these two guys went to the same f***ing games. I was astonished. "You're kidding me on," I replied. "Naw," he says, "Tam does the hame team, Nobby the away wan." I asked him if they'd arrived by mistake. No, he said. Apparently they travelled down in the same motor!'

Presumably, the mode of transport was not a Jaguar.

CHAPTER 20

The Boogie Man Cometh

I'm driving up from glasgow for an interview with Andrew Considine, but right now I'm concentrating more on my transport than my meeting with a man who has donated body, heart and soul to the club for God knows how many years. My vehicle is a two-year-old BMW 7 series, with only 14,000 miles on the clock, and it's a dark blue beauty. I've always loved cars. At 17, I dodged a maths lesson at Aberdeen Academy and sat my driving test. A pass led to my best-ever summer holiday job – working for the snooty Campbell and Sellar taxi firm in the West End. Boy, did I have some laughs! One day, I'm asked to report to the bothy, where the austere, sock-less Mr Sellar hands out the assignments. He tells me to pick up a couple of ageing spinster sisters and take them on their weekly jaunt around the city – at the most sedate of paces. It's a sixties prequel to Driving Miss Daisy. *I do as I'm bid, subdue my boy racer instincts and ferry them all over the place, including the cobbled streets of Old Aberdeen, at 20mph. They alight, back at their terraced house, give me a small tip and express their delight. One, in fact, takes it further. 'Driver – that's the best ride we've ever had!'*

I'm not sure the clients in my next story could say the same thing. My last day at the taxi firm is a Saturday and there's a game on at Pittodrie. Nothing comes between me and my football at this stage of my life. So, I'm going, whatever happens. I'm due off at two o'clock, but there's a problem. Mr Sellar says it's imperative I take the Austin Sheerline – the poor man's Rolls Royce – and ferry the best man and bridesmaid to and from a wedding. The service begins at the time I'm due to finish. F*** it! I'm going to miss the first half. But Sellar doesn't want to hear sports-oriented protestations. Reluctantly, I perform my duties and hang around anxiously during the nuptials. After they come out for the obligatory photo session, I usher my clients into the car and attempt to drive dutifully behind the bridal car to the reception, which is being held near the Fountain in Great Northern Road. Progress, for some reason, is abysmally slow, but now we're going down Argyle Crescent and into Westburn Drive. There are no oncoming cars, so I put my foot down and we go hurtling by a startled bride and groom and on up to the Six Roads and beyond. The best man and bridesmaid are not exactly doing cartwheels, for I've upset delicate stomachs *and also protocol in arriving at the reception ahead of the bridal car. But I can't give credence to their disapproval: I'm already late for my beloved Dons.*

Talking of weddings, I'm nearing Aberdeen and am now concentrating on Considine, the well-spoken, conservative, fairly undemonstrative guy who has been at Pittodrie apparently since Wee Alickie *made his* Green Final *debut. At some point, I'm going to ask this well-spoken, conservative, fairly undemonstrative guy about that infamous stag-do video – the one in which he cross-dressed, danced and lip-synched to 'Yes, Sir, I Can Boogie.' I imagine it's probably best to warm him up first.*

THERE'S NO DENYING THAT Douglas Mackay Considine left only a shallow footprint in the history of Aberdeen FC. The defender, signed from Huntly as the Alex Ferguson narrative began to formulate, played on 48 occasions in a career that began late in 1978 and ended abruptly three years later. It was claimed that he had defied his boss by wearing long sleeves instead of the more fashionable short ones. This may well have been accurate. But perhaps an even more compelling reason for the departure was the allegation that he attempted to back heel the ball across his penalty area on one occasion – breaking a Ferguson taboo – and the show-pony trick backfired. It's claimed a vexed manager decided there and then he would not play for the club again.

Considine was fashioned from durable material, however: if his Aberdeen career was over, the next life was a street corner away. He duly went to Dunfermline, where he played a couple of years, before retiring at the ridiculously early age of 26 and setting up an ultra successful dry-cleaning business that today has an enviable client list: The Queen uses his laundry services when she is in residence at Balmoral. Considine lives in some style in the beautiful Royal Deeside town of Banchory and, in spite of the nature of his departure, his love of Aberdeen insists on burning brightly, as his Pittodrie season ticket suggests. There is, of course, another incentive for regular attendance: these days, son Andy is in charge of the family football escutcheon. And it seems that the baton of durability and stubbornness has been passed on. His Pittodrie sojourn has not been easy, either. Fans have not always been supportive and have accused him of various malfunctions, including a lack of pace. But now, at 29, Considine has discovered maturity and is enjoying some of his finest moments, even though he is often played out of position at left back.

If you were to assess people in terms of loyalty, this extremely amenable young man would imitate Len Goodman and merit a straight ten. At Pittodrie since he was 11 years old, he has suffered all the slings and arrows of becoming what is known as a fixture and fitting. The point is fixtures and fittings are not always appreciated and consequently are not rewarded for their worth to the team. Considine, admittedly, has never been a spectacular player, in the mould of a Hayes or a McGinn. Nevertheless, he has seen players of far less stature and commitment come in for far more reward. But, as the winter of 2016 progressed into 2017, he decided that he'd been compliant for too long. As speculation abounded that his next destination would be either Inverness CT, in a swap deal, or even Rangers, he was offered a new contract to take him through to the summer of 2019. It was believed to be an increase of £100 a week – in other words, a smack in the face and considerably below what he considered to be his worth to the team. So, for once in his uncomplaining life, he dug his heels so fiercely into the ground that earth clung to his uppers.

The average wage was £133,000 per year and this offered a genuine yardstick. Andy's agent predicated a counter bid with this sum in mind and, after a due process of haggling, a new, improved contract was agreed. Consequently, I'm sitting in the Willie Miller Suite beside someone who's settled, secure and delighted that everything has worked out so positively.

'It took a good six or seven weeks to get where we wanted to be,' he says. 'I think I've always felt that growing up through the club, you almost don't get paid as much as a new signing. That's really it. I felt I had been unfairly treated in that sense over the years after all the service I'd given – and that I had almost to ask for a contract on the last occasion. The fact that they came to me this time made me think I had every right to ask to be on par with the majority (of players). That was only fair. As I sit here speaking to you, it's amazing how quickly time goes. I can remember signing at 17, remember so many youth games and your life goes by like a finger snap. It's been wonderful, though. I can imagine the amount of folk who'd give anything to be able to walk through the doors of Pittodrie and play football for a living. It's the best job in the world; I'd like to think that everyone who plays the game would agree with that. To have the love of the game and to play for your boyhood heroes is the icing on the cake.'

Now, that's what an Aberdeen fan wants to hear. There is an abundance of mercenaries in this game, but Considine is the ideal template and in more ways than one. An admission hereabouts: it used to be a pleasure to interview footballers when money and greed did not dictate their every movement. I feel I'm being returned to more equable days in this chat with a guy who is unfailingly polite and disarmingly open. His one demand is that people are fair with him. You can't arraign a man for that. He learned this at the age of 16 when Aberdeen didn't seem to know whether they should offer him a contract or not. Rangers were also interested. Suddenly, on a day of expectation, there was no contract on the Pittodrie table. Considine was distraught.

'I remember speaking to my mum and dad and wondering where I went from here. It was a real sore one. The thought of going down the road to Rangers – there was more chance of getting a game at Aberdeen than Rangers at that time.

But then, suddenly, they (Aberdeen) phoned and gave me a year's contract. Now all this had all happened between midday and dinner time, just a few hours, so they must have gone back and thought they'd give me a chance. Relief! I've had a fantastic time and, to get to where I am today, it's forever been a privilege to be putting on the red shirt. And now, of course, we're showing our true colours again under Derek McInnnes. That's wonderful, because we've come through some difficult times. And, believe me, I've seen some horrible times and dark days.'

Since he has brought up the subject, it's only polite to ask him to carry the torchlight through the darkest days. 'I would say there were two: the first was losing to Queen of the South in the Scottish Cup semi-final, under Jimmy Calderwood. I think that was, in effect, the last straw for him. And I also remember just as Craig Brown and Archie Knox joined, we were playing Hearts down at Tynecastle. Simmy (Neil Simpson) and Neil Cooper took the team and we got absolutely battered. I was walking from Tynecastle to the bus, which was a good hundred yards away, when this fan came up to me and you could see in his eyes that he was borderline tears. "Please tell me, Andy, that we're not getting relegated. We CAN'T get relegated!"

'Hey, it's easy for players to forget how much it means to supporters; guys with Aberdeen blood through them since the day they were born; trying to explain how big a club this is. The tradition is huge. Look at the wall here with Willie Miller on it – 797 appearances, 65 Scotland caps. Just look at what he's won.'

The dark days were offset, in many ways, by those nights under lights that were positively effulgent: Aberdeen surprised everyone, even themselves, by reaching the last 32 of the Europa League. 'I think Calderwood was a great manager. Over the five or six years he was here, putting the cups aside, the last 32 of the Europa League, as it is now, was a huge feat. Okay, we scraped through, third in the league out of four, but we gained so much experience playing against some of the World Cup legends. We got Bayern Munich and the game here was just incredible. The place was full and bouncing, and that's what you want as a player and dream of as a kid. It's why you play football – to be part of these moments.'

The humbling of FC Copenhagen supplied another special night. A freezing night, Considine reminds me. Not in the upper section of the Richard Donald stand it wasn't, I reply. He laughs. 'I can imagine it wasn't. A lot of these teams probably came here and thought, "Aberdeen, who are they?" But we took them by surprise, got in their faces and to come away with four goals was something special. It was summed up with Jamie Smith's volley. The tactics were right that night. Obviously, the Rangers connection doesn't go down well when you come here, but Jimmy was a nice guy. So was Jimmy Nicholl. They would tell jokes and stories that were hilarious and you had real respect for them. I don't know if it's just these days, but you see some younger lads lacking respect. I've seen it here, young boys coming in and showing coaches very little respect. Before you know, they're out the door. Career over. I'm sure it happens at every club.

'Yeah, football's come on a lot recently. You've got the likes of Pep Guardiola and the Barcelona and Real Madrid way of playing football. A lot of teams are trying to emulate that style and they're trying to ingrain it in young boys. You can see that here but, at the same time, you've got to remember the principles of football. What's the point of not being able to attack a cross? You're on the 18-yard box and instead of clearing it... you've been taught to take a couple of touches and find a pass. There's still the principles of the game and I suppose I've grown up with old-school football. It helped me. It was always: get your head on the end of that cross, don't take too many touches, and let the ball do the work kind of thing. I've not been blessed with pace as a player, but I find my positional sense is very good. If I can read the game, it makes my life a lot easier.'

So, here is the thinking footballer, even if he's one who finds the old principles difficult to jettison. He stresses he does not take his work home with him to his wife of two years, Madeleine. You can almost touch the pride he has in her: she has been his rock and instrumental to how he has progressed as a footballer over the five years they have been together.

'She's really settled me down. She's always there to listen and to give advice. We have a two year old son, Harry, and a six-month-old son, Teddy. To go home to them and see their smiling faces, it brings me on as a dad and as a person: it lights up your life having such a lovely family and I do everything for them. It's all about them at the end of the day. They've made me a better person.'

I ask him if he needed settling down. 'Before I met her, I'd been single for a couple of years – I don't love a night out; that's not what I'm getting at. One or two does me for a month. But I wasn't preparing in the right way to be a footballer, probably not giving myself the best chance. You know, I almost lost myself in the gym for a good number of years. I didn't have a lot of guidance when it came to that. I was taking protein shakes left, right and centre, and lifting heavy weights which weren't benefiting me whatsoever as a footballer. I was just getting big and heavy and it was affecting my football. I remember when Mark McGhee came in, I was sitting at 14 stone. I'd ballooned.'

McGhee and his assistant, Scott Leitch, weaned Considine off the weights; and now sports scientist Graham Kirk has taken him down other avenues of fitness. He is eternally grateful to them for their assistance. 'Don't get me wrong, the additional weight helped me in a sense because I was able to stand up to the big strikers. I could handle myself. But, if I could go back, I wouldn't lift a weight. I became too big and bulky. When Jimmy Calderwood was manager, I played a few games at left back and I found it very hard to get up and down the line because I was a size too big. I wish I'd had a bit more guidance when it came to that. If I hadn't gone near the gym, I might have been able to blossom a bit more as a young player. Maybe it held me back a bit.'

We are moving inexorably into the part of the interview where things could easily go awry. This is not the time to be injudicious but, nevertheless, I have to ask Considine about his dad's departure. He claims his father had a wonderful time at Pittodrie and, indeed, offers an alternative explanation as to why he left. It is one, considering all factors, that is totally believable. 'Dad would only have been 21 or 22 when he signed, so I can imagine it would have been pretty daunting going into a dressing room like that with a lot of egos and strong personalities. He loved his time here, but it came down to the fact that he wasn't getting a (regular) game and I think he'd maybe gone above Fergie to get some answers. Fergie found out and that was it. Then he went to Dunfermline. But the advice I get from him about football is invaluable.'

That advice has turned Considine into a well-rounded young man who recognises, unlike many others, his limitations. He confesses that he went through a long period of failing to learn from his mistakes. 'That will probably stick with me until I stop playing. I wish I had learned from them. It's not that I didn't try to; it's just that I went through a spell where I just lost concentration at corners or free kicks. I remember the very first one and I think it probably killed my confidence for a number of years. We played Dundee United in the first game of the season at Tannadice, and it was in the last five minutes. The corner came in and I don't know why, but I tried to chest the ball back to the goalkeeper. A United player suddenly nipped in and scored and they won 1-0. It hurt massively because I was sitting in the dressing room, thinking, "What on earth was I doing? How could I be so stupid?" Calderwood and the players had a go at me and they had every right. I don't really think I had a leg to stand on. I was out in the real world. I wish I did have a thicker skin back then as I do now. I've grown that skin over the years, but it does take time. I'm not saying I no longer care what people say, but at the same time I'm able to block it out. Social media can be nasty. I've read numerous horrible things directed at players and it's disgusting, really. Some people just go way over the top. But football's a tough school and you need some seriously thick skin. The advice I'd give to young players is they need to grow that skin, because you just can't tippy toe your way through football.'

We're back to emotions and to times when it's beneficial to be able to return to a solid family life and the welcome of a good woman. Not that Considine takes his work home with him. Besides, there are some things that are difficult to explain, like post-match friction in the tunnel. He remembers two such occasions in recent years. One was a 1-0 victory over Hearts. 'I'm trying to remember their striker's name (might it have been Christian Nade?) Something kicked off and he was in the midst of it. He was just throwing people about as if they were toys. I don't think you'd want to be involved in that.'

More recently, it was difficult for Considine not to be involved when 'afters' were high on the agenda. The Dons had dispensed with St Johnstone in the Scottish League Cup quarter-final, a last-minute goal from Adam Rooney putting bitter rivals in their place. The Dons celebrated loudly and pointedly, with the door of the home dressing room open and the victory music pounding out. Former Don Steven MacLean allegedly took exception to the tone of the celebration and entered the changing room and switched off the music. The ghetto blaster was switched back on immediately, whereupon MacLean re-entered foreign territory. On this occasion, he faced the interrogation technique of Mark Reynolds. 'What the hell do you think you're doing?' McLean and Reynolds became involved in a skirmish which travelled outside the dressing room. 'Well, everyone just rushed out and just about everyone was involved. You couldn't move in the tunnel. Oh, God, it just kicked off. But, listen, it's part of the game.'

The clock is declaring that we are almost at the end of the interview. If Considine proved that he could fight, he had demonstrated back in 2015 that he was a multi-layered character; that he could dispense with the conservatism and send himself up. Yes, we have now arrived at that controversial video which went viral. That video – in which his father and a few friends made sterling contributions – was filmed during what was one of the more bizarre stag weekends. Considine does not flinch when I raise the subject. Instead, he extends warm thanks to his good friend Nick Sangster, who organised it.

'We went to London for my stag do. It was one of the funniest, most hilarious afternoons of my life. We flew down on the Friday, went out that night and did it on the Saturday. I think we'd been drinking since half past ten that morning. We all congregated in someone's room and played drinking games. We kind of made our way to the studio as the day wore on, stopping off at a few bars. So, we were well tanked up at this point. We were also allowed to drink during the making of it. I had a face full of make-up and the gear on. My dad was involved, my uncles, too. I wish it hadn't got out, really, because it was everywhere. So it wasn't kind of nice to see. But, hey, it was banter and I'm sure a lot worse goes on in stag do's. It was brilliant.'

And how did it go up here at Pittodrie? 'Oh, I think every new player who comes in gets shown the video. I wouldn't have changed it. It was a cracking idea and a wonderful weekend. I'll always be reminded of it.'

Andy Considine, perhaps not as conservative and undemonstrative as previously imagined, will stay in the memories of all Dons fans. He is the Player of the Year for the season 2016-17. He scored a hat-trick against Dundee at Dens Park. The Boogie Man has cometh and no mistake.

CHAPTER 21

Milne and Fergie Mk 11

The following is an extract from the Cooney and Black website which I once shared with my business partner, Jim Black. 'This somewhat deranged world of Scottish football occasionally predisposes itself towards wild exaggeration. The Highland News, for instance, recently reported that Inverness CT manager John Hughes had drawn comparisons between his prolific striker, Billy McKay, and the little guy employed to do similar business for FC Barcelona: Lionel Messi.

'No, this is not a misprint. You can visualise McKay pulling the duck-feather duvet over his head when he read that one. Can you imagine the stick he received when he next popped that head around the dressing room door at the Tulloch Caledonian Stadium? Anyway, a similar form of hyperbole was employed in Aberdeen recently when Stewart Milne and some of his acquaintances from the business community toasted the club's 2014 League Cup victory.

'Now, aside from an impressive flourish of solidarity from over 40,000 fans, it had been a less than convincing conclusion at Hampden. The Dons just about crawled over the line, extra time and penalties being required to deny the muscular challenge of the aforementioned Inverness. Yet, the jubilation within Milne, no doubt encouraged by the massive turn-out in the city for the homecoming, was unconfined. I understand he astounded his chums by announcing that, in Derek McInnes, he'd found a manager who belonged to the same league as Alex Ferguson. That statement put the chairman so far over the top that he effectively joined the space race. Had he totally lost his senses? Or, might he have been positively pixilated at the time of speaking?'

IF MY MEMORY IS EFFICIENT, securing access to hombres like Maradona, Pele, Beckenbauer and Cruyff was relatively easy. It was a case of asking and being given – if, of course, those subjects felt kindly disposed towards yours truly. Stewart Milne represented a far sterner challenge. He and I were introduced outside the Mansfield Traquair, at Eddie Turnbull's funeral, on 9 May, 2011. I asked him if an interview could be arranged and he provided me with a contact number for his personal assistant. The dear lady must have held a proficiency certificate in obfuscation: there was to be no interview, despite numerous phone calls and entreaties. Milne's mind, to be fair, was monopolised by more important matters – a vast building empire to sustain during the most damaging of economic times; and a football club that occasionally needed the assistance of a life-support machine.

Almost six years later, I have been invited to join him at his beautiful home, Dalhebity House, in Bieldside. Set in 14 acres of prime Deeside land, the original building was the birthplace of Princess Diana's maternal grandmother, but it needed fortunes spent on it. Milne decided to rebuild it along classical lines but with the requisite modernity. When planning permission was granted, the bulldozers were summoned and tasked with reducing the old place to rubble. The timber-framed mansion took the best part of three years to complete, but now it offers eco-friendly, virtually zero carbon living. How big is it? When I use the toilet facilities, I lose myself in the labyrinth of rooms and corridors and have to be redirected back to our meeting place.

Dalhebity House aside, Milne is currently enjoying the benefits of Cloud Nine football living. He has secured the services of a well-regarded manager and the team is moving along nicely, with only the occasional urge to self immolate. But the chairman could not always declare a state of personal equilibrium at Pittodrie. After taking over from Ian Donald as chairman, he found himself the first and instinctive reference point of irate supporters. When things went wrong – and they often did in those days – Milne was targeted for abuse. Indeed, as fortunes slalomed, sometimes crazily, the more mischievous elements would throw their scarves at him in the directors' box, some of them hoping they would dislodge the wig that had become not only a fascination for them but also an object of their derision. Close to his 20th anniversary as chairman, he talks of his role in less than glowing terms. 'It's been pretty demanding at times and it can take its toll. On the face of it, there is precious little reward being chairman, so you need a real passion for the game and the club. That's probably the major driving force. If I wisna a fan, I'd have given up a long time ago.'

It wouldn't be difficult to go along with the banter that once surrounded him: some folk contended he was an electrician who essentially got lucky. Success such as this, of course, requires far more than an association with Lady Luck: the distance he has travelled from the humble beginnings of childhood is considerable. He was brought up in the tiny village of Tough, near Alford. There was no electricity in the house, so the radio had limited reception and relied on batteries that had to be recharged twice a week. Today, this is an industrious man whose personal batteries might carry the Duracell branding. All this industry has delivered dividends: unlike many of its competitors, the Stewart Milne Group has negotiated a difficult and treacherous path through the fiscal wastelands of 2008. It emerged far from unscathed yet still competitive, and retains its position as one of the UK's leading independent home builders. And now, of course, it's grappling with the damaging effects of the downturn in the local oil and gas economy. In the year 2015-16, the firm has reported pre-tax losses totalling £26.1million. He has the additional worry of building a new home for the club – and ensuring that the club keeps pace with the ever-changing dynamics of the European game. Superficially, anyway, it appears to be grist to the Milne mill.

Of course, I'm here to discuss football and the past rather than the future, and I'm anxious to ask him about that announcement he made to his business associates regarding comparisons between McInnes and Ferguson. But history tells you he isn't comfortable with interviews and it may be appropriate to bide my time until we have established some form of rapport. What pleases me is that I'm meeting another genuine died-in-the-sheep's wool Dandy. Milne became chairman of Aberdeen FC in 1998, some years after his firm built the Richard Donald stand, but his love of the club had been established far in advance of this. He attended his first game at Pittodrie in 1963, in the days of Tommy Pearson. Initially, he could go to matches only in midweek (he played football on Saturdays) and then only when there was a spare seat in a neighbour's car. It was when he moved into Aberdeen at the age of 16 that he began to assume diehard status.

Milne, dressed in black and looking far younger than his 66 years, sits to my right at the long, polished table. The hairpiece was jettisoned years ago and he looks all the better for its removal. He's pleasant and personable and therefore the antithesis of the stereotypical football chairman. Many are abrasive, demanding, autocratic, ego-driven and comprehensively ruthless. You suspect the only box Milne ticks is ruthlessness – he is currently on his ninth manager in virtually 20 years. But even this is partially ameliorated: any urge to kick the victim when he's down is resisted. Thus, if the chairman gets the appointment wrong, there is no reneging on contractual obligations. He pays up without a murmur.

And, crucially, his heart is not of caraway seed proportions, like so many of his ilk who turn their backs on direct confrontation. Roy Aitken can surely offer confirmation of this. On 9 November, 1997, he became the first manager to be sacked by Milne, who was preparing to take on the role of chairman at the time. Call it a dress rehearsal for what was ahead. It wasn't by any means a conventional sacking, yet it was destined to become the most difficult of all. After a traumatic Sunday – a 5-0 defeat by Dundee United at Tannadice; Dean Windass sent off – Milne summoned the directors to his home. When the axe was being sharpened, it was agreed that he be appointed executioner.

'The difficulty was because I'd such a belief in Roy and he was such a committed guy and so determined to succeed. I like to think we gave him every chance and backed him in every way (remember, Aitken had been given £1million to spend on Paul Bernard). The sad thing in football is that when somebody goes so low, everyone jumped on his bandwagon and it was very difficult for him to climb back up again. That was the point we reached with Roy. I'll always remember that night, because he stayed just 200 yards down the road from here. I walked down and was faced by him and his wife. She wanted to stay in the room and that made it harder. I can assure you it was an emotional experience. But we got through it.'

I ask Milne if he needed fortification beforehand. 'No. I was in the house for probably over an hour. Mind you, I think he gave us a drink. Aye, we had a drink together. He's a guy I still have the utmost respect for.'

And so the managers came and the managers went with a regularity that became almost monotonous: Alex Miller, Paul Hegarty, Ebbe Skovdahl, Steve Paterson, Jimmy Calderwood, Mark McGhee and Craig Brown. Milne, who favours discretion rather transparency in these matters, is reluctant to talk about any of them in any specific detail. He says of the intriguing Skovdahl, 'He was a strong character and I found him to be a good guy. I did like working with him. When it came to parting company, that wisna overly difficult. We had all come to the same conclusion that the time was right. It (the sacking) happened here. No blood on the carpet. But I don't think any of them were overly difficult or angry. Some were more difficult than others.'

I ask him to talk about the Steve Paterson situation and suddenly Milne becomes curiously vague. It appears the chairman wants to empty his mind of that debacle. 'I can't actually remember how it started off. But we thought – out of all the managers we've ever taken on – that (he) was probably the biggest risk. But we genuinely believed he had the potential to make that step up to the next level. He may have done so if he hadn't had all these other issues.'

But he knew about those issues, didn't he? 'Yeah. Yeah. Well, being honest, not to the extent that eventually came through.'

We already have identified the man behind the Paterson appointment: Keith Wyness. Milne tells me Wyness was engaged as a wise counsel rather than a chief executive – although this is his job description on Wikipedia. He had been hired on the recommendation of Alex Ferguson, after Milne had intimated that the Dons needed someone who had a wide knowledge of the game and an enviable contact network. So, with regards to Paterson, what happened to due diligence? 'I'm sure you never know the full picture about people. I'm nae trying to defend the decision. We got that wrong. It didn't work out and was a step too far for Steve. We knew there was risk with that appointment.'

What, because of the drinking? 'Well, I wouldn't want to get personal. I don't see merit in being specific. I could be critical about different aspects of every manager that's been here, but I wouldna want that because in most cases there was a lot more good than was bad. I dinna employ anyone in the Stewart Milne Group that disna have faults and downsides. But if there are enough strengths that you can work with, you can manage.'

So, how did he feel as chairman when the whole mess was unravelling in the national press? Until now, Milne has been the displaying the apprehension of the guy in the dentist's chair, just waiting for the drill to locate a nerve. But, suddenly, he becomes more voluble. 'Lots of things. Angry for one. He let the club down and he also let himself down. Also, a bit of sympathy for his condition. The weakness was obviously there and it was a big struggle for him at the time to keep on top of it. I gave him credit; he worked hard to make sure it wisna to the forefront. But it was obviously taking its toll as well. He just reached a point where he could no longer manage it. But this is the big thing that I struggle to square within football. You can be up there for a short time and then, with not a great deal changing, you can be right down there again. I think one of the examples this year has been Mark Warburton, where, at times, he's been destroyed by the press and at other times he's got things going. One bad defeat and that suddenly changes again. Real life is not like that. No. F*** me, if I was to get down every time something bad happens in SMG, I'd have been buried a long time ago. The reality of life, whether it's your working life, your personal life or your football life, is if you can get 60-70 per cent of it good and you learn to manage the 30-40 per cent bad, you're doing well. If it's the other way around, then you're in trouble.'

It's an admirable speech, and one very much applicable to the business of hiring and firing. But I cannot quite fathom what it has to do with Steve Paterson. His demise had no associations with vicarious decision making: he was given every chance; it was he who insisted on the suicide option. And yet, results-wise, he had a better record than that of Mark McGhee.

McGhee, whose win ratio was a pitiful 24 per cent, holds the unenviable record of being the least successful of all Aberdeen's managers. In his 17-month spell, he allegedly gained a reputation for arrogance in the club and subsequently lost the respect and confidence of many people very quickly. Without going into further excruciating detail, I also know, from what he told me in the Lanes of Brighton, that he planned on making sweeping changes in his backroom staff, particularly in the area of the physio department. Milne refuses to comment on any aspect of this, but significantly draws my attention to Derek McInnes' standing. 'Derek has worked so hard from day one to connect with everyone within the club, both upstairs and downstairs. As a result, he could get anyone to burst a gut to get something done for him. If someone does something for him, he shows an appreciation. Mark didn't connect with anyone, whether it was upstairs or downstairs. Derek speaks to whoever he meets in the corridor. It's all about connecting. It's nae just the manager who delivers success within a club; he has a vital role, but if you hidna everybody else behind the scenes making contributions... that's why with Mark it was such a short reign.'

Milne talks about the time, during the McGhee period, when they went to Celtic Park and came away with the mother and father of all spankings: 9-0. I remember this day with great clarity. It was November 6 2010 – my birthday. Mind you, I had to be somewhere else and therefore suffered the humiliation almost second hand. Milne sat in the directors' box and experienced every second of it. 'Oh, it was just horrendous and it was embarrassing for Celtic as well. Just part of the tapestry, though.'

How long had he stayed in the boardroom after the match? 'Just normal. That's the difference. You accept that something's gone wrong, but you dinna abandon the role that you've got. To me, the meeting of people after a game is an important part of it all. You work hard at building relations with other clubs and we had people supporting Aberdeen in the boardroom that day. If I just f***ed off to my car after the game, you're letting them down as well. Probably the one thing I've got out of football is that it prepares you for life. I've taken things out of the game that's benefited me and the Stewart Milne Group.'

Had he received an apology from the manager? 'He was out here on the Sunday – at my request. But it wisna really an apology. No, Mark felt really bad about that, but to me, it didna have the impact. I think there was an opportunity that day to get a lot of lessons out of that. I think a manager must be involved in honest, open discussions. I think Mark is one of those individuals; he cannae admit to anything 'cos he sees it as a sign of real weakness.'

Milne, I suspect, would rather be talking about the future and Aberdeen's plans for a new home, but I insist on pinning him to the past. Nine managers in 19 years: that is Aberdeen FC's answer to a turkey shoot. It puts him in line with Tottenham's Daniel Levy and Hibernian's Rod Petrie. How does he feel when he reads criticism of himself? Is it fair or palpably unfair? 'It's a bit of both. We are critical of ourselves sometimes if things don't go to expectations. But the difference is there's constructive criticism like trying to find out what's gone wrong and if it could have been dealt with in a different way. In football, it's often very severe criticism based on quite a narrow agenda. You get murdered if you get anything wrong, severely and publicly. And there's no recognition for all the things that are going on in the background. I can understand that and it's one of the things I've learned over the years. I've learned to cope with it. But, when the media is having a go at the club or me, it's the people within that feel it as well. Over the years, we've been extremely lucky that we've got so many loyal people working in the background. So you can come in on a Monday morning and we're maybe in the middle of a bad period, they've got the guts to plough on. They get hurt as well with a lot of the severe criticism because they think it's reflecting on their performance. I'm nae sure if I've answered your question, but I'm just trying to give a bit of an understanding.'

And here was me thinking that the chairman was going to restrict himself to short, staccato bursts of dialogue. He's now talking as if he's been familiar with a microphone all his life. But, it seems, he's only just begun. 'If you took Aberdeen from 2008 to now, with regards to managers, I don't think that you'd find we're too much out of line with most of the other clubs. I believe and the board believes that every decision we've made to part with managers has been done for the right reasons. And I'd like to think we've always carried it out the right way. We've been very fair with those we've parted company with. I strongly believe that. The one that gets thrown back to me a lot is Ebbe Skovdahl, which was an unusual appointment. But we did a lot of work before we appointed him. His club, Brondby, was very similar to Aberdeen and he did a fantastic job there. They spoke very highly of him and we genuinely believed that he could come in and do a real job for us. Maybe under different circumstances, he might have done that, but it didn't work out. You could go through all the managers and pick out the good and the bad.

'Same with Craig and Archie. They came in and did a good job – no, a fantastic job – at a time we needed a bit of stability. That gave us a bit of a platform to move forward and build a squad. Craig might have a go at me for saying this, but he was at an age when it doesn't matter how good and able you are, the years take their toll. We felt that we needed some new energy into the club, somebody who was capable of making a real commitment over those next four or five years, picking up the journey that Craig and Archie had started. People were critical when we decided that they'd done the job they'd come in to do and when we appointed Derek. But I think that was one of the best moves that we made over the years. Derek and Tony have injected a new energy and new thinking into the club. They've played a huge part and allowed us to build a very strong infrastructure. We genuinely believe we're going to be able to sustain it.'

Milne is quick to trample on any theory that he is a dictator, benevolent or otherwise. But he also points out that he should never been dismissed as a soft touch. 'I don't think I'm a dictator. I've always worked this way in business: I'm a great believer that you achieve things through other people. A good leader sets out what we're going to do, and everybody understands what's got to be delivered. Then you use the talent around you. It's those people who deliver the bulk of whatever happens. Sure, I get involved, but one of my best qualities is that I'm a good delegator. I strongly believe in allowing people to get on with their jobs. There's a way to do things when people are nae performing. You've got to be honest with them, but it disna need to be in a destructive way. If you destroy people, you've got to spend a lot of time rebuilding them. But there's also a need for very blunt and direct discussions. That's the way I've operated with all the managers.'

Milne favours spending time with his lieutenants away from the workplace. He asks them to visit him at Dalhebity House or at his office. He and McInnes spend a lot of time together, talking not just about day-to-day issues but also focussing on forward planning. 'If things are not going right, then you've got to be asking the direct questions. To me, that's something that should build a relationship. If I believe people are on the right track, I'll back them 100 per cent. If not, I'll be equally blunt and making them aware of the consequences.'

Remembering that he said he shipped some criticism when he appointed McInnes, I ask him if he sacked Brown. The eyes tell you he's almost outraged by the question. But a definitive explanation is forthcoming. 'No, no. We spoke about it for a few months as part of looking forward and developing a momentum. Craig was very much part of the decision making process. We could have left it a wee bit longer but, on balance, it was the right time to make a move. If we'd sacked Craig, he wouldna still be here. We said, "This is a decision we've come to very much with your input, Craig. We want you to remain very much part of the club. There is more you can contribute to the next stage of the development." That's worked out. I think he genuinely enjoys being part of it. You know, Craig's one of the nicest and best people I've worked with; he's so committed. He never had any real connect to Aberdeen before, but in the role he fulfils, he's probably our best ambassador. He does an immense amount of work and will do anything for the club. Our corporate support has a great affection (for him). I think you could always argue that we could have left it another year before we brought somebody else in, but we felt it was the right time to make the move. If we could bring the right person in, with the right attitude, a person who wisna going to come and destroy everything that Craig had built. I think that was a good starting point. And then we would move it on to the next level.'

Whilst Aberdeen strive to reach the next stage of their development, I'm arriving at the next stage of this interview. I've more or less allowed Milne to run the show up so far, but now that he's settled and perhaps trusts me more, it's time to ask the real questions. The right person, as far as the board of directors was concerned, was Derek McInnes. But I put it to him that I'm not sure that he was first choice.

Those eyes are drilling into me again. 'He was.'

'Derek Adams was interviewed.'

'He was never interviewed.'

It's all about semantics here. 'Not officially, maybe.'

'I have chats with lots of people.'

'Well, I was told he was offered the job. And your vice chairman (George Yule) was behind him.

'I can sit here and put my right hand up to God and categorically state that Derek Adams was never offered the manager's job at Pittodrie. Never.'

'He was in your thoughts, though.'

'There was a number of people... but there was a reason we spoke with Derek. It was never an interview.'

'So what was it, then?'

'It was a discussion because I was asked to have it by somebody.'

'Your vice chairman?'

'Yeah. I met with Derek and Derek's father – it was Derek's father who asked me. But he was never offered the job. Derek McInnes was the number one choice.'

My information – and, admittedly, this might have contained a strain of prejudice – was that Adams could have had the job, but he allegedly insisted that the backroom staff had to change, which would have engendered a considerable pay-out. But who am I to contradict the man who is giving me a couple of hours of his time on a Friday morning? I back off the Adams line and concentrate on McInnes.

What was the one thing Milne identified in him that he knew would make him a good Aberdeen manager? He insists that former St Johnstone chairman Geoff Brown spoke very highly of his former employee, and that Brown had played an integral part in shaping the McInnes approach to management. 'He's got natural leadership skills. When we met with him, at our house in Gleneagles, we spent about three hours with him. But I knew within the first hour that he was our guy. I was convinced that he could come in here and pick up what Craig and Archie had started off. He was 100 per cent committed. There was a determination to deliver success that I'd never seen in any other manager. You could see the desire, the commitment, the thinking as to how he was going to approach the job. Then, the following night, we got him up here to meet the rest of the board.'

So McInnes was given two helpings of sybaritic living on consecutive days? Milne laughs. 'We were impressed... by the time he left here on the Friday night, we were all 100 per cent behind him. It was just getting to know him and giving him the opportunity to put his thinking on the table. I was convinced he was somebody I could build a strong relationship with. There was an openness and an honesty, a directness and a determination. And a work ethic that was absolutely essential.'

Right, let's finally cut to the chase and I'm not talking about the ITV one that involves anyone answering to the name of Iron Knickers. I put it to Milne that sometime after the Dons' League Cup victory over Inverness CT, he had paid McInnes the ultimate compliment – that he'd more or less said that he'd found Alex Ferguson, Mark 11. Milne attempts to spoil the moment. 'I'm trying to think where that would have been.'

His memory returns almost immediately. 'No, in fact, Alex Ferguson was there. I think there are a lot of comparisons (between the two men). That was the first time that Derek had met Sir Alex. They struck up a great understanding and you could see they have a lot of the same qualities.'

'It was one helluva endorsement.'

'Well, he's got to prove it. I used the opportunity to throw the challenge down to Derek: this is what you can aspire to.'

'Did you have a wee drink in?'

The Milne smile returns. 'I think Sir Alex has a very high regard for Derek as an individual and how he sets about doing his job. Look, I think he's capable of continuing to deliver success for Aberdeen. He's never content with what we've already done. He's always trying to move on to that next stage. The big test for Derek and the club is we've got to deliver another trophy and get into the group stages of the Europa Cup. That's what the drive is for. Everyone within the club believes that we've got a fighting chance of achieving that with Derek at the helm.'

There is a time for everything, they say. This is the time for direct speech. Putting my fan's hat on and trying not to be blinded by the light that surrounds McInnes, I suggest that the last two January transfer windows have been much more than disappointing. First, there was the Tansey affair (Milne doesn't wish to discuss that, but my informants tell me that the then manager, John Hughes, allegedly threatened to walk out if the player was sold). Tansey, of course, has signed a pre-contract and will be an Aberdeen player by the time this book is published. But what about the Ash Taylor question and whether he is a bone fide centre half or an unofficial bomb scare?

Remember we are talking prior to the Tansey situation changing. I believe Aberdeen are possibly two players away from becoming a really good side. The hopeful thing is that Milne is aware of these recruitment problems. 'January is a very disruptive window for a lot of clubs. It suits those that have a lot of money to go out there and put pressure on and destabilise players. The reality is at clubs like ours there's not a lot of players who are available then. But I wouldn't necessarily disagree with you. If we could get a top-notch central defender and a top-notch midfield player who would fit into that squad, yeah, but it's finding them and finding them within the parameters that we can afford. We are continually looking and when we come round to the summer, there will no doubt be other changes. But, by the time we get in a central defender and a midfielder, some of the existing players will have moved on.'

It's time to move the interview into uncharted waters and discuss the David Goodwillie affair. I warn Milne that he is not going to like the question. Now, in my opinion, this 2014 signing from Blackburn Rovers should never have taken place. In 2011, the Dundee United player and his colleague David Robertson had been charged with raping a young woman, Denise Clair, at a flat in Armadale, West Lothian. The case against both men was dropped before it reached court. There was always the possibility that there would be a civil case against them. (Ultimately, this happened, with Miss Clair winning her case this year and being awarded £100,000 in compensation from Goodwillie and his co-defendant. Please note that the court ruling came after he had left Aberdeen). I understand there was at least one member of the Pittodrie boardroom who predicted that the move was unwise. So, I ask Milne why, in light of all the controversy and uncertainty, the player was signed.

'At the end of the day, as far as we can, we back the manager's judgment of players. Everyone around that boardroom table has a real belief in Derek's judgment. Derek had worked with the player before and knew him well. He was prepared to take on the challenge of getting Goodwillie back to where he once was. There was no certainty that there would be a (civil) case. Derek weighed everything up – we weighed everything up. The decision was made that we'd take him to the club. I'm not aware that anybody seriously questioned whether it was the right decision.'

I point out that there was one director who said there was a good chance of the player being summoned and how would this look for Aberdeen? Milne's response is unconvincing. 'Yeah, I'm not saying that... we challenged Derek in lots of different areas. And that whole thing was challenged. There's nae one player we bring into the club that there's not something that casts a bit of doubt. But it comes to this: at the end of the day, you've got to make a judgment. If 70-80 per cent is good, can we manage the other 20 per cent? The decision wisna made blindly. We knew there was an issue here... '

But wasn't it more like 50-50 than 80-20? 'No, if it had been like that, we wouldna have made that decision. It might have been 70-30. The thing is I don't think we got out of him what he had the potential to deliver. It didna work out as we all hoped it might.'

Okay, we'll leave that one in the pigeon hole labelled 'unsatisfactory'. I hit him with a question about his wealth. It was only a few years ago that the Sunday Times Rich List put his fortune at £300-million plus. He laughs, I suspect out of relief that we have now left the subject of Goodwillie. 'I thought in your wisdom you'd never have believed that, especially other people's newspapers.'

I persist. There was lots of gossip that Milne's millions had dwindled and there was even a suspicion that his company might have gone bust. Was there any chance of that happening? 'No, the reality is that the world changed in 2008 and since then it's been a pretty challenging environment. Particularly in our sector. Aberdeen recovered a bit quicker than the rest of the world, but then, when the rest of the country starts to come back, what happens to Aberdeen and the economy up here? Before the crash, our turnover was close to £500 million. Now we're back to half of that. That's just the cycle you come through. It's like everything else: you've just got to adjust to the environment you're in. It's been a very painful process and it's cost of a lot of money to come through it. But you've got to learn from that and we're a stronger organisation going forward.'

We're on to the last question and you see a floodwater of relief on his face. I tell him that Joe Harper once told me that he'd paid for so many things out of his pocket, yet never told anyone about it. Harper couldn't understand that and neither could I. Particularly after the vilification to which he'd been subjected. 'Listen, it's nae just what I've done. Lots of people have made sacrifices. If we'd published what we'd had to do just to keep things going over the past period, most people wouldna believe it. I've always been a great believer that if you feel you need to go out and shout about things, it's not the right thing to be doing. It's more important to be discreet. Let people judge on the outcome, as opposed to what you've done and havenae done.'

And how long will his leadership last? The smile is back. 'Put it this way: I have no plans to abdicate.'

It took me years to secure a meeting with Stewart Milne. It took me minutes to make my mind up about him. I think, contrary to what many people believe, that my club is in bloody good hands. He may not be a scholar, but he is a gentleman of the boardroom. He doesn't get everything right, but he's only human. He escorts me to the door and we exchange pleasantries.

I tell him I hope I haven't been too intrusive. 'No, no. You say it in a nice way.' I'm not sure I wanted to hear that.

CHAPTER 22

McInnes Bites Back

INTERVIEWING SPORTS PERSONALITIES has monopolised much of my profession-al life, but there have been inevitable qualifications to the rules of engagement. For instance, I make it an imperative to identify the carefully-coded messag-es sent out by vexed interviewees. A certain look, the odd sigh or overt con-sultation of the wristwatch indicate that your victim believes you're abusing your welcome and that he's nearing exhaustion, if not slipping into full-blown catatonia. We may be close to this situation today, in the Willie Miller Suite at Pittodrie: after approximately one hour and 36 minutes of comparatively respectful questioning, Derek McInnes is betraying small signs of impatience, but these are about to morph into significant signs of irritation. Mind you, that's a considerable improvement on catatonia.

McInnes travels down this avenue on only rare occasions, his lack of enthu-siasm for one-to-one interviews almost equalling Sir Phillip Green's initial reluc-tance to open his wallet to BHS pensioners. It's said his admiration for some members of my profession could be diagnosed as slim going on anorexic. Thus, the barriers have been erected: Aberdeen FC, whether they agree or not, have established themselves as a form of sporting politburo, where everything is con-trolled, in the manner reminiscent of a Glaswegian manager who is long gone but far from forgotten. You suspect that newspapers, bar the local ones, are considered almost an irrelevance and most news of any import is released on the club's website, occasionally at the ungodly hour of midnight. It's probable I would have challenged this state of affairs back in my sports-editing pomp, but retirement has emancipated me from all that, thank God.

Before we return to McInnes, let me stress that strategies are essential for interviews with football managers, taking into consideration the levels of their paranoia and indeed senses of their own importance. So, you work out the var-ious game plans according to quotients of temperament, ego, belligerence, etc.

Sir Alf Ramsey didn't like Scotsmen, but he did love a gin and tonic. So, I plied him with enough drink to make his eyes spin. We got on famously.

Alex Ferguson was an awesome project, far more intimidating than Ramsey. The trick was to try not to be intimidated. After absorbing the ritualistic bollocking and then fronting him up, our early relationship flourished.

Bill Shankly could be a likeable, if crusty, old stick, but if you fed his ego a little and resisted the temptation to say anything provocative or silly, it was possible to harmonise with him.

The disturbing thing is I cannot really work out a strategy for McInnes.

It's evident he is a good football manager and an ambitious and perhaps arrogant one at that. As far as I know, ambition and arrogance have not yet been classified as crimes. They are an essential part of the weaponry for anyone wanting to leave an imprint on life. An open book he is not, though. He seems reluctant to lift the trap door and reveal his real personality. I am well aware that he has done me a considerable favour by agreeing to see me and I'm not going to forget it any time soon. But it's understood that much of this game will be played according to his rules. You therefore honour the fact that confidences concerning all sorts of subjects – including James Maddison, Miles Storey and even television's Eilidh Barbour – must not be broken. But, as far as I am aware, no sycophancy agreement has been signed. It is not written in stone that I must agree with everything he says.

Now, something about Aberdeen FC has been troubling me for 18 months and today I'm attempting to pinpoint that trouble spot. You no doubt remember the team's performances in 2015-16, the season it was suggested that the Dons might have won the Premiership title. It's inarguable that they were given every possible chance as Celtic, under Ronny Deila, were anaemic representatives of their true selves. But, in the end, some mystifying and unaccountable lapses of concentration, both in October and near the chequered flag, meant that the Dons finished second, 15 points behind the Glaswegians.

The depressing trend began in a September League Cup evening at Easter Road; the Dons had recorded eight straight victories in the League, but lost 2-0 to the local heroes of Hibernian. This precipitated a disastrous five-game run, in which we picked up only one point out of 15, before relatively normal service was resumed. Social media, in particular, identified the defeat by Hibs as the reason for the collapse, and indeed all sorts of rumours abounded about friction in the dressing room that night. I put it to McInnes that it had all gone wrong in Edinburgh. Up until this point, he has been the essence of warmth and hospitality. But now it's as if someone has opened the front doors of Pittodrie and a cruel, cold wind is blowing in off the North Sea.

'What, away back in October?' he asks, incredulously. Actually, it was 23 September. 'No, I don't think that's fair because we were only three points behind in January. I think, even your question has really kinda annoyed me because you're so wrong. Our start meant that we broke a club record. Alex Ferguson and all, no other manager had won eight league games in a row, as good as the teams had been. So, there was so much that was right. As soon as we dipped below that, it went from this to that. It can sometimes happen, but to imply that there was something sinister and untoward other than that the team had lost a few games… even your line of questioning, as a respected journalist, to even question something that's picked up from social media is wrong.'

It's my turn to experience irritation. I tell McInnes that social media was not the sole provider of the information; besides, I'm old enough to form my own conclusions. His fight against perceived injustice, however, has only just begun.

'Aye, but if you're asking me about a league challenge, that was real. There was three points in it in January (he's conveniently forgetting that the Dons might have been comfortably ahead of Celtic by then if they hadn't lost four games and drawn one). That was three or four months after the Easter Road game. We were trying to bring another striker to the club to take the weight off Adam Rooney – but then we picked up injuries to (Willo) Flood and (Ryan) Jack in January, And all of a sudden, the priority changed. We needed a midfielder in. I then got a call from Liverpool one Sunday morning, taking Danny Ward back. I thought, "F***, here we go." At last I've found myself a keeper who's capable. Then it was a case of can we get a keeper in? You're not going to get one of any real note in January. I don't want to disparage anyone, but…' (he stipulates that the next five words are off the record).

'We lost Rooney in the first week of February and then Danny Ward. Now, you lose your No. 9 and your goalkeeper and all of a sudden, we were weaker in two major positions. I brought Simon Church in to play alongside Rooney: the two games they played together, we beat Celtic and Partick Thistle. Goodwillie went to Ross County, so we had one striker in the building. We thought Rooney and Church on the pitch at the same time equals goals. We thought, if he's no' scoring, the other will. If Leigh Griffiths had got injured at the same time with the same injury, that would have impacted hugely on Celtic. They were so dependent on him. Celtic lost four games last season. People say this to me all the time: "Aw, you'll never have a better chance. Youse blew it – the best chance to win the league." Nonsense! Even if we had kept up the levels of what we were doing, we still needed other teams to beat Celtic. We beat them twice, Motherwell beat them at Parkhead and St Johnstone beat them 2-1. Their points tally was on a par with most championship winning teams.

'So criticise Deila, criticise how unconvincing Celtic were at times. I understand that. But the points they got in the league still had to be applauded. They still done the job. So, even if we'd been better and took it to the last game, instead of the last three or four games, we'd have had to keep our standards up. And the wheels came off at Motherwell. Robson sent off. We were 1-0 up but lost two late goals. They (Celtic) got the last-minute winner at Kilmarnock – Rogic. If they'd not won that game and we had won ours, I think we'd have been level with them in March/April. That was a defining moment, no' losing a league cup-tie at Hibs.'

Now, I must admit that I'm impressed with the passion and fluency of the this human word processor: the outburst puts you in mind of that genius of statistics and speedy speechifying, Jeff Stelling. I congratulate McInnes on his memory, but I don't believe he's listening. The rant is some way from its conclusion.

'We lost at Inverness before Hibs (actually it was after the Hibs match). It was our third game in six days. I thought we looked leggy and they overpowered us, Ryan Christie scores a wonderful goal, so there was a fantastic goal and a slightly below-par performance. It was difficult to say we didn't deserve to lose the game – I thought they were just a wee bit hungrier than us. It was the first defeat in nine league games. It happens. I don't think you can win every game. We went to Hibs and this is another thing. I thought they were a decent side. They went 5-4-1 at home and allowed us to have all the ball. We picked up two injuries in the first 20 minutes. See, nobody will even look at that: Shinnie and Flood come off and we end up a wee bit disjointed. We were 0-0 until the 83rd minute and we huffed and puffed. And Cummings scored out of nothing in a counter attack. Then they scored in injury time when we were chasing the game. So, if you actually look back, we've actually lost two keys players, mainstays, playing every week, in the first 20 minutes. There was never the same rhythm to our play. [We were] still better than Hibs, though. But they've done us on the counter attack and won the game. Let's not forget, they won the Scottish Cup as well: they werenae a bad team. This was our fourth game in 11 days. Then it was St Johnstone at home – and we lost 5-1. Everyone went into overdrive. What the f***'s going on? We lost 5-1. It was just one of thae games. Even when I look back, we actually played well, but that result was in total isolation. We've never lost a game like that. Never. Just so you know. I'm no' going into this – I don't want any of that being spoken about, to be honest.'

I cannot believe McInnes has just said that he expects this to be treated as a private conversation. It's perfectly clear that he's on the record until he talks about a particular facet of the goalkeeping situation. But now that he's reached the end of his peroration, he realises there's been too much transparency and seeks to retract. He's not on. I remember being told that Shay Logan had once allegedly disrespected Celtic in the press conference, likening them to a team in the bottom reaches of England. When McInnes heard, he raced down to the media room and persuaded journalists against using the Logan material. As far as today is concerned, in my estimation, there's little in what he's said that should worry him. So, I remind him that the book is meant to be about the truth and congratulate him on putting up a pretty impressive defence of his team. Why the hell would he not want that to go out to the fans? He softens his stance.

'But that was the reality. We lost to Hibs in the League Cup, then a freak-ish game here and we lost three games in a row. All of a sudden, it was a case of what's going on? It happens. Players go through good spells of form; we're a team that normally go on winning runs three or four times a season; strong runs. And, if we have a bad result, we just jump straight back on. You can say that's where we lost the league, but were only three points behind in January. No, criticism is what it is. If it's constructive, if it's warranted, okay. Nobody is beyond criticism. Every decision I make has a consequence. If you win a game, you're deemed to have picked the right team and made the right decision. That's not always the truth.'

The storm of indignation abates. If anything untoward occurred at Easter Road that night – and, without wishing to be sinister, I'm still convinced that something did occur – it's not going to be McInnes who deposits it in the public domain. Having said all that, this is just a small segment of discord in what has been a vastly enjoyable interview. I've known a host of managers and most of them suffer from justifiable paranoia: they're correct in their thinking that many people are out to get them. But I'm not out to 'get' McInnes. There are some things he's done in his time of which I have not approved: his penchant for the lone striker; the apparent lack of a back-up plan when things are going awry; the incomprehensible signings of Josh Parker, Alan Tate. Andrew Driver, Calvin Zola and Gregg Wylde; his insistence that David Goodwillie would be good for Aberdeen; and his perseverance with Ash Taylor at centre half; his reluctance to play Niall McGinn in his best and most productive position – through the mid-dle. But I'm a fan who pays his money and thus is entitled to carp: I also recog-nise that it's all too simplistic to be right from the vantage points of an armchair or a terracing. Nothing is ever straightforward and nobody is perfect, not even the greatest of managers. So, an understanding of McInnes' inner being, not only his *moedus operandi*, is what I want. And this is what I'm given.

He asks me why I'm writing the book. The explanation is simple: there's the age factor, the fact that I have a heart condition and that I also suffer from pros-tate cancer. Time is not my best friend. Besides, I've lived my life through this club for more than six decades. I would like to make a meaningful contribution to it. McInnes responds with compassion: he tells me he has a friend who's been refusing to acknowledge the obvious regarding prostate cancer and that the doctors believed they might have been too late in catching it. 'Anyway, they cut it away and he phoned me on Friday and said he's got the all clear. Fantastic. It was worrying him sick for the last couple of months.'

I can sympathise with that feeling. Our conversation progresses smoothly. McInnes was born in Paisley, birthplace of so many gifted men, including the subject of my earlier ebook, *Gerry Rafferty: Renegade Heart*. His mother still lives in the same house in which he was born. His father, a one-time transport manager in Chivas Regal, died, aged 61, of a perforated bowel. He had been suffering from Non-Hodgkin Lymphoma and had experienced the debilitating effects of chemotherapy. McInnes, playing for Toulouse at the time, was called by his Uncle James and told that his father was gravely ill. He flew back imme-diately and was able to spend a few hours at his father's bedside. 'He wasn't responsive but he knew I was there. He died at a quarter to midnight, almost a year to my wee boy's first birthday – 24th of March. Jack was born on the 25th. It was so sad: he was away too early. He had been always very healthy up until a year or two before he was diagnosed. He'd served in the military, then come back into civil life and worked hard. He used to come to all my games. He was a brilliant supporter. He'd never go overboard if I'd done well, but equally never criticise me if I hadn't. He was always the first person I spoke to after a game and, although it diminishes after a time, his opinion still matters. I think of him every day. I just feel it was unfair that he missed out on so much. I got three boys: they're all different, but he would have loved them.'

The McInnes playing career was eclectic: Morton, Rangers, Stockport County, Toulouse, West Brom, Dundee United, Millwall and St Johnstone. He had been captain at Morton, but it was at West Brom where he learned the true meaning of accountability. He remembers manager Gary Megson handing him the players' complimentary tickets. 'He was making the point that I was there to lead, I loved the responsibility of that. That's me. As soon as I'm involved, I give everything.'

In his second season, the love affair intensified. West Brom were promoted to the Premier League, but McInnes experienced the dubious distinction of being the first Baggie to be sent off in this elite division. There was a compensatory factor: he was playing at Old Trafford at the time – against Beckham, Scholes, Giggs and Co – and he was kicking Nicky Butt. He was slightly aggrieved. Min-utes earlier, he had been on the end of a similar challenge from Roy Keane. 'But it was brilliant just taking the team out.'

McInnes had completed all his coaching badges by the time he moved to Dundee United in 2003, but his eyes were riveted on management. 'I didn't want to be a coach.'

As he entered the twilight zone of his playing career, he dabbled in youth coaching with both Millwall and then St Johnstone. He made the conversion to management after Owen Coyle left to go to Burnley. When chairman Geoff Brown offered him the job, he was scarcely surprised but felt it was right. His relationship with Brown meant that he could become familiar with the ropes without having directorial hassle. He was still playing at the time, but after a few games he acknowledged the reality of his situation. 'My head was like a toy shop. I realised I couldnae do it. You either need to be a player, or a manager, unless you've got a huge support network behind you. It's just too much of a challenge. Now, I was close to a lot of my players: they were my team mates and I travelled with them. All that had to stop. I needed to become the guy who was seen as a manager, no' just Del the team mate or the guy who picks the team. As much as I felt I could still contribute on the pitch, they needed me to contribute more as a manager. And I made that decision to stop playing.'

I ask him if the conversion had precipitated any resentment. 'No. I've always been close to my players. I still speak to my St Johnstone players and they still text me. I still speak to my Bristol City players. Even when guys leave from Aberdeen squads that I've had, you cannae be buddy-buddy or best pals, but you can still have an influence on them and be close to them.'

And so we arrive at the moment that possibly influenced the McInnes managerial career more than any other. Saints had fallen just short of promotion in his first year: they were desperate to swim with the dolphins in the SPL, but both crowds and budgets were small. Tough decisions were required. There were two options for centre half: one a youngster, the other Alan McManus, a fellow Paisleyite and a good friend with whom he travelled. Who should go? McManus was the unfortunate one. And, as McInnes recalls, 'He never saw it coming. I always remember thinking that this would be the toughest one I'd ever done. But it was the right decision – 100 per cent right. No, he never agreed with that decision and I didn't expect him to. We never spoke for a number of years. There was no need to speak. But I speak to him now. He's fine. It's the same with anything I do, regarding football. The overriding decision has got to be right. As soon you try to compromise, it leaves you nowhere. I said to him the way I wanted to press the game and play with a high line – at his age, the tendency was to go a bit deeper, and that wouldn't have allowed me to play how I wanted to. He disagreed, as he would, but I was ready for that. It wasn't easy. But I think that every time when I go to release players and tell them they're no longer part of the plans, I always remind myself of that one. It's never easy, but it's been easier since then. He's still a pal. He'll no' admit it, but now he'll know I was right.'

McInnes' successful spell in Perth brought him to the attention of Bristol City. He might not care to confess it, but deep down it might have been better for him had he escaped that attention. Before McInnes' arrival, a cursory glance of City history tells you that those in charge would have experienced difficulty spotting a solar eclipse, never mind a manager who delivered satisfaction. Eighteen – that's correct: 18 – had come and gone from 1980 to 2011, which was when McInnes arrived. In fact, he was their fourth boss in 19 months. Distress signals were everywhere. October saw City at the bottom of the league, ten points below the second-bottom team. McInnes and his first lieutenant, Tony Docherty, brought out the repair kit and went to work. The club was haemorrhaging money and the wage bill had to be halved by that Christmas, but in spite of the stifling prohibition, the two Scots kept the club in the Championship. McInnes' status was at its zenith at this point and he admits now, 'In hindsight, we should have been kicking and screaming to get things done: we needed a huge recruitment drive to get better players in and get some out. We did neither, really. But the answers weren't in the building.'

The fact that McInnes did not act at the optimum moment came back to persecute him. The next season, the team began positively and were high in the league when the transfer window closed, having sorted out Cardiff, Crystal Palace and Southampton along the way. But it was evident that they were going to fall short, certainly defensively. McInnes does not exonerate himself from culpability. 'Hey, I've got my part to play in that, but I think there were others there who had a part to play. I loved the club, loved living in the city. The supporters were always very fair with me and I was desperate to be the one who changed their fortunes and bring them stability. But, unfortunately, I never got the opportunity to finish the job.'

He did, however, have the opportunity to play the Good Samaritan. One evening, after a defeat at Birmingham, he was approached by a group of supporters. Ironically, they didn't want to demonstrate their anger at defeat, but to relate a hard-luck tale: the tyres on their mini-bus had been slashed, they were clearly distressed, had no money and were wondering how they would get home. McInnes contributed the contents of his own pocket and urged his players to make their contributions. They gave the beleaguered fans £300. 'We weren't legally allowed to take them on our bus, 'cos of the numbers already on it. So, we managed to get them home. It didnae seem anything out of the ordinary at the time. It was the right thing to do. I remember there were teenage boys and I've got teenage boys – I wouldnae have wanted them stuck so far away from home.'

Charity often goes unrewarded. In January of 2013, after only 16 months in charge, McInnes was climbing into his car and heading for Paisley and the comforting arms of his wife Nicola. His team had lost 4-1 to Leicester. McInnes had felt protected. 'The language from the people above was, "We need to sort out this mess. If we go down with Derek McInnes, we go back with Derek McInnes." I felt my relationship was so strong with the people there that we'd work our way through this. Obviously, when you're at the bottom end of the table, you're never ever safe, but it was actually a shock when they did it. I think it was quite a reactive decision. But, there again, I totally understood that they wanted to go in another direction. I felt we would have stayed up that year; I'd never had a relegation on my name – I'd only had success. And I felt, having shown an ability to keep them up from a far worse situation the year before, we'd have done it again. We'd have definitely done it – kicking and screaming.'

The next question is simple: was there a sense of betrayal within him? 'Och, I don't want to… I felt a bit let down because of what I was getting told, really. I'm trying to offload a lot of the high earners and trying to bring in players on far less money, which is difficult when you're trying to raise standards. But the importance of reducing the wage bill was stressed to me on a daily basis. I think betrayal is too strong a word. I like Steve Lansdown, the owner, and I know he gave me such a good reference to my current chairman, Stewart Milne. I always felt that he was someone I could have worked with. He was a very wealthy man who lived in Guernsey for tax reasons. He'd fly in and fly out for games and I really had no relationship with him because of that.'

The 313-mile journey from Bristol provided McInnes with a lot of thinking time. Much of this, I imagine, was devoted to the Arnold Schwarzenegger man-tra: I'll be Back. McInnes agrees. 'Yes, it was. Better managers than me have lost their jobs and people say you don't become a proper manager until you've been sacked. But it wisnae nice at the time – I cannot pretend otherwise. I thought it important just to immerse myself in the family again. I loved seeing my wife and kids on a daily basis. But people just think I had such a bad experience at Bristol City. It's so wrong. Yeah, the last two months were difficult because results weren't there. But I was talking to Walter Smith not long ago and he was speaking about Everton. I actually feel like him: I done some of my best work as manager at Bristol. The results don't always come with that. You're having to manage a situation rather than just the team, and you're having to put out fires. If things transmit to wins on a Saturday, you're no' doing it because you've got good players or there's a decent manager, it's because everything else is running right. There's got to be an infrastructure and a solidness about how you work throughout your club for that to manifest on the pitch. That, for me, was what we had at St Johnstone – one chairman, one decision maker. It's similar here. We've got a board, but Stewart's the main decision maker. I like the simplicity of that. It's yes or no when you want to do something. There's no dancing around things with promises and false promises, or things like that.'

So, the spring of 2013 saw McInnes taking stock and preparing himself for the next challenge. He has rarely encouraged interviewers to dwell overly long on those months in England. 'Obviously, there had to be a period of reflection. I always think you can come across as bitter and twisted. But I believe we should have stayed up and that I should have stayed in the job. I'd have bettered them, the way I bettered St Johnstone, the way I bettered this club. I believe my way of working and how we work as a staff gets results. But I totally understand. The nature of Championship football is that of the 24 managers who started 2016, 15 lost their jobs before the end of the year. That's down to the nature of what's at stake. I've got no axe to grind. We live, we learn.'

Stewart Milne learned enough about McInnes from both Brown and Lansdown to appoint him on 25 March, 2013. At his interview, he told them that he didn't know what they were looking for, but he illustrated his methodology. 'I told them what I expected; told them I would set the pace, drive the club on. I had certain standards and knew how I wanted my team to play. I more or less said, if that's what you expect from your manager, here I am. But I also told them I couldnae be someone I'm not. I wanted the job; Aberdeen felt right, right from the start. I got a good feeling. A lot of time your gut tells you. Don't get me wrong, there was work to be done: this is a demanding club. But now I think we've put a squad together and a team that keeps pace with that demand. How the club was operating and how it was working, we were never giving ourselves a chance to compete. Now, we're a totally different animal. We've got our respect back in Scotland, which I wanted to do. We're now competing in Europe every year and trying to get some respect from that. Domestically, teams worry about playing Aberdeen and that wisnae always the case.'

We Aberdeen fans, perhaps like most football fans, are an idiosyncratic lot. Some of us adhere to reason and common sense, others are insatiable in their demands. The latter is not always possible. McInnes said originally that he didn't want fans coming along through a sense of duty or because their dads had taken them to games. 'I wanted them to wake up on match days, home and away, and feel the way I did about the team; wake up with that excitement in their stomachs. So, first of all, we had to get the hardest working team, an energetic team, an honest team. We had that through our first signings in Willo Flood and Barry Robson. These were people who could handle being Aberdeen players.

Believe me, it's no' an easy club to manage or to play for. But the rewards are everything.

'Say it was 0-0 at home to Kilmarnock and the fans were baying for blood, I needed players who would give more, no' go under with the pressure of it all. I look at the squad now and we have a team of value. There's money in that squad. We've got players who every other team in Scotland – well, the majority, anyway – would love in their team. And we've got a connection with the supporters, even though we cannae be good all the time. We try to be good, the aim being to win every game, but there are acceptable ways of losing and the supporters identify with that.'

I would imagine that Craig Brown might take exception to some of the McInnes reasoning, particularly the insistence that he and Docherty would have had no chance of competing with the structure that was in place. It was Brown, after all, who was obliged to sell all his important players. And it was Brown, indeed, who urged his successor to forge close links with the chairman and avoid what he termed the line-manager system. Curiously, McInnes never mentions the name of the former Aberdeen manager in the 11,500 words that are exchanged on this day. But you suspect nothing stands in way of progress, McInnes-style.

'When I came to Aberdeen, I consciously made sure that the guy who makes the decisions and helps me do the job better is the guy I'm close to and work closely with. I involved Stewart with everything. Every couple of weeks, I go out to his house and we sit for three or four hours, and that, effectively for me, is a board meeting. It's relaxed and we get up to date with staffing and recruitment issues. It's always transparent and open. There's no point me forming relationships with other people (I take it he's referring to Duncan Fraser and George Yule) if the guy I need to be working closely to is the chairman. I didn't want to hear things second hand. It's always better to look people in the eyes and express my concerns, whatever. And I think that being honest, abrupt at times and transparent is always the best way, rather than let anything fester. I phone the chairman on a Friday and give him the team. I think that's his right to know it and why I've picked it. I'll speak to him briefly after the game. I was out to dinner with him last night. He's a very busy man and his love for the club is clear. The time he puts in outwith his own business to make Aberdeen as strong as we can isn't always documented. He works so hard, and any time I get with him to talk about our plans is always invaluable to me.'

I can understand why McInnes reputedly blew the directors away at his interview. He comes at you like a steamroller and leaves you to decide whether it's sensible to jump out of the way or accept the consequences. You get the feeling he doesn't mind, either way. He's remorseless and ruthless, just how a good football manager should be. And abrupt when the occasion demands it. 'You've just got to see it as it is. If things need changed, I like that frankness that you can have, rather than dancing about things.'

I ask him where he would put himself if they were a league table for ruthlessness. He doesn't answer directly but does not leave you in any doubt that he would be up there hoping to win a league title. 'I think I know what I want and I'm prepared to give people opportunities. I don't like being about lazy people and don't want them in my club. I don't want negative people in my club. Radiators and drainers… I'd rather work with people who are uplifting and positive and ready to get busy, make the situation better rather than mump and moan. I cannae be around people like that. I think it's important that you never allow bad practice. As soon as you allow things to creep in, you're gone. Never have a lazy day; some days are more demanding than others, but we're here to work and I know how I want it to work and how it has to work. I think, in terms of ruthlessness, it's being like a parent: you've got to chastise, but you've also got to give players a cuddle and show compassion at the right time. It's about getting good people in the building and knowing that, if mistakes are made or performances are low, it's not through lack of professionalism or neglect, it's through honesty. We all make mistakes and you can't expect to be brilliant every day, but you can be honest every day. And hard working. I've made some quick decisions after bringing players in and I've moved them on in the next window. I knew they werenae right, werenae good for me.'

We could start with Josh Parker, I suggest. 'There have been others. You don't need to mention names, but they were mentally weak. You bring them in but you know quickly they're no' going to do a job. So you move them out, rather than persevere and hope it goes all right.'

So, what about Miles Storey? Here's a man who has sat on the subs' bench so many times there must be a ridge across his backside. Heartbreak Ridge, perhaps? Does McInnes have any compassion for him, or does such a feeling never enter his head? 'I think every time you make a decision on a match day, you're doing all you can to help the players win the game, so you do whatever is required. Sometimes, it's an obvious decision. I don't like going like for like. I always feel that the team that was picked to start is the one I thought could win the game. So I give them every opportunity to show them I was right. There'll be times, not loads of times, when I make changes at half-time.'

McInnes delivers a fairly detailed summation of Storey's time at Aberdeen, but insists that it remains off the record. The suspicion is that the player will not be at Pittodrie when the 2017-18 begins and indeed when this book is published. Peter Pawlett, however, is a different proposition. Perhaps the fact that he's signed a pre-contract with MK Dons enables the manager to talk more freely. He begins by admitting that, when he arrived at Pittodrie, he found Pawlett to be drifting. 'He'd been out on loan and had some decent moments, but nobody was convinced about Peter. We came in, played him in the No. 10 position, centrally. Because of his pace, everyone thought he was a winger, but actually he's no' very good there. He's good working from central areas. He was explosive and eliminated people and had a big influence in our games. He was part of our DNA. You could hear other managers talking about us. "Oh, the pace of Aberdeen – McGinn, Hayes, Pawlett." We were a counter-attacking team in that first season. It was a new team and a bit of an unknown. Peter Pawlett is as good a counter attacking player as you'll get.

'But, when teams started to recognise the strength of what he's got in that position, you've then got to work harder for solutions. Peter, in those first 18 months, was dynamic for us, a big influence. For the next 18, he was in and out and never had the same influence. Mind you, I think there's still more to come from him. He's chosen to go down to England. I felt the best way of progressing his career was at Aberdeen. But he's took the opportunity to go. I have to think he's made the wrong decision, but I totally respect what he'd decided. Looking back, certainly in my time, he was one of the constants in those four years. He's stronger now and more robust – you have to be playing in that central area.'

The rumour mill, a flourishing business concerning all things Aberdeen FC, says that Pawlett had an altercation with Anthony O'Connor in training and had deposited the Irishman on the floor. I ask McInnes if there is any truth in this. He takes a political sidestep. 'I think you see the physical shape of Peter: he's bought in what we're trying to do here. I think we're strong, quick and powerful at times. Peter's not one to go about kicking people, but he can look after himself. See his shoulders – I think that's down to the work he does and to the sports scientist, Graham Kirk.'

We move on to an afternoon that holds painful memories for both of us: the League Cup final, against Celtic. I've already elucidated my feelings at the beginning of this book. McInnes joins me in my disappointment and stresses the obvious: the team never played to their normal level. They needed to be more aggressive and impose themselves on the game, but it didn't materialise. But, he wonders, even if they had done these things, if the result would have been any different. 'I don't know. People go on that I picked the wrong team: O'Connor played instead of Reynolds and Maddison instead of McGinn. Everything else was the same. I think most Aberdeen fans would have said O'Connor was our best centre half at the time – and Maddison our biggest attacking threat. A few weeks before this, we left Maddison out against Celtic, and it was a case of,

"What's he doing?" Leaving Niall out was a tough decision, but I just felt his intensity levels were catching up with him: he hadn't had a break. It's difficult leaving him out of any team, but in my four years here, I think he's started more games than anybody. I still think the team was right – if it played to form. The players know themselves that we didn't perform to our level. All the work, during the week, had been about coming forward and being aggressive; all the language was about stepping forward. To be honest, in the league game at Parkhead, we lost 1-0 to a free kick. We were that team then. We closed them. That's how the final needed to be, but we still needed to find the quality on the back of that to score.'

But McInnes cautions that maybe the critical fans like myself should stop and think before we take the road to perdition and throw ourselves into the inferno. Only a few days after the Hampden debacle, he received a most welcome phone call from the de facto patron of Aberdeen. Sir Alex Ferguson offered advice that only he can offer.

'You know how many cup finals I lost?'

McInnes was thinking perhaps one or two. He was stunned by the answer.

'Eleven! Everyone talks about the ones I won, but I lost 11.'

McInnes recalls, 'He said two or three of those he questioned himself: made his subs too early, made his subs too late and beat himself up over it. He says, "Ah, I could have been better myself." But for the other seven or eight of them, the players just didnae turn up. And he was talking about guys with 60 caps and 600 League games – Scholes, Carrick and the rest. He told me, "Sometimes, finals can do that to you. It's only by revisiting them that you get used to the situation." His analogy was that it was like a one-way street. At first you don't know where you're going, but you keep going down the street until you get your bearings.'

I imagine the signing of David Goodwillie must have been equally frustrating to McInnes. He doesn't disagree. 'I knew David from when he was a young boy at Dundee United and I knew his qualities. He'd been drifting for two or three years and hadn't done really anything. Like any manager, you're thinking, "We'll be the ones to get him going: this'll be good." And it didnae work out. I think he had some good moments for us and some of his better games were in European competition when it was about retention of the ball. He was a better all-round player than the one I played with at United, But, for me, I thought he had lost that instinct to score goals. I felt he'd forgotten what he was – a centre forward. He was doing much of his good work 30 yards from goal. The instinct to put himself in a position for goal just wasn't there, Rooney will go and miss; he's constantly on the move in the box; that's his strongest environment; he's got the predatory instinct. We wanted Adam to be more like Goodwillie, and Goodwillie to be more like Adam. We thought the combination of both might be able to work at times, but it didn't go well for him.'

McInnes is sending out a carefully-coded message: he's looking at his watch, informing you that your time is limited. But I want to know why Goodwillie came in the first place, considering the background of the rape charge. 'But he'd been found not guilty.' McInnes protests. I point out there was a civil case coming up. 'Yeah, but that wasn't prominent at the time... I don't really want to go into it.'

I'm not surprised he doesn't wish to proceed. In my book, as a fan, it would be difficult for him to justify the signing of Goodwillie. I suspect it subtracted from Aberdeen FC's image both on and off the park. And managers, however accomplished they are, must be held accountable. But I know from experience and the temperature in the Willie Miller Suite that there is little point in pursuing this line of questioning. When the rant concerning Hibs in the League Cup is over, I have occupied McInnes' time and territory for nearly two hours and the unspoken agreement is that the occupation must end. Although his mood has deteriorated slightly in the last half-hour, he nevertheless remains courteous and escorts me to the front door. Here, however, the man whom Stewart Milne believes to be a facsimile of Fergie asks if I'll send him a copy of the interview. A thought occurs: he is the first famous manager to ask for a preview of my finished work.

Epilogue

THE INTENTION WAS TO WRITE an objective account of a football club that has dominated my dreams for the best part of seven decades. The work is nearing completion and I should be exultant but, as with most things pertaining to Aberdeen FC, there are qualifications. Take today's 2017 Scottish Cup final, for example: sadly, my expectations are those of a Zen Buddhist seeking serenity in the Oval Office. Aberdeen are encountering a Celtic team that inflicts grievous bodily harm on anyone unlucky enough to be blocking out its sun. We could be in an accident and emergency unit before the end of the day, much like we were last November.

Underpinning the pessimism is the fact that this has been a week unlike any other. Focus – it's a word cherished, championed and almost colonised by Derek McInnes – has been difficult, if not impossible, to implement. Sunderland, seeking a replacement after David Moyes' resignation, are looking north and the bookies believe our manager will be appreciative of their interest. Pittodrie is in its usual state of denial. Surely the directors are discussing a managerial Plan B? Apparently, this has not even occurred to them. Ryan Jack, meanwhile, seems destined to model the light blue jersey of Rangers; McInnes is said to be incandescent with rage because he claims Jack told him Rangers would not be a consideration. He's now stripped him of the captaincy. Ironically, the incandescence stops short of dropping him. Jack plays today. Furthermore, it's said that Kenny McLean's sat nav could be directing him back to Ibrox. Ironically, Sunderland have been all but stalking him these last few months. In addition, there are rumours about the futures of Jonny Hayes, Graeme Shinnie and Joe Lewis. Aberdeen FC are obligated to put their best foot forward today; the trouble is this foot is dangling perilously close to a f***ing banana skin. Couldn't all the rumour and innuendo have been delayed by a week? Of course not. Football does not countenance waiting for sentiment. And now, against this formidable combination of odds, we are obliged to confront by far the best team in Scotland.

As I assume my seat in the North stand, together with two of my sons, I seek refuge from all this pessimism and return to that little bubble of fifties nostalgia with the man who gave me life and introduced me to football. Everything is defined as if in ultra high density. John Joseph Cooney, tending to his beloved

garden, is a face pressed against the front window; it's the face of parental
concern as I wildly celebrate Paddy Buckley's goal against Celtic. Dad can't
appreciate the delirium of his son and fears he's experiencing convulsions. If I
only could articulate to him the importance of it all, but a nine-year-old does
not have the necessary articulacy. Celtic eventually triumph by two goals to one.
A little boy cries in Hilton Drive in 1954; now, an old man's cheeks are moist
in 2017. Only the years are subject to change. I realise now that football is not
more vital than life and death, but I submit that it comes a close third.

The tears are not the sole product of sport. Bill Duff, an Aberdeen Academy
schoolmate whom I remember standing alongside on the South terracing in the
early sixties, died last month. A former prison governor, he had been suffering
from prostate cancer, but was reassured everything was under control. Occasionally, he and I would share our respective histories of the disease. He seemed
to be handling it better. In April, he went snorkelling whilst on holiday in Bris-
bane. A few days later, he complained of shoulder pain; it's said he entered the
hospital as an ostensibly young man and emerged some days later as an old one.
He'd been diagnosed with terminal cancer of the bladder and stomach. Segrega-
tion of our respective fates is difficult. I shut moist eyes and picture the Saturday
congregation of school friends and fellow Dons fans: Bill Duff, Gordon Donald,
Ivor Finnie, Ian Thompson, and John Dingwall. The full package is there: the
pals, the bugle, the songs, and the passion redolent of youth. God, if we could
only rewind the years. The Hampden pitch is now a f***ing blur.

I shake myself out of the past, engage in the glorious and ritualistic red
and white flag display put together by a group of selfless souls, and wonder
whether there will be cause for any further celebration today. How much faith
can be invested in a team that has a proclivity for malfunction in show games?
And what of McInnes? He is a good, invariably capable manager, certainly, but
does he have the necessary wherewithal to be any more than that? There again,
what do I know? A fortnight ago, Brendan Rogers delivered an unequivocal
endorsement of his ability – ahead of his side's 3-1 victory at Pittodrie. Rogers
declared that McInnes had performed so magnificently that he deserved a second chance in English football. This reminded me that more homework was
necessary. I sought an independent view of that Bristol City failure, so I called
an old journalistic colleague who is close to the English club. Ralph Ellis's
response was initially favourable: McInnes had impressed by being very stu-
dious and analytical, but had been grievously hampered by the imperative to
reduce the wage bill. In fairness, this was an approximation of what McInnes
had told me. Consequently, some senior players destined for departure not
only tended to down tools but also influenced the younger ones to join them
in industrial action.

But I was equally anxious to know what our manager hadn't imparted. Unsurprisingly, football bosses favour reticence regarding their deficiencies. My informant came quickly to the point. 'McInnes signed a number of players from Scotland who, basically, weren't up to the task. Richard Foster gained the unfortunate reputation of allegedly being just about the worst right back ever to wear a Bristol City shirt.'

Also featuring on the debit side was the claim that McInnes attempted to change things dramatically. 'Somebody who had one bad game wouldn't be seen in the team for a month. That didn't go down well with the players. Neither did the very detailed accounts of the opposition. McInnes spent a lot of time talking about how good they were. Players got bored with that. The bottom line was that while he could handle the technical side of it fairly well, what he didn't handle was the management side of it, particularly with the David James's of this world. It was a new thing for him to handle big players, and they wondered why he spent so much time talking the opposition up, whereas he could have talked his own men up.'

All this is filtering through my mind as the teams take the field, particularly the segment about McInnes talking up the opposition. There has been evidence of this during his Pittodrie tenure. Does he have recidivist tendencies? We are about to find out. But the thought occurs that I'm maybe being too inflexible, too intolerant, too unforgiving: young managers are entitled to make mistakes; this is their way of learning. And the early indications, on this afternoon of May 27, are that McInnes has absorbed the lessons of the past. Today's mindset appears to be radically different. In November, our heroes stood off the opposition as if they felt threatened by collective halitosis. Now we're right in Celtic faces and looking to slit throats. A Hayes goal puts us into the unexpected territory of supremacy but, a minute later, we are reminded of the laws of trespass: Stuart Armstrong equalises, emphasising inadequacies in our defence. Celtic occasionally seem capable of putting us to the broadsword, but if we fear steel, there is no notion of apprehension in our eyes. We are the better team for 59 minutes, in spite of all their millions. Then, Adam Rooney, who has been sacrificed for the effective muscle of Jayden Stockley, is brought on as substitute. Rooney's predatory skills are a wonder, but they are confined to the penalty box. I foresee problems. Aberdeen's pressing game has had a deleterious effect on legs; we need pace. Now, we're bringing on a striker who, according to these old eyes, has difficulty running onto the park, let alone around it. Niall McGinn is then substituted by Anthony O'Connor: is this a message to Celtic that we're contemplating unfurling the white flag? For a few brief but exciting moments, Hayes and McLean submit that they don't believe in capitulation, but an inadequate final ball belies an impressive build-up. The green and white thumb screws are applied. Now, with seconds left, Tom Rogic goes on a run. O'Connor cannot compete with nimble Australian feet; nor can Andy Considine; Joe Lewis sees the ball beat him at the near post. It's all over. Time to experience that familiar feeling of desolation.

The despond fades, however, as self absorption yields to common sense. Our pride has undergone a 90-minute restoration programme. It was said no-one could breathe the same rarefied air favoured by high-flying Celtic. The accusation is not applicable any more. McInnes' initial tactics were all about aggression and denying the Glaswegians time and space to weave their intricate and incisive patterns. Our punching power might not have been concussive, but we bloody well bloodied their noses. We competed and did so with a bit of style, the unfortunate option of surrender blissfully absent. Importantly, defeat has left no detritus. For me, it's an epiphanal moment: even at this septuagenarian age, I'm recognising that there are penalties for delusion. I realise I have predicated my evaluation of the manager on times gone by. The days of Turnbull and Ferguson belong to yesteryear and they ain't coming back: the playing fields back then were so level that they would have been fit for crown green bowling. We could afford to challenge Celtic and Rangers. Now, there's not so much a gap as a chasm between my team and the Glaswegian double act: money influences, money dictates, money decides. McInnes, stripped of the necessary fiscal ammunition, has made my team seem important again. It's time to give him due credit and to be realistic. Now, it's as if I'm intoxicated by the spirit of compromise. I'm a fan and I'll very possibly debate his methodology in the future if I'm lucky enough to be around, but not right now. No, right now even in defeat, his status if that of a hero. There is, of course, one concerning thought to all this: will he be the manager when the sandstorm of adrenaline abates and the new season begins? The epiphany is already losing its sheen: I fear we are about to lose him.

* *

ALMOST THREE WEEKS LATER – an inordinately long time in football – the matter is still unresolved. Sunderland and chief executive Martin Bain have made their intentions clear: they wish to purchase the McInnes magic. Our leader has gone to Florida to rest his body, if not a fevered mind. Should he stick with Stewart Milne, who is not so much a chairman as a personal cheer leader? Milne represents solidity, succour and safety. Sunderland, meanwhile, might be representative of insanity. They have collapsed in the manner of a weekend inebriate, with debts of mega millions and an odds-on chance of a new ownership. Offsetting such negativity is the thought that McInnes would be earning three times his current salary should he choose the north-east of

England. But where would he be if the new incumbents didn't fancy the cut of his bewhiskered jib?

Uncertainty, however, closely allied to chaos, is not confined to Wearside: Aberdeen FC are threatening a dramatic implosion. They have lost Peter Pawlett, Niall McGinn, Ash Taylor, and Ryan Jack, and are about to lose Jonny Hayes to Celtic. But at least there is an assembly of wits. Bill Shankly once specialised in vituperative one-liners. One footballer angered the Liverpool manager and thus encouraged his sarcastic side. 'Listen, if his brains were gunpowder, he widnae hae enough to blaw the cap aff his heid!' There have been many moments in history when the fans of Aberdeen FC have aimed similar sentiments at the club's board of directors. But this time, the board, recognising that it could soon stripped of a vital asset, is putting its act together and discussing replacements. Tommy Wright and Alex Neill are in its thoughts. So, too, perhaps briefly, is David Moyes. But time is of the essence: the team is due to play a Europa League qualifier on 13 July. New players are required to restore the depleted framework. However, there is some positive news in that a potential sugar daddy has arrived promising to distribute his candy. Dave Cormack, a former chief executive, sold his software company for £630 million. A portion of that sum makes him a major shareholder and a man who might just make the difference.

Today, on 15 June 2017, Sunderland's Chief Executive Martin Bain is scheduled to meet McInnes in Florida. A former male model, Bain is a fashion-conscious dude who was known to heft two mobile phones while trying to make sense of Rangers in the David Murray era. He is so conscious of hygiene that he tends to change shirts between meetings. He allegedly has tapped into Walter Smith's experience and come out holding McInnes' name above all others. It is imperative that he gets his man. And it looks like he has. Sunderland, after initial reluctance, agree to compensate Aberdeen by close to a million pounds and therefore he is given permission to speak to McInnes, whose face now sports a Floridian tan to complement the fashionable beard.

The next part is purely a hypothethis, but I suspect it is adjacent to the truth. McInnes is understandably conflicted, but Bain may be talking to the beard. A fretting Milne has phoned his lawyer, Les Dalgarno, who also acts for Sir Alex Ferguson. 'Can you ask Alex to have a word with Derek?' Ferguson is a maestro at the art of recommendation. Apparently, his wisdom was crucial last season in Robbie Neilson's decision to leave Hearts and join MK Dons. 'Do you have any further advice?' Neilson queried. 'Aye,' said Sir Alex, 'get a wee bit closer to your razor, son!'

This particular situation is as close to the razor's edge as it gets. Ferguson and McInnes have already formed an alliance, as you will have read in the last chapter. It's my guess that he is the crowning factor in this matter. McInnes tells

Bain he is sticking with the granite of Aberdeen. He was probably almost there in his own mind, but the words of Fergie would have reinforced the situation. I suspect Bain has to change more than his shirt when he absorbs this negative news; after all, he must report back to a brooding master in American Ellis Short.

Whatever, my estimation of the McInnes performance in this instance has swollen exponentially. He is one smart fella. He may have put the Aberdeen FC support through six degrees of hell, but by making the decision to stay, he has greatly extended the perimeters of his power base on so many levels. For instance, Rangers put in a bid of £300,000 for Kenny McLean and are rewarded with the sound of derision from the Aberdeen boardroom. McInnes has assurances that no further players will be sold in this transfer window. This smacks of hypocrisy, considering that the manager was scarcely thinking of his players when he was debating whether to decamp to England. But, hey, this is football: hypocrisy is almost encouraged. Furthermore, McInnes has told fans that while his ambitions are with the Dons for the moment, there may come a day when this is not the case. This tells potential suitors in England that they may not be wasting their time, like Sunderland. His name is out there in neon. Finally, he has won further handsome remuneration for himself and his exemplary lieutenant, Tony Docherty. It would not surprise me if he earned close to £500,000 in the next 12 months.

The pain of uncertainty has disappeared. All is well again with my red and white world. Players, classy players, are arriving to replace those whose sense of adventure spirited them away. The images of Leggat, Cooke and Harper will never fade, but their modern-day equivalents are far from being inadequate. Only a foolhardy man would predict that everything will be well with the Dons from here on in, but it's my fervent wish that they continue to progress and that their carefully-laid plans of a new home at Kingsford are realised. And while I look forward enthusiastically to the investment of Dave Cormack, I must admit to a grievous omission. I forgot to thank Aberdeen's benefactors of 2014. A major investment by Willie and Elaine Donald helped to eradicate Aberdeen's massive debt, thereby giving the club the opportunity and platform to prosper. They are entitled to a unique place in history: it is to be hoped that their legacy is not squandered.

It is almost time, then, to close the word processor. I hope the invective in this book has not offended but, as football life is rawer than a newly peeled onion, I'll exonerate myself by emphasising that the language needed to be in its most elemental form. The writing of it, meanwhile, has certainly proved a great release for me. Prostate cancer is a tyrant which can dominate your life if it is allowed freedom of expression. The six-month long odyssey for Dons nostalgia proved therapeutic and somehow derailed the bouts of introspection that tend to accompany the illness.

There is one real concern, however, and it's something for which there is no answer: would this book have won the approbation of my father? He was an autodidact and, when he was absent from his beautiful garden, his head would be lost in the works of Shakespeare, Tolstoy or Steinbeck. But I remember one particular day that he wasn't consumed by such heavy literature. Shortly after I had joined the *Press & Journal*, I sat at home and assumed the guise of the then Sports Editor, Norman MacDonald. I had so much to thank that man for - he gave me my first job in journalism and you do not forget people like that. So, with Mr MacDonald in mind, I wrote an imaginary match report about the Dons. Dad spotted it and queried the authorship. When I told him, a shake of the head was accompanied by a slightly sardonic smile. He told me he never believed me to be capable of such scribbling. It was a back-handed compliment, of course, but one I shall never forget. Coming from a man who unwittingly opened up the wonderful vista of Aberdeen FC to me, it came to mean almost as much as anything else I have achieved in this sporting life.

We should conclude, of course, with an emphasis on football rather than emotions. I met Derek McInnes at the football writers' awards dinner in Glasgow in May of this year and we talked briefly and warmly. I told him I would send that chapter to him, but warned not all of it would be to his liking. Soon I was regretting my actions. I was informed that the manager wasn't 'exactly over the moon' about my interpretation of him. I pointed out that I had written a chronology of events and therefore it would be unwise to draw any precipitate conclusions. I was told that McInnes would telephone me. This did not happen. It was further claimed he was going to email me. This didn't happen, either. Then I was informed he wanted to see me in person. No date was forthcoming. I can only imagine that he rationalised the situation and decided to wait until he had read the whole book before acting upon it.

So to date, we have not tumbled into dispute and I hope it doesn't happen. My initial scepticism of him, as already stated, has gradually vanished. There are a whole lot of wannabe football managers out there, but few have the requisite credentials to be good football managers. Without doubt, McInnes possesses those credentials. But, aside from being a sports journalist (retired) and a writer, I'm also a fanatical fan – and fans have opinions that will not always coincide with those in charge. No doubt there will be moments of conflict in the future – in my opinion, the centre of defence still looks porous and Ryan Christie should not be played on the right wing. But, at the time of writing, despite not playing to our potential, we are at the summit of the Scottish Premiership and the squad is, if anything, stronger than its predecessor. The manager? Eddie Turnbull once placed in a nutshell the essence of football management. 'You're either a hero or a hoo-er.' McInnes, currently anyway, is that hero.

Luath Press Limited

committed to publishing well written books worth reading

LUATH PRESS takes its name from Robert Burns, whose little collie Luath (*Gael.*, swift or nimble) tripped up Jean Armour at a wedding and gave him the chance to speak to the woman who was to be his wife and the abiding love of his life. Burns called one of the 'Twa Dogs' Luath after Cuchullin's hunting dog in Ossian's *Fingal*. Luath Press was established in 1981 in the heart of Burns country, and is now based a few steps up the road from Burns' first lodgings on Edinburgh's Royal Mile. Luath offers you distinctive writing with a hint of unexpected pleasures.

Most bookshops in the UK, the US, Canada, Australia, New Zealand and parts of Europe, either carry our books in stock or can order them for you. To order direct from us, please send a £sterling cheque, postal order, international money order or your credit card details (number, address of cardholder and expiry date) to us at the address below. Please add post and packing as follows: UK – £1.00 per delivery address; overseas surface mail – £2.50 per delivery address; overseas airmail – £3.50 for the first book to each delivery address, plus £1.00 for each additional book by airmail to the same address. If your order is a gift, we will happily enclose your card or message at no extra charge.

Luath Press Limited
543/2 Castlehill
The Royal Mile
Edinburgh EH1 2ND
Scotland
Telephone: +44 (0)131 225 4326 (24 hours)
email: sales@luath. co.uk
Website: www. luath.co.uk